# Orality and Literacy

Walter J. Ong's classic work provides a fascinating insight into the social effects of oral, written, printed and electronic technologies, and their impact on philosophical, theological, scientific and literary thought.

This thirtieth anniversary edition – coinciding with Ong's centenary year – reproduces his best-known and most influential book in full and brings it up to date with two new exploratory essays by cultural writer and critic John Hartley.

Hartley provides:

- a scene-setting chapter that situates Ong's work within the historical and disciplinary context of post-war Americanism and the rise of communication and media studies
- a closing chapter that follows up Ong's work on orality and literacy in relation to evolving media forms, with a discussion of recent criticisms of Ong's approach, and an assessment of his concept of the 'evolution of consciousness'
- extensive references to recent scholarship on orality, literacy and the study of knowledge technologies, tracing changes in *how* we know *what* we know.

These illuminating essays contextualize Ong within recent intellectual history and display his work's continuing force in the ongoing study of the relationship between literature and the media, as well as that of psychology, education and sociological thought.

**Walter J. Ong** (November 30 1912–August 12 2003) was University Professor Emeritus at Saint Louis University, USA, where he was previously Professor of English and Professor of Humanities in Psychiatry. His many publications have been highly influential for studies in the evolution of consciousness.

**John Hartley** is an educator, author, researcher and commentator on the history and cultural impact of television, journalism, popular media and creative industries. He is Professor of Cultural Science and Director of the Centre for Culture and Technology at Curtin University, Western Australia.

# IN THE SAME SERIES

Walter J.
# Ong

## Orality and Literacy

The Technologizing of the Word

**30th Anniversary Edition**

With additional chapters by John Hartley

Routledge
Taylor & Francis Group

LONDON AND NEW YORK

First published in 1982 by Methuen & Co. Ltd

New edition published 2002 by Routledge

This 30th anniversary edition published 2012 by Routledge
2 Park Square, Milton Park, Abingdon, Oxon OX14 4RN

Simultaneously published in the USA and Canada
by Routledge
711 Third Avenue, New York, NY 10017

*Routledge is an imprint of the Taylor & Francis Group, an informa business*

*British Library Cataloguing in Publication Data*
A catalogue record for this book is available from the British Library

*Library of Congress Cataloging in Publication Data*
Ong, Walter J.
Orality and literacy : the technologizing of the word / Walter J. Ong,
with additional chapters by John Hartley.
p. cm. – (30th anniversary ed.) (3rd ed.)
Includes bibliographical references and indexes.
1. Language and culture. 2. Oral tradition. 3. Writing. 4. Written communication.
I. Hartley, John, 1948- II. Title.
P35.O5 2013
306.44–dc23
2012005539


ISBN 978–0–415–53837–4 (hbk)
ISBN 978–0–415–53838–1 (pbk)
ISBN 978–0–203–10325–8 (ebk)

Typeset in Joanna
by RefineCatch Limited, Bungay, Suffolk

# CONTENTS

# GENERAL EDITOR'S PREFACE

No doubt a third General Editor's Preface to *New Accents* seems hard to justify. What is there left to say? Twenty-five years ago, the series began with a very clear purpose. Its major concern was the newly perplexed world of academic literary studies, where hectic monsters called 'Theory', 'Linguistics' and 'Politics' ranged. In particular, it aimed itself at those undergraduates or beginning postgraduate students who were either learning to come to terms with the new developments or were being sternly warned against them.

*New Accents* deliberately took sides. Thus the first Preface spoke darkly, in 1977, of 'a time of rapid and radical social change', of the 'erosion of the assumptions and presuppositions' central to the study of literature. 'Modes and categories inherited from the past' it announced, 'no longer seem to fit the reality experienced by a new generation'. The aim of each volume would be to 'encourage rather than resist the process of change' by combining nuts-and-bolts exposition of new ideas with clear and detailed explanation of related conceptual developments. If mystification (or downright demonization) was the enemy, lucidity (with a nod to the compromises inevitably at stake there) became a friend. If a 'distinctive discourse of the future' beckoned, we wanted at least to be able to understand it.

With the apocalypse duly noted, the second Preface proceeded piously to fret over the nature of whatever rough beast might stagger portentously from the rubble. 'How can we recognise or deal with the new?', it complained, reporting nevertheless the dismaying advance of 'a host of barely respectable activities for which we have no reassuring names' and promising a programme of wary surveillance at 'the boundaries of the precedented and at the limit of the thinkable'. Its conclusion, 'the unthinkable, after all, is that which covertly shapes our thoughts' may rank as a truism. But in so far as it offered some sort of useable purchase on a world of crumbling certainties, it is not to be blushed for.

In the circumstances, any subsequent, and surely final, effort can only modestly look back, marvelling that the series is still here, and not unreasonably congratulating itself on having provided an initial outlet for what turned, over the years, into some of the distinctive voices and topics in literary studies. But the volumes now re-presented have more than a mere historical interest. As their authors indicate, the issues they raised are still potent, the arguments with which they engaged are still disturbing. In short, we weren't wrong. Academic study did change rapidly and radically to match, even to help to generate, wide reaching social changes. A new set of discourses was developed to negotiate those upheavals. Nor has the process ceased. In our deliquescent world, what was unthinkable inside and outside the academy all those years ago now seems regularly to come to pass.

Whether the *New Accents* volumes provided adequate warning of, maps for, guides to, or nudges in the direction of this new terrain is scarcely for me to say. Perhaps our best achievement lay in cultivating the sense that it was there. The only justification for a reluctant third attempt at a Preface is the belief that it still is.

TERENCE HAWKES

# BEFORE ONGISM

"To become what we want to be, we have to decide what we were."[1]

## John Hartley

## "Friends, Romans, countrymen, lend me your ears"[2]

2012 marks the centenary of the birth of Walter J. Ong, SJ (November 30), but he is still read and regarded as a contemporary scholar. Something that he wrote about his own one-time teacher, Marshall McLuhan, resonates for Ong's own scholarly time travels: His "voice is always the voice of the present calling into the past, a past that he teases into reacting ebulliently and tellingly with present actuality in his readers' minds" (Ong 2002: 307). Walter Ong's own publications spanned 70 years, continuing to 2003, the year of his death.[3] His interests ranged from ancient Sumerian writing systems to modern computers – both using digital code, he noted (2002: 527–49). He was immersed in historical scholarship, but remained forward-looking throughout. His last book (Ong 2002), published as he approached his 90th birthday, is jauntily subtitled *"Challenges for Further Inquiry."*

This is not the place for an appraisal of Ong's life and works. For the enthusiast and the specialist, there are good accounts readily to hand, including Thomas Farrell's Introduction to the collection already mentioned (Ong 2002: 1–68; and see Soukup 2007). In bringing to your attention a new edition of Ong's best-known book, *Orality and Literacy*, I seek neither to bury nor to praise him. Instead, I want to address the non-specialist *reader* of his book, for whom – judging by customer reviews on Amazon.com – the coherence underlying his historical and intellectual trajectories may not be immediately evident.[4] For newly minted "readers' minds," perhaps, there's a need to reconnect that "ebullient and telling" link between present actuality and past ideas, a connection I'm going to call "Ongism."[5]

Given his free-ranging time travels, it may be helpful to trace a line that connects Ongism with various historical periods in the broader history of ideas; the history of *systems of thought* and concomitant media of expression through which ideas have been organised, as follows:

– *Ancient and medieval rhetoric* (roughly 500 bce to 1500 ce),
  o   because it was rhetoric – an oral art – that "ultimately took all knowledge as its province" (Ong 1971: vii); via
– the European *Reformation* (1500–1700),
  o   where print-based Ramism (Ong 1958) reformed knowledge as well as religion; a move that linked religion with the rise of capitalism (Tawney 1998), and created a path-dependency for (Protestant) Methodism and (scientific) method alike (Ong 1953); and
– the ensuing *Enlightenment* (1700–1900),
  o   both scientific and Scottish (see Berry 1997; Phillipson 2010);
– as these impacted the growth of the *American Republic*,
  o   directly through Benjamin Franklin (Atiyah 2006) and indirectly though Thomas Jefferson (McLean 2011); thence to
– the technological determinations of *modern knowledge* (1900–date),
  o   where, according to the Ong line of thought, writing and print-literacy have "transformed" human consciousness as a whole, while a "secondary orality" has emerged with digital media.

*Orality and Literacy*, the summation of 30 years of his work, brought Ong's thought to wide attention, striking a chord with those who were curious about the impact of communication technologies – speech, writing, print, screen, computer – on how humans think and know. That curiosity was not always benignly motivated, because some feared that contemporary technologies, especially the most popular broadcast and screen media (television in particular), were destroyers rather than creators of knowledge, especially in comparison to the empire of print, which was the unchallenged medium of communication for all of the great realist knowledge systems of modernity – science (the paper), journalism (the press) and imaginative fiction (the novel).

This tripartite division of the real corresponded with much older classifications. These emerged at the very time when print's ascendancy as a medium began to be asserted in late sixteenth and early seventeenth-century Europe: very much Ong's preferred stamping ground. It was Sir Francis Bacon (1605), founding philosopher of modern empirical science (dubbed by some the "father of inductive reasoning"),[6] and urgent advocate of the "advancement of learning," who tried to classify knowledge on the basis of the relationship between forms of communication and human faculties. As Diana Altegoer writes: "Bacon claimed that all human learning flows from the three fountains of *memory, imagination and reason*, from which emanate *history, poesy, and philosophy*; there can be no others" (Altegoer 2000: 22). Bacon saw what he called "the faculties of the mind of man" as of two kinds: "the one respecting his *understanding and reason*, and the other his *will, appetite, and affection*"; and it was *imagination* that acted as an "agent or nuntius" [messenger] between the two (Bacon 1605: Book II, section XII). Thus, "poesy, aligned with the imagination, held a pivotal place in Bacon's scheme to advance learning; by linking reason with the will and appetite" (Altegoer 2000: 22).

Bacon's schema was inherited from earlier, oral traditions of rhetoric and logic, not least via Peter Ramus, the central figure in Ong's scholarship. Perhaps unselfconsciously or unwittingly,[7] it has continued to serve as the underlying epistemology of modern print culture's three realist textual systems, which we might spatialise as follows:

| HUMAN FACULTY (BACON) | | | |
|---|---|---|---|
| MEMORY | IMAGINATION | REASON | } TRUTH |
| WILL | APPETITE | UNDERSTANDING | } TRUTH |

| | FORM OF KNOWLEDGE | | | |
|---|---|---|---|---|
| PRE-MODERN | HISTORY | POESY | PHILOSOPHY | } LEARNING |
| MODERN | JOURNALISM | FICTION | SCIENCE | } REALISM |

| | MEDIUM OF COMMUNICATION (ONG) | | | |
|---|---|---|---|---|
| PRE-MODERN | RHETORIC | SONG | DIALOGUE/ Lecture | } ORAL/ Chirographic |
| MODERN | THE PRESS | THE NOVEL | THE PAPER | } PRINT-LITERATE |

Be it noted that Bacon's schema saw *truth* as the prize of all three of these forms of knowledge, history, poesy and philosophy, working together. Later specialisation forced "science" and "fiction" ever further apart, at least in principle, but Bacon wanted to broker a "symbiotic relationship between scientific understanding and affective poetics" (Altegoer: 23) – an aspiration to which contemporary science is slowly returning, as for instance in E.O. Wilson's call for "consilience" (1998) between the creative humanities and natural sciences.

Ong's expertise lay in using the skills of literary-historical research and textual criticism to tease out the way that the pre-modern arts of knowledge – logic, rhetoric, and dialectics – were transformed following the emergence of print. These arts (which don't quite map onto the schema above, tempting though it may be to assign them to the respective columns), were deployed in the medieval period for the serious business of organising and distributing knowledge. Ong's work was an early example of what is now called the "science of science" – an investigation not into *what* but *how* we know. Along with his contemporary, Marshall McLuhan,[8] who coined the slogan "the medium is the message," Ong popularised the idea that knowledge is a product of language, and that the medium in which language is communicated – by voice, writing, print – makes us think along certain path-dependent lines. Ong went further: he contended that "writing *restructures consciousness*" (*Orality and Literacy*: Chapter 4).

Thus "Ongism" is the place where mind is determined by medium. Methodologically, it uses *linguistic analysis* – something that "from the time of the medieval scholastics, the Anglo-Saxon world has been generating a good deal of thought around" (Ong 1958: 4). Such analysis reconnects rhetoric with science (knowledge). Further, although he was interested in the invention of writing, going back several millennia, Ong's own scholarship was chiefly preoccupied with the Renaissance and Reformation periods, during which European culture was convulsed with religious conflict internally, and accelerating expansionism externally. At such a time, "linguistic analysis" connects with the great themes of religion and empire (power) in the modernising West. Ongism used the seemingly arcane past to cast unexpected light on the long present, "ebulliently and tellingly" using textual studies to link power and knowledge, across "historical continuities (which are also psychological continuities)," far exceeding those theorised by Foucault (*Orality and Literacy*: 162), certainly in Ong's own estimation.

This is the context for *Orality and Literacy*'s extraordinary contemporary reach and for Ong's influence across many interdisciplinary domains. The latter are listed by Lance Strate as: "rhetoric, communication, education, media studies, English, literary criticism, classics, biblical studies, theology, philosophy, psychology, anthropology, cultural studies, history, medieval studies, Renaissance studies, American studies, gender studies, biology, and computer science" (foreword to Ong 2002: ix). Strate puts that range of influence down to Ong's mastery of "noetics, of knowledge and our ways of knowing," a scholarly pursuit where "expertise encompasses expertise itself." That's a canny observation, but there are at least two further reasons for Ong's influence. The first, *historical*, is less often commented on – although it may tell us more – than the second, *disciplinary*.

## Intellectual origins of Americanism

Historically, Ong's scholarship emerged in an era when the USA reached for and achieved world leadership; explicitly after World War II with the so-called *pax americana*. US global hegemonic status was assumed (in both senses – taken on and taken for granted) not directly through imperial conquest, but through ideas, on the presumption of those ideas' moral and democratic superiority, which only had to be promulgated to be binding on all, whether you were American or . . .

say . . . Vietnamese. Thus, the "ways of knowing" and the "expertise" that Ong investigated were not just of historical interest; they were newly important because they had become *American*.

*Americanists* sought the intellectual origins of US superiority in what Ong's own academic mentor, Perry Miller (1939; 1953), called "the New England Mind" – a Protestant, "downright," democratic, "plain-style" mind. Inspired by Miller, Ong traced that way of thinking directly back to the sixteenth-century French dialectician Peter Ramus (Ong 1958: 4–7). His work on Ramism is a major achievement, but it might not have escaped the seminar – or seminary – had it not been for the context of its composition at Harvard, the American Republic's first university.

Perry Miller returned to Harvard after secret wartime service in Britain, thought to be connected with developing American capabilities in the new art of psychological warfare.[9] He supervised Ong's doctorate (1948–54), which was published by Harvard University Press. Ong acknowledges Miller there (1958: x), and makes the connections between Harvard, Americanism, and Ramism:

> The present [1958] wave of interest [in Ramus] dates from 1935 and 1936, when Professor Samuel Eliot Morison published his tercentennial Harvard volumes, *The Founding of Harvard College* and *Harvard in the Seventeenth Century*. Morison . . . traced New England's first fruits back to branches on the tree of knowledge long forgotten in the traditional accounts of America's heritage.
>
> (1958: 3)

Within a page or so, this "American heritage" has become universal: "Before Morison's and Miller's works, there was not much written concerning the fuller implications of Ramism in the history of the human mind" (1958: 5, my emphasis). Thus, for Ong, "Present-day interest in Ramism in the English-speaking world is . . . communal; it tends to regard Ramism . . . as a phenomenon or symptom which . . . may yield helpful and even startling information concerning intellectual history and the formation of the modern mind" (1958: 6 my emphasis).

Harvard is not just the oldest institution of higher education in the USA (founded in 1636 at the height of Ramist method); it is also the richest and has almost routinely been rated as the top-ranking university in the world.[10] It was and remains a kind of megaphone for Americanism, not least through Harvard Business Publishing, whose mission is "to influence real-world change by maximizing the reach and impact of its essential offering – ideas."[11] Among the latter was the idea that the "formation of the modern mind" occurs in the crucible of language – a crucible heated by literature and drama even as it is cooled by "plain style" and "downrightness."

For instance, working for many years at Harvard, contemporaneously with Ong, was Alfred Harbage (1941; 1947). A notable literary historian, Harbage saw *Shakespeare's audience* as the precursor and model of modern American democracy, because his plays addressed all sections of society, from courtier to courtesan to cobbler.[12] Over time, the Globe and other theatres attracted a sizable proportion of the entire population. Andrew Gurr (2004: 50) estimates 25,000 visitors a week, totalling 50 million admissions from 1580 to 1640. The popular audience in the "wooden O" was literally enacting a modern polity forming itself – in the minds of apprentices and artisans – even as the plays onstage wrestled with the pains and tensions of emergent modernity, to which American democracy is the heir.

Without wanting to overstate it (as American supremacism, for instance), there is a vein of *political philosophy* running through the literary-historical scholarship of mid-century America. The mood extended well beyond Harvard. Across the country, literary scholarship seemed determined to give substance to Walt Whitman's post-Civil War vision for America's "democratic vistas";[13] a vision newly urgent in a post-World War II world. Richard Altick at Ohio (*The English Common Reader*, 1957) and R. F. Jones at Stanford (*The Triumph of the English Language*, 1953) come to mind.[14] Most notable, perhaps, was Yale, where American Studies was established in the same period, not least for political reasons. American Studies was:

> an enterprise that would be, among other things, an instrument for ideological struggle in what some among them termed the American crusade in the Cold War, and what others among them saw as virtually a second civil war.
>
> (Holzman 1999: 71)

A leading figure in this enterprise was Norman Holmes Pearson, who, like Perry Miller at Harvard, was a secret agent for the OSS (Office of Strategic Services) – precursor of the CIA – during World War II. Where Perry's protégés at Harvard included the Jesuit priest Walter Ong, Pearson's at Yale included James Jesus Angleton, who learnt there the craft of practical criticism of decontextualised documents. Angleton went on to apply it as chief of counter-intelligence at the CIA, where he remained for a generation (Holzman 2008). While at Yale, as Terence Hawkes has pointed out, Angleton was much influenced by the New Criticism, especially as practised by William Empson (1930), whose theory of the irreducible ambiguity of expression served Angleton well in his search for double meanings as evidence of Soviet "double agents," within the CIA itself. His obsessive search for spies turned to domestic suspects during the Johnson and Nixon presidencies, among them the liberal and countercultural elite of American society, including Martin Luther King and Edward Kennedy. Hawkes draws the parallel between literary criticism and counter-intelligence:

> When agents may be recognized as "turned" . . . they themselves become "texts" which demand complex analysis. A sensitivity to ambiguity then becomes a crucial weapon. The improbable but undeniable impact of modern literary criticism on practical politics has no better model, and Angleton later described his work in counter-intelligence as "the practical criticism of ambiguity."
>
> (Hawkes 2009)

Strangely, it seems, the study of rhetoric, of literary theory, and the practical criticism of arcane texts at Ivy-league colleges, intersected both personally and institutionally with the career of high-stakes political Americanism during the crucial period of its global ascendancy. As a Jesuit, presumably Ong was not involved in the counter-espionage shenanigans of active spy-masters like Perry, Pearson and Angleton, but he was brought to prominence in an intellectual environment where literary history, linguistic analysis and an expanded doctrine of the USA's "manifest destiny" were brought into alignment.

This was a philosophy that sought to revive or maintain (i.e. to construct) a bond between Classical Ciceronian rhetoric, modern mass democracy, and the American Republic, much as US ex-President John Quincy Adams had done in the early nineteenth century – as the occupant of Harvard's first chair in Rhetoric (Rathbun 2000).[15] Ong himself yoked the literary and rhetorical traditions of Harvard scholarship together, and perhaps learnt the habit of universalising and Americanising pre-modern European cultural forms, by following the work of Milman Parry and Albert Lord, both extensively cited in *Orality and Literacy*. As Thomas Farrell has noted:

> Parry was a classicist at Harvard University who undertook field studies of Yugoslavian singers of tales in the 1930s. Lord was a graduate student who worked with Parry and later wrote his doctoral dissertation on the findings of their field studies . . . subsequently published in 1960 as *The Singer of Tales*, a landmark study.
>
> (Farrell, in Ong 2002: 2)

Seeking to answer the question "what is new in our understanding of orality?" (where "orality" should be understood as a *human* characteristic, not one belonging to a given culture, time or place), Ong writes that: "More than any earlier scholar, the American classicist Milman Parry . . . succeeded in undercutting . . . cultural chauvinism so as to get into the 'primitive' Homeric poetry on this poetry's own terms. . ." (*Orality and Literacy*: 18). As for Albert Lord, he "carried through and extended Parry's work with convincing finesse"; moreover, "those who studied with him [Milman Parry] and Lord at Harvard . . . were already applying Parry's ideas to the study of Old English Poetry" (*Orality and Literacy*: 27). Ong thus places his own work in a *Harvard* tradition of scholarship, where the *American* discovery of an "oral-aural cast of mind" (Ong 2002: 301) among preliterate poets, both ancient (Homer) and modern (Serbo-Croat), is rapidly applied to Anglophone canonical literature and thence to culture and civilisation in general; and to rhetoric and thence to philosophy and knowledge in general. The presumption is that the "American mind, although a many-faceted thing" (Ong 2002: 294) can be equated with the human mind. This logic is clear in *Orality and Literacy*, where Ong concludes his chapter on "The modern discovery of primary oral cultures" (Chapter 2). He extrapolates directly from Milman Parry's discovery of oral methods of composition in Homer (*Orality and Literacy*: 21), via Lord, Havelock and others (27–8), to McLuhan and Ong's own work (28–9), thence in turn to the study of human consciousness in general through the work of the psychologist Julian Jaynes (29–30). Jaynes, of course, had studied as an undergraduate at Harvard before taking his doctorate in psychology at Yale.[16]

This tradition, however occluded by changing circumstance and academic fashion, was institutionalised not just in American Studies, but more fundamentally in the uniquely American (Ong 2002: 74) schools of "Speech," "Rhetoric" and "Communications" that spread literary criticism along with the "plain style" of protestant, scientific and persuasive prose across the campuses of the expanding West, to places like St. Louis, for instance, where Walter Ong studied for his MA and subsequently taught.[17] Rhetoric was valued in order to prepare citizens for public life as lawyers, clergy or politicians, and to underpin the general education of a commercial and scientific population (Bedford 1984). How to pervade the polity with both democratic principles and the ability to marshal and deploy knowledge effectively, for civic as well as private purposes? In a society increasingly organised through knowledge and dependent on the technologisation of the communications media, this question was never far from the surface; and for Ong's generation the answer was never far away either: the "informed citizen" (Schudson 1998) must understand rhetoric. As Ong wrote in 1970, "To this day most of the work on the history of rhetoric is still done by Americans, who in their extreme commitment to literacy have been far enough removed from the old rhetorical or oratorical culture underlying European education to find its phenomena intriguing" (Ong 2002: 74; and see Ong 2002: 294).

For the World Wide Web generation, as opposed to the World War II one, some of this intellectual provenance needs to be reconstructed. "Freedom" – the "American way" – was built on the capability of winning an argument. The science of noetics, then, of "knowing how we know," was at the top of the Cold War agenda, in both its paranoid forms (counter-intelligence) and its optimistic forms, which included knowing how to demonstrate the superiority of Americanism over, say, Khrushchev's Russia.[18]

At the macro level, American hegemony was founded as much on the power of its media, culture and science as on its military might. As the Cold War heated up, hearts and minds across the world were wooed with mediated visions of Americanism, in the convincing – the Shakespearean – disguise of mass entertainment. This is now called "soft power"; and the Chinese Communist Party not only espouses it, at the highest level of diplomacy and statecraft, but also reckons that the Americans are still up to it too:

> In the latest issue of the ruling Communist Party's top theoretical journal, "Qiushi," which means "Seeking Truth," President Hu [Jintao] warned that the country must promote its own culture over "western-ization" promoted by hostile forces. "We must clearly be aware that international enemy forces are stepping up their strategic plots to westernize and split our country," he wrote. "The fields of thought and culture are important sectors they are using for this long-term infiltra-tion. We must clearly recognize the seriousness and difficulty of this struggle, sound the alarm bell . . . and take effective measures to deal with it."
>
> (Reuters 2012)

This is China's (ostensible) rationale for imposing strict import quotas on Hollywood films. Harmless entertainment to some is hostile infiltra-tion to others. "Democratic vistas" are "strategic plots," precisely because, as Walt Whitman had put it back in 1871, "I shall use the words America and democracy as convertible terms."[19]

At the micro level, the individual citizen needed mental software to engage in an increasingly textualised world; one where knowing relied on technologically transported information that was abstracted from its contextual roots, just as writing and print are abstracted from the situ-ated immediacy of speech. Perhaps such abstraction suited the migrant and settler society of the Americas more comfortably than it did the autochthonous cultures of Old Europe. Certainly, it wasn't only lawyers and leaders who required rhetorical skills to manipulate ideas and knowledge, and skills in "the practical criticism of ambiguity" to resist manipulation in the messages of others. To be successful citizens and consumers, to sustain an enterprising economy, and to know how to tell our entertaining and enlightening social media from their hostile and invasive spam, everyone must exercise the "soft power" of knowledge.

## Contemporary communication and cultural studies

Turning from historical to disciplinary reasons for the influence of Ongism, this same "noetic" tradition was, of course, one of the great taproots of contemporary communication studies. Here, the germinal figure is not Ong's doctoral supervisor at Harvard but his master's supervisor at St Louis – a Canadian professor of English, much the same age as Ong,[20] who came to St Louis, hotfoot from Cambridge, to teach Shakespeare. His name was Herbert Marshall McLuhan. McLuhan provided a different rationale for taking an interest in rhetoric; one that extended its influence from the historical and political "New England mind" to the mind in general, linking the study of technologies of communication to individual (and universal) cognitive psychology, without abandoning the progressivist grand narrative of "manifest destiny", but simply projecting it backward in time and outward to humanity as a whole.

This even more abstract and ambitious agenda suited the sixties very well, as the subsequent career of Marshall McLuhan demonstrated (Wolfe 2000). Indeed, because military triumphalism was decisively defeated in Vietnam, it was only in the realm of ideas, knowledge, media and culture that Americanism could prevail. In the era of Vietnam, Americanism shifted across from patriotism to protest; from "the American way" to critique of "Amerika"[21] – and this conquered the world, through popular music, subcultures, and the "new social movements" of the 1960s. Recasting the human mind as a product of media took medieval rhetoric out of the seminary and put it in the world of what are now known as "Mad Men" (advertisers from Madison Avenue).[22] It is in this context that the idea of a medium being able to shape and transform consciousness took popular hold, just as Vietnam, sex and drugs and rock'n'roll were setting campuses alight with the idea that consciousness ought to be changed in various ways, as soon as possible and with whatever semiotic or chemical assistance was to hand.

It's hard to see Walter Ong, SJ, as a prophet of what is now summed up in the term "the sixties" (Gitlin 1987). Nonetheless, his closing statement in *Orality and Literacy* is that "orality-literacy dynamics enter integrally into the modern evolution of consciousness toward both greater *interiorization* and greater *openness*" (*Orality and Literacy*: 176). This might be heard as intensely meaningful equally by the Haight-Ashbury generation (Timothy Leary, *Playpower* and Yoko Ono with a stiffening of Illich) *and* the entrepreneurs of global media expansion (Wolfe 2000). Philosophy, protest, mind-expansion and commercial popular culture were all of a piece at this time, which partly accounts for the topic of orality being seen as "cool" (not quite as McLuhan might have put it). It was Ong himself who accused Derrida's logic of being "*psychedelic*," its effects being "due to sensory distortions" (*Orality and Literacy*: 76), in a chapter on "psychodynamics." But his real influence wasn't on Derrida; it was on *the youth of the day*:

> At the same time that the electronic stage is extending man's exploration outside the body, it is creating a desire for exploration of the individual's inner world. One example is the widespread interest in psychedelic substances. Many Americans, having ingested these chemicals, echo McLuhan's and Ong's theories. They state that their psychedelic episodes bring about "a sense of simultaneity in time and space," and "a sense of solidarity with all the people in the world." Others gather into drug or "hippie" subcultures, in which tribal rites are enacted, in which bright Indian clothes and primitive body markings are worn, and in which an intense sense of community often develops.
>
> (Krippner 1970)

In *Orality and Literacy* Ong deals with some of the other cool theory of the time – cool theory being the *raison d'être* of the New Accents series in which the book appeared – by seeking to negotiate his own position in relation to formalism, structuralism, deconstruction, etc., as well as certain approaches from linguistics and the social sciences. These positions, debates, and theoretical approaches form a significant part of the intellectual provenance of contemporary media and communication studies.

Ong's reach and impact are at least partly explicable by his ability to navigate contemporary currents of literary theory and postmodern philosophy (without drowning in "Theory"). He managed this by calling on his own unrivalled expertise in the history of knowledge, while maintaining a course that seemed to lead directly from these scholarly heights into the midst of the noisy melee of contemporary popular media. His insights provided both explanation and alibi for the immediate sensory experience of the tuned in, turned on, dropped out student, whose intellectual landmarks were more likely to come from music, movies, media and medications than from Latinate literature or intellectual traditions. Without a whiff of psychedelia in his own writings, Ong presided over a mind-altering moment in modern media studies. Perhaps this is what made his theory seem so cool at the time – it messed enlighteningly with *readers' minds*. Whether it explained the transformation of the *human mind* – in general – is another question, to which I shall return in my second additional chapter below, following Ong's *Orality and Literacy*.

## Notes

1  Quotation from Neil MacGregor, Director of the British Museum (MacGregor 2010: 409).
2  William Shakespeare (1599) *Julius Caesar*, III.ii.52. Online: shakespeare.mit.edu/julius_caesar/julius_caesar.3.2.html; and see note 12, p. 221, below.
3  From 1929 till after his death in 2003: see a full bibliography at: academic.slu.edu/ong/Full_Ong_bib_complete_Oct2008.pdf.
4  Amazon.com customer reviews range from one to five stars: "Read this book only if you are forced to do so by someone. Even that didn't do it for me . . . If you want an expensive fire starter or something to stop the teetering of some annoying table then buy this" (one star); "As a reader or literate I never considered the differences inherent in a primarily oral world. This book explains them. What a wonderful new way to see things" (five stars): www.amazon.com/Orality-Literacy-New-Accents-Walter/dp/0415027969 (accessed Jan 2012).
5  "Ongism" is not my neologism. It may have been coined by Dell Hymes (1996: 34), who used it to refer to technological determinism

in communication theory. See also: lulu101.typepad.com/theory_i_f08/2008/09/walter-ongism-w.html, where it backs the claim that "Words are things, typography as alive" (Design Theory at CalArts).

6   See for instance this classic entry in the *Short Biographical Dictionary of English Literature* (Cousins 1910): "The intellect of Bacon was one of the most powerful and searching ever possessed by man, and his developments of the inductive philosophy revolutionised the future thought of the human race." This habit of extrapolating from the known (Bacon's publications) to the unknown ("the future thought of the human race") is an old problem, from which Walter Ong was not exempt: see new chapter "After Ongism".

7   The word I'm looking for here is "insensibly," as used frequently by Edward Gibbon throughout *The Decline and Fall of the Roman Empire* to describe historical change that occurs slowly, beneath the threshold of conscious will; for instance where he writes how the "natives of [different parts of] Italy . . . *insensibly coalesced* into one great nation. . ." (1910: Vol 1, Ch II, p. 41).

8   Ong (1958: x) credited McLuhan with inspiring his interest in Ramus; and Farrell (Ong 2002: 12) claims that Ong's book prompted McLuhan to write *The Gutenberg Galaxy* (1962). Thus although Ong was formally McLuhan's MA student, their mutual influence was that of peers.

9   "In 1942 Miller resigned his post at Harvard to join the U.S. Army; he was stationed in Great Britain for the duration of the war, where he worked for the Office of Strategic Services. Miller may have been instrumental in creating the Psychological Warfare Branch of the O.S.S.; certainly he worked for the PWB for the duration of the war. (Precisely what he did and how he spent his time has never been disclosed; it may have been regarded in the postwar world by government officials as a matter of national security.) After 1945 Miller returned to teaching at Harvard." (*Wikipedia*: "Perry Miller".)

10   Harvard is only newsworthy when it *loses* the #1 spot. See, e.g.: www.bloomberg.com/news/2011–10–06/harvard-loses-top-world-ranking-to-caltech.html.

11   See: harvardbusiness.org/about.

12   Harbage clearly felt the need to press this point home for American readers, adding a foreword to the US edition of *As They Liked It*: "Shakespeare's audience was large and heterogeneous, drawn from

the general public, but a selective principle was at work. There were other theatres than the Globe, and other writers for the Globe itself. Shakespeare and his audience found each other, in a measure created each other. He was a quality writer for a quality audience. It is difficult to see how we can reach any other conclusion. The great Shakespearean discovery was that quality extended vertically through the social scale, not horizontally at the upper genteel, economic, and academic levels. ... To a greater extent than we are aware, Shakespeare and his audience created the humane climate of subsequent generations, including, one hopes, our own" (Harbage 1947; foreword to the 1961 US edition).

13   See xroads.virginia.edu/~hyper/whitman/vistas/vistas.html.
14   See: histsoc.stanford.edu/pdfmem/JonesRF.pdf; and: www. telegraph.co.uk/news/obituaries/1584760/Richard-D-Altick.html.
15   See also: www.shakespeareinamericanlife.org/identity/politicians/presidents/pick/jqadams.cfm; and note that Joseph Quincy Adams Jr., a scion of the Presidential family, was founding director of the Folger Shakespeare Library in Washington: www.folger.edu/template.cfm?cid=795.
16   See: www.julianjaynes.org/about-jaynes.php.
17   SLU still offers a master's program in "Communication Studies + Speech Communication & Rhetoric": "A program that focuses on the scientific, humanistic, and critical study of human communication in a variety of formats, media, and contexts. Includes instruction in the theory and practice of interpersonal, group, organizational, professional, and intercultural communication; speaking and listening; verbal and nonverbal interaction; rhetorical theory and criticism; performance studies; argumentation and persuasion; technologically mediated communication; popular culture; and various contextual applications" (www.universities.com/edu/Masters_degree_in_Communication_Studies_Speech_Communication_and_Rhetoric_at_Saint_Louis_University_Main_Campus.html).
18   Most notoriously perhaps in the "Kitchen Debate" between US Vice-President Nixon and Soviet Premier Khrushchev, in July 1959. See: watergate.info/nixon/1959_nixon-khrushchev-kitchen-debate.shtml.
19   See: http://xroads.virginia.edu/~hyper/whitman/vistas/vistas.html.
20   McLuhan was born in 1911, Ong in 1912.
21   A coinage associated with Jerry Rubin, Abbie Hoffman and the Yippies (Youth International Party): see for instance: www1.american.edu/bgriff/H207web/sixties/rubinchildofAmerika.htm.

22    McLuhan's axiom "the medium is the message" was used in *Mad Men*: see here for the clip: www.videohippy.com/video/5901/MAD-MEN-The-medium-is-the-message-106; and here for a discussion of its anachronistic placement in the series: www.nytimes.com/2010/07/25/magazine/25FOB-onlanguage-t.html; and here for a re-enactment of its emergence and uptake – as part of "Canadian heritage": www.youtube.com/watch?v=RtycdRBAbXk.

# ORALITY AND LITERACY

## Walter J. Ong

# ACKNOWLEDGEMENTS

Anthony C. Daly and Claude Pavur have been very generous in reading and commenting on drafts of this book, and the author wishes to thank them.

The author and publisher would like to thank the British Library for permission to reproduce Figure 1, the title page of Sir Thomas Elyot's *The Boke Named the Gouernour*.

# INTRODUCTION

In recent years certain basic differences have been discovered between the ways of managing knowledge and verbalization in primary oral cultures (cultures with no knowledge at all of writing) and in cultures deeply affected by the use of writing. The implications of the new discoveries have been startling. Many of the features we have taken for granted in thought and expression in literature, philosophy and science, and even in oral discourse among literates, are not directly native to human existence as such but have come into being because of the resources which the technology of writing makes available to human consciousness. We have had to revise our understanding of human identity.

The subject of this book is the differences between orality and literacy. Or, rather, since readers of this or any book by definition are acquainted with literate culture from the inside, the subject is, first, thought and its verbal expression in oral culture, which is strange and at times bizarre to us, and, second, literate thought and expression in terms of their emergence from and relation to orality.

The subject of this book is not any 'school' of interpretation. There is no 'school' of orality and literacy, nothing that would be the equivalent of Formalism or New Criticism or Structuralism or Deconstructionism, although awareness of the interrelationship of orality and literacy can affect what is done in these as well as various other 'schools' or 'movements' all through the humanities and social sciences. Knowledge of orality-literacy contrasts and relationships does not normally generate impassioned allegiances to theories but rather encourages reflection on aspects of the human condition far too numerous ever to be fully enumerated. This book will undertake to treat a reasonable number of those aspects. Exhaustive treatment would demand many volumes.

It is useful to approach orality and literacy synchronically, by comparing oral cultures and chirographic (i.e., writing) cultures that coexist at a given period of time. But it is absolutely essential to approach them also diachronically or historically, by comparing successive periods with one another. Human society first formed itself with the aid of oral speech, becoming literate very late in its history, and at first only in certain groups. *Homo sapiens* has been in existence for between 30,000 and 50,000 years. The earliest script dates from only 6000 years ago. Diachronic study of orality and literacy and of the various stages in the evolution from one to the other sets up a frame of reference in which it is possible to understand better not only pristine oral culture and subsequent writing culture, but also the print culture that brings writing to a new peak and the electronic culture which builds on both writing and print. In this diachronic framework, past and present, Homer and television, can illuminate one another.

But the illumination does not come easily. Understanding the relations of orality and literacy and the implications of the relations is not a matter of instant psychohistory or instant phenomenology. It calls for wide, even vast, learning, painstaking thought and careful statement. Not only are the issues deep and complex, but they also engage our own biases. We – readers of books such as this – are so literate that it is very difficult for us to conceive of an oral universe of communication or thought except as a variant of a literate universe. This book will attempt to overcome our biases in some degree and to open new ways to understanding.

It focuses on the relations between orality and writing. Literacy began with writing but, at a later stage of course, also involves print. This book thus attends somewhat to print as well as to writing. It also makes some passing mention of the electronic processing of the word and of thought, as on radio and television and via satellite. Our understanding of the differences between orality and literacy developed only in the electronic age, not earlier. Contrasts between electronic media and print have sensitized us to the earlier contrast between writing and orality. The electronic age is also an age of 'secondary orality', the orality of telephones, radio, and television, which depends on writing and print for its existence.

The shift from orality to literacy and on to electronic processing engages social, economic, political, religious and other structures. These, however, are only indirect concerns of the present book, which treats rather the differences in 'mentality' between oral and writing cultures.

Almost all the work thus far contrasting oral cultures and chirographic cultures has contrasted orality with alphabetic writing rather than with other writing systems (cuneiform, Chinese characters, the Japanese syllabary, Mayan script and so on) and has been concerned with the alphabet as used in the West (the alphabet is also at home in the East, as in India, Southeast Asia or Korea). Here discussion will follow the major lines of extant scholarship, although some attention will also be given, at relevant points, to scripts other than the alphabet and to cultures other than just those of the West.

W. J. O.
Saint Louis University

# 1

# THE ORALITY OF LANGUAGE

## THE LITERATE MIND AND THE ORAL PAST

In the past few decades the scholarly world has newly awakened to the oral character of language and to some of the deeper implications of the contrasts between orality and writing. Anthropologists and sociologists and psychologists have reported on fieldwork in oral societies. Cultural historians have delved more and more into prehistory, that is, human existence before writing made verbalized records possible. Ferdinand de Saussure (1857–1913), the father of modern linguistics, had called attention to the primacy of oral speech, which underpins all verbal communication, as well as to the persistent tendency, even among scholars, to think of writing as the basic form of language. Writing, he noted, has simultaneously 'usefulness, shortcomings and dangers' (1959, pp. 23–4). Still he thought of writing as a kind of complement to oral speech, not as a transformer of verbalization (Saussure 1959, pp. 23–4).

Since Saussure, linguistics has developed highly sophisticated studies of phonemics, the way language is nested in sound. Saussure's contemporary, the Englishman Henry Sweet (1845–1912), had early insisted that words are made up not of letters but of functional sound units or phonemes. But, for all their attention to the sounds of speech, modern schools of linguistics until very recently have attended only incidentally, if at all, to ways in which primary orality, the orality of cultures untouched by literacy, contrasts with literacy (Sampson 1980). Structuralists have analyzed oral tradition in detail, but for the most part without explicitly contrasting it with written compositions (Maranda and Maranda 1971). There is a sizable literature on differences between written and spoken language which compares the written and spoken language of persons who can read and write (Gumperz, Kaltmann and O'Connor 1982 or 1983, bibliography). These are not the differences that the present study is centrally concerned with. The orality centrally treated here is primary orality, that of persons totally unfamiliar with writing.

Recently, however, applied linguistics and sociolinguistics have been comparing more and more the dynamics of primary oral verbalization and those of written verbalization. Jack Goody's book, *The Domestication of the Savage Mind* (1977), and his earlier collection of his own and others' work, *Literacy in Traditional Societies* (1968), still provide invaluable descriptions and analyses of changes in mental and social structures incident to the use of writing. Chaytor very early (1945), Ong (1958b, 1967b), McLuhan (1962), Haugen (1966), Chafe (1982), Tannen (1980a) and others provide further linguistic and cultural data and analyses. Foley's expertly focused survey (1980b) includes an extensive bibliography.

The greatest awakening to the contrast between oral modes of thought and expression and written modes took place not in linguistics, descriptive or cultural, but in literary studies, beginning clearly with the work of Milman Parry (1902–35) on the text of the *Iliad* and the *Odyssey*, brought to completion after Parry's untimely death by Albert B. Lord, and supplemented by later work of Eric A. Havelock and others. Publications in applied linguistics and sociolinguistics dealing with orality literacy contrasts, theoretically or in fieldwork, regularly cite these and related works (Parry 1971; Lord 1960; Havelock 1963; McLuhan 1962; Okpewho 1979; etc.).

Before taking up Parry's discoveries in detail, it will be well to set the stage here by asking why the scholarly world had to reawaken to the oral character of language. It would seem inescapably obvious that language is an oral phenomenon. Human beings communicate in countless ways, making use of all their senses, touch, taste, smell, and especially sight, as well as hearing (Ong 1967b, pp. 1–9). Some non-oral communication is exceedingly rich – gesture, for example. Yet in a deep sense language, articulated sound, is paramount. Not only communication, but thought itself relates in an altogether special way to sound. We have all heard it said that one picture is worth a thousand words. Yet, if this statement is true, why does it have to be a saying? Because a picture is worth a thousand words only under special conditions – which commonly include a context of words in which the picture is set.

Wherever human beings exist they have a language, and in every instance a language that exists basically as spoken and heard, in the world of sound (Siertsema 1955). Despite the richness of gesture, elaborated sign languages are substitutes for speech and dependent on oral speech systems, even when used by the congenitally deaf (Kroeber 1972; Mallery 1972; Stokoe 1972). Indeed, language is so overwhelmingly oral that of all the many thousands of languages – possibly tens of thousands – spoken in the course of human history only around 106 have ever been committed to writing to a degree sufficient to have produced literature, and most have never been written at all. Of the some 3000 languages spoken that exist today only some 78 have a literature (Edmonson 1971, pp. 323, 332). There is as yet no way to calculate how many languages have disappeared or been transmuted into other languages before writing came along. Even now hundreds of languages in active use are never written at all: no one has worked out an effective way to write them. The basic orality of language is permanent.

We are not here concerned with so-called computer 'languages', which resemble human languages (English, Sanskrit, Malayalam, Mandarin Chinese, Twi or Shoshone etc.) in some ways but are forever totally unlike human languages in that they do not grow out of the unconscious but directly out of consciousness. Computer language rules ('grammar') are stated first and thereafter used. The 'rules' of grammar in natural human languages are used first and can be abstracted from usage and stated explicitly in words only with difficulty and never completely.

Writing, commitment of the word to space, enlarges the potentiality of language almost beyond measure, restructures thought, and in the process converts a certain few dialects into 'grapholects' (Haugen 1966; Hirsh 1977, pp. 43–8). A grapholect is a transdialectal language formed by deep commitment to writing. Writing gives a grapholect a power far exceeding that of any purely oral dialect. The grapholect known as standard English has accessible for use a recorded vocabulary of at least a million and a half words, of which not only the present meanings but also hundreds of thousands of past meanings are known. A simply oral dialect will commonly have resources of only a few thousand words, and its users will have virtually no knowledge of the real semantic history of any of these words.

But, in all the wonderful worlds that writing opens, the spoken word still resides and lives. Written texts all have to be related somehow, directly or indirectly, to the world of sound, the natural habitat of language, to yield their meanings. 'Reading' a text means converting it to sound, aloud or in the imagination, syllable-by-syllable in slow reading or sketchily in the rapid reading common to high-technology cultures. Writing can never dispense with orality. Adapting a term used for slightly different purposes by Jurij Lotman (1977, pp. 21, 48–61; see also Champagne 1977–8), we can style writing a 'secondary modeling system', dependent on a prior primary system, spoken language. Oral expression can exist and mostly has existed without any writing at all, writing never without orality.

Yet, despite the oral roots of all verbalization, the scientific and literary study of language and literature has for centuries, until quite recent years, shied away from orality. Texts have clamored for attention so peremptorily that oral creations have tended to be regarded generally as variants of written productions or, if not this, as beneath serious scholarly attention. Only relatively recently have we become impatient with our obtuseness here (Finnegan 1977, pp. 1–7).

Language study in all but recent decades has focused on written texts rather than on orality for a readily assignable reason: the relationship of study itself to writing. All thought, including that in primary oral cultures, is to some degree analytic: it breaks its materials into various components. But abstractly sequential, classificatory, explanatory examination of phenomena or of stated truths is impossible without writing and reading. Human beings in primary oral cultures, those untouched by writing in any form, learn a great deal and possess and practice great wisdom, but they do not 'study'.

They learn by apprenticeship – hunting with experienced hunters, for example – by discipleship, which is a kind of apprenticeship, by listening, by repeating what they hear, by mastering proverbs and ways of combining and recombining them, by assimilating other formulary materials, by participation in a kind of corporate retrospection – not by study in the strict sense.

When study in the strict sense of extended sequential analysis becomes possible with the interiorization of writing, one of the first things that literates often study is language itself and its uses. Speech is inseparable from our consciousness and it has fascinated human beings, elicited serious reflection about itself, from the very early stages of consciousness, long before writing came into existence. Proverbs from all over the world are rich with observations about this over-whelmingly human phenomenon of speech in its native oral form, about its powers, its beauties, its dangers. The same fascination with oral speech continues unabated for centuries after writing comes into use.

In the West among the ancient Greeks the fascination showed in the elaboration of the vast, meticulously worked-out art of rhetoric, the most comprehensive academic subject in all western culture for two thousand years. In its Greek original, *technē rhētorikē*, 'speech art' (commonly abridged to just *rhētorikē*) referred essentially to oral speaking, even though as a reflective, organized 'art' or science – for example, in Aristotle's *Art of Rhetoric* – rhetoric was and had to be a product of writing. *Rhētorikē*, or rhetoric, basically meant public speaking or oratory, which for centuries even in literate and typographic cultures remained unreflexively pretty much the paradigm of all discourse, including that of writing (Ong 1967b, pp. 58–63; Ong 1971, pp. 27–8). Thus writing from the beginning did not reduce orality but enhanced it, making it possible to organize the 'principles' or constituents of oratory into a scientific 'art', a sequentially ordered body of explanation that showed how and why oratory achieved and could be made to achieve its various specific effects.

But the speeches – or any other oral performances – that were studied as part of rhetoric could hardly be speeches as these were being orally delivered. After the speech was delivered, nothing of it remained to work over. What you used for 'study' had to be the text of speeches that had been written down – commonly after delivery and often long after (in antiquity it was not common practice for any but disgracefully incompetent orators to speak from a text prepared verbatim in advance – Ong 1967b, pp. 56–8). In this way, even orally composed speeches were studied not as speeches but as written texts.

Moreover, besides transcription of oral performances such as orations, writing eventually produced strictly written compositions, designed for assimilation directly from the written surface. Such written compositions enforced attention to texts even more, for truly written compositions came into being as texts only, even though many of them were commonly listened to rather than silently read, from Livy's histories to Dante's *Comedia* and beyond (Nelson 1976–7; Bäuml 1980; Goldin 1973; Cormier 1974; Ahern 1982).

## DID YOU SAY 'ORAL LITERATURE'?

The scholarly focus on texts had ideological consequences. With their attention directed to texts, scholars often went on to assume, often without reflection, that oral verbalization was essentially the same as the written verbalization they normally dealt with, and that oral art forms were to all intents and purposes simply texts, except for the fact that they were not written down. The impression grew that, apart from the oration (governed by written rhetorical rules), oral art forms were essentially unskillful and not worth serious study.

Not all, however, lived by these assumptions. From the mid-sixteenth century on, a sense of the complex relationships of writing and speech grew stronger (Cohen 1977). But the relentless dominance of textuality in the scholarly mind is shown by the fact that to this day no concepts have yet been formed for effectively, let alone gracefully, conceiving of oral art as such without reference, conscious or unconscious, to writing. This is so even though the oral art forms which developed during the tens of thousands of years before writing obviously had no connection with writing at all. We have the term 'literature', which essentially means 'writings' (Latin *literatura*, from *litera*, letter of the alphabet), to cover a given body of written materials – English literature, children's literature – but no comparably satisfactory term or concept to refer to a purely oral heritage, such as the traditional oral stories, proverbs, prayers, formulaic expressions (Chadwick 1932–40, *passim*), or other oral productions of, say, the Lakota Sioux in North America or the Mande in West Africa or of the Homeric Greeks.

As noted above, I style the orality of a culture totally untouched by any knowledge of writing or print, 'primary orality'. It is 'primary' by contrast with the 'secondary orality' of present-day high-technology culture, in which a new orality is sustained by telephone, radio, television, and other electronic devices that depend for their existence and functioning on writing and print. Today primary oral culture in the strict sense hardly exists, since every culture knows of writing and has some experience of its effects. Still, to varying degrees many cultures and subcultures, even in a high-technology ambiance, preserve much of the mind-set of primary orality.

The purely oral tradition or primary orality is not easy to conceive of accurately and meaningfully. Writing makes 'words' appear similar to things because we think of words as the visible marks signaling words to decoders: we can see and touch such inscribed 'words' in texts and books. Written words are residue. Oral tradition has no such residue or deposit. When an often-told oral story is not actually being told, all that exists of it is the potential in certain human beings to tell it. We (those who read texts such as this) are for the most part so resolutely literate that we seldom feel comfortable with a situation in which verbalization is so little thing-like as it is in oral tradition. As a result – though at a slightly reduced frequency now – scholarship in the past has generated such monstrous concepts as 'oral literature'. This strictly preposterous term remains in circulation today even among scholars now more and more acutely aware how embarrassingly it reveals our inability to represent to our own minds a heritage of verbally organized materials except as some variant of writing, even when they have nothing to do with writing at all. The title of the great Milman Parry Collection of Oral Literature at Harvard University monumentalizes the state of awareness of an earlier generation of scholars rather than that of its recent curators.

One might argue (as does Finnegan 1977, p. 16) that the term 'literature', though devised primarily for works in writing, has simply been extended to include related phenomena such as traditional oral narrative in cultures untouched by writing. Many originally specific terms have been so generalized in this way. But concepts have a way of carrying their etymologies with them forever. The elements out of which a term is originally built usually, and probably always, linger somehow in subsequent meanings, perhaps obscurely but often powerfully and even irreducibly. Writing, moreover, as will be seen later in detail, is a particularly pre-emptive and imperialist activity that tends to assimilate other things to itself even without the aid of etymologies.

Though words are grounded in oral speech, writing tyrannically locks them into a visual field forever. A literate person, asked to think of the word 'nevertheless', will normally (and I strongly suspect always) have some image, at least vague, of the spelled-out word and be quite unable ever to think of the word 'nevertheless' for, let us say, 60 seconds without adverting to any lettering but only to the sound. This is to say, a literate person cannot fully recover a sense of what the word is to purely oral people. In view of this pre-emptiveness of literacy, it appears quite impossible to use the term 'literature' to include oral tradition and performance without subtly but irremediably reducing these somehow to variants of writing.

Thinking of oral tradition or a heritage of oral performance, genres and styles as 'oral literature' is rather like thinking of horses as automobiles without wheels. You can, of course, undertake to do this. Imagine writing a treatise on horses (for people who have never seen a horse) which starts with the concept not of horse but of 'automobile', built on the readers' direct experience of automobiles. It proceeds to discourse on horses by always referring to them as 'wheelless automobiles', explaining to highly automobilized readers who have never seen a horse all the points of difference in an effort to excise all idea of 'automobile' out of the concept 'wheelless automobile' so as to invest the term with a purely equine meaning. Instead of wheels, the wheelless automobiles have enlarged toenails called hooves; instead of headlights or perhaps rear-vision mirrors, eyes; instead of a coat of lacquer, something called hair; instead of gasoline for fuel, hay, and so on. In the end, horses are only what they are not. No matter how accurate and thorough such apophatic description, automobile-driving readers who have never seen a horse and who hear only of 'wheelless automobiles' would be sure to come away with a strange concept of a horse. The same is true of those who deal in terms of 'oral literature', that is, 'oral writing'. You cannot without serious and disabling distortion describe a primary phenomenon by starting with a subsequent secondary phenomenon and paring away the differences. Indeed, starting backwards in this way – putting the car before the horse – you can never become aware of the real differences at all.

Although the term 'preliterate' itself is useful and at times necessary, if used unreflectively it also presents problems which are the same as those presented by the term 'oral literature', if not quite so assertive. 'Preliterate' presents orality – the 'primary modeling system' – as an anachronistic deviant from the 'secondary modeling system' that followed it.

In concert with the terms 'oral literature' and 'preliterate', we hear mention also of the 'text' of an oral utterance. 'Text', from a root meaning 'to weave', is, in absolute terms, more compatible etymologically with oral utterance than is 'literature', which refers to letters etymologically/(literae) of the alphabet. Oral discourse has commonly been thought of even in oral milieus as weaving or stitching – rhapsōidein, to 'rhapsodize', basically means in Greek 'to stitch songs together'. But in fact, when literates today use the term 'text' to refer to oral performance, they are thinking of it by analogy with writing. In the literate's vocabulary, the 'text' of a narrative by a person from a primary oral culture represents a back-formation: the horse as an automobile without wheels again.

Given the vast difference between speech and writing, what can be done to devise an alternative for the anachronistic and self-contradictory term 'oral literature'? Adapting a proposal made by Northrop Frye for epic poetry in The Anatomy of Criticism (1957, pp. 248–50, 293–303), we might refer to all purely oral art as 'epos', which has the same Proto-IndoEuropean root, wekw-, as the Latin word vox and its English equivalent 'voice', and thus is grounded firmly in the vocal, the oral. Oral performances would thus be felt as 'voicings', which is what they are. But the more usual meaning of the term epos, (oral) epic poetry (see Bynum 1967), would somewhat interfere with an assigned generic meaning referring to all oral creations. 'Voicings' seems to have too many competing associations, though if anyone thinks the term buoyant enough to launch, I will certainly aid efforts to keep it afloat. But we would still be without a more generic term to include both purely oral art and literature. Here I shall continue a practice common among informed persons and resort, as necessary, to self-explanatory circumlocutions – 'purely oral art forms', 'verbal art forms' (which would include both oral forms and those composed in writing, and everything in between), and the like.

At present the term 'oral literature' is, fortunately, losing ground, but it may well be that any battle to eliminate it totally will never be completely won. For most literates, to think of words as totally dissociated from writing is simply too arduous a task to undertake, even when specialized linguistic or anthropological work may demand it. The words keep coming to you in writing, no matter what you do. Moreover, to dissociate words from writing is psychologically threatening, for literates' sense of control over language is closely tied to the visual transformations of language: without dictionaries, written grammar rules, punctuation, and all the rest of the apparatus that makes words into something you can 'look' up, how can literates live? Literate users of a grapholect such as standard English have access to vocabularies hundreds of times larger than any oral language can manage. In such a linguistic world dictionaries are essential. It is demoralizing to remind oneself that there is no dictionary in the mind, that lexicographical apparatus is a very late accretion to language as language, that all languages have elaborate grammars and have developed their elaborations with no help from writing at all, and that outside of relatively high-technology cultures most users of languages have always got along pretty well without any visual transformations whatsoever of vocal sound.

Oral cultures indeed produce powerful and beautiful verbal performances of high artistic and human worth, which are no longer even possible once writing has taken possession of the psyche. Nevertheless, without writing, human consciousness cannot achieve its fuller potentials, cannot produce other beautiful and powerful creations. In this sense, orality needs to produce and is destined to produce writing. Literacy, as will be seen, is absolutely necessary for the development

not only of science but also of history, philosophy, explicative understanding of literature and of any art, and indeed for the explanation of
language (including oral speech) itself. There is hardly an oral culture
or a predominantly oral culture left in the world today that is not
somehow aware of the vast complex of powers forever inaccessible
without literacy. This awareness is agony for persons rooted in primary
orality, who want literacy passionately but who also know very well
that moving into the exciting world of literacy means leaving behind
much that is exciting and deeply loved in the earlier oral world. We
have to die to continue living.

Fortunately, literacy, though it consumes its own oral antecedents
and, unless it is carefully monitored, even destroys their memory, is
also infinitely adaptable. It can restore their memory, too. Literacy can
be used to reconstruct for ourselves the pristine human consciousness
which was not literate at all — at least to reconstruct this consciousness
pretty well, though not perfectly (we can never forget enough of our
familiar present to reconstitute in our minds any past in its full integrity). Such reconstruction can bring a better understanding of what
literacy itself has meant in shaping man's consciousness toward and in
high-technology cultures. Such understanding of both orality and
literacy is what this book, which is of necessity a literate work and not
an oral performance, attempts in some degree to achieve.

# 2

## THE MODERN DISCOVERY OF PRIMARY ORAL CULTURES

### EARLY AWARENESS OF ORAL TRADITION

The new awakening in recent years to the orality of speech was not without antecedents. Several centuries before Christ, the pseudonymous author of the Old Testament book that goes by his Hebrew *nom de plume*, Qoheleth ('assembly speaker'), or its Greek equivalent, Ecclesiastes, clearly adverts to the oral tradition on which his writing draws: 'Besides being wise, Qoheleth taught the people knowledge, and weighed, scrutinized, and arranged many proverbs. Qoheleth sought to find pleasing sayings, and to write down true sayings with precision' (Ecclesiastes 12:9–10).

'Write down . . . sayings.' Literate persons, from medieval florilegia collectors to Erasmus (1466–1536) or Vicesimus Knox (1752–1821) and beyond, have continued to put into texts sayings from oral tradition, though it is significant that at least from the Middle Ages and Erasmus' age, in western culture at least, most collectors culled the 'sayings' not directly from spoken utterance but from other writings. The Romantic Movement was marked by concern with the distant past and with folk culture. Since then, hundreds of collectors, beginning with James McPherson (1736–96) in Scotland, Thomas Percy

(1729–1811) in England, the Grimm brothers Jacob (1785–1863) and Wilhelm (1786–1859) in Germany, or Francis James Child (1825–96) in the United States, have worked over parts of oral or quasi-oral or near-oral tradition more or less directly, giving it new respectability. By the start of the twentieth century, the Scottish scholar Andrew Lang (1844–1912) and others had pretty well discredited the view that oral folklore was simply the left-over debris of a 'higher' literary mythology – a view generated quite naturally by the chirographic and typographic bias discussed in the preceding chapter.

Earlier linguists had resisted the idea of the distinctiveness of spoken and written languages. Despite his new insights into orality, or perhaps because of them, Saussure takes the view that writing simply represents spoken language in visible form (1959, pp. 23–4) as do Edward Sapir, C. Hockett and Leonard Bloomfield. The Prague Linguistic Circle, especially J. Vachek and Ernst Pulgram, noted some distinction between written and spoken language, although in concentrating on linguistic universals rather than developmental factors they made little use of this distinction (Goody 1977, p. 77).

## THE HOMERIC QUESTION

Given a long-standing awareness of oral tradition among literates and given Lang's and others' demonstration that purely oral cultures could generate sophisticated verbal art forms, what is new in our new understanding of orality?

The new understanding developed over various routes, but it can perhaps best be followed in the history of the 'Homeric question'. For over two millennia literates have devoted themselves to the study of Homer, with varying mixtures of insight, misinformation and prejudice, conscious and unconscious. Nowhere do the contrasts between orality and literacy or the blind spots of the unreflective chirographic or typographic mind show in a richer context.

The 'Homeric question' as such grew out of the nineteenth-century higher criticism of Homer which had matured together with the higher criticism of the Bible, but it had roots reaching back to classical antiquity. (See Adam Parry 1971, drawn on heavily here in the next few pages.) Men of letters in western classical antiquity had occasionally shown some awareness that the Iliad and the Odyssey differed from other Greek poetry and that their origins were obscure. Cicero suggested that the extant text of the two Homeric poems was a revision by Pisistratus of Homer's work (which Cicero thought of, however, as itself a text), and Josephus even suggested that Homer could not write, but he did so in order to argue that Hebrew culture was superior to very ancient Greek culture because it knew writing, rather than to account for anything about the style or other features in the Homeric works.

From the beginning, deep inhibitions have interfered with our seeing the Homeric poems for what they in fact are. The Iliad and the Odyssey have been commonly regarded from antiquity to the present as the most exemplary, the truest and the most inspired secular poems in the western heritage. To account for their received excellence, each age has been inclined to interpret them as doing better what it conceived its poets to be doing or aiming at. Even when the Romantic Movement had reinterpreted the 'primitive' as a good rather than a regrettable stage of culture, scholars and readers generally still tended to impute to primitive poetry qualities that their own age found fundamentally congenial. More than any earlier scholar, the American classicist Milman Parry (1902–35) succeeded in undercutting this cultural chauvinism so as to get into the 'primitive' Homeric poetry on this poetry's own terms, even when these ran counter to the received view of what poetry and poets ought to be.

Earlier work had vaguely adumbrated Parry's in that the general adulation of the Homeric poems had often been accompanied by some uneasiness. Often the poems were felt to be somehow out of line. In the seventeenth century François Hédelin, Abbé d'Aubignac et de Meimac (1604–76), in a spirit more of rhetorical polemic than of true learning, attacked the Iliad and the Odyssey as badly plotted, poor in characterization, and ethically and theologically despicable, going on to argue that there never had been a Homer and that the epics attributed to him were no more than collections of rhapsodies by others. The classical scholar Richard Bentley (1662–1742), famous for proving that the so-called Epistles of Phalaris were spurious and for indirectly occasioning Swift's antitypographic satire, The Battle of the Books, thought that there was indeed a man named Homer but that the various songs that he 'wrote' were not put together into the epic poems until about 500 years later in the time of Pisistratus. The Italian philosopher of history, Giambattista Vico (1668–1744),believed that there had been no Homer but that the Homeric epics were somehow the creations of a whole people.

Robert Wood (c. 1717–71), an English diplomat and archaeologist, who carefully identified some of the places referred to in the Iliad and the Odyssey, was apparently the first whose conjectures came close to what Parry finally demonstrated. Wood believed that Homer was not literate and that it was the power of memory that enabled him to produce this poetry. Wood strikingly suggests that memory played a quite different role in oral culture from that which it played in literate culture. Although Wood could not explain just how Homer's mnemonics worked, he does suggest that the ethos of Homeric verse was popular rather than learned. Jean Jacques Rousseau (1821, pp. 163–4), citing Père Hardouin (neither mentioned by Adam Parry) thought it most likely that Homer and his contemporaries among the Greeks had no writing. Rousseau does, however, see as a problem the message on a tablet which, in Book VI of the Iliad, Belerephon carried to the King of Lycia. But there is no evidence that the 'signs' on the tablet calling for Belerephon's own execution were in a true script (see below, pp. 83–5). In fact, in the Homeric account they sound like some sort of crude ideographs.

The nineteenth century saw the development of the Homeric theories of the so-called Analysts, initiated by Friedrich August Wolf (1759–1824), in his 1795 Prolegomena. The Analysts saw the texts of the Iliad and the Odyssey as combinations of earlier poems or fragments, and set out to determine by analysis what the bits were and how they had been layered together. But, as Adam Parry notes (1971, pp. xiv–xvii), the Analysts assumed that the bits being put together were simply texts, no alternative having suggested itself to their minds. Inevitably, the Analysts were succeeded in the early twentieth century by the Unitarians, often literary pietists, insecure cultists grasping at straws, who maintained that the Iliad and the Odyssey were so well structured, so consistent in characterization, and in general such high art that they could not be the work of an unorganized succession of redactors but must be the creation of one man. This was more or less the predominant opinion when Parry was a student and beginning to form his own opinions.

## MILMAN PARRY'S DISCOVERY

Like much trail-blazing intellectual work, Milman Parry's grew out of insights as deep and sure as they were difficult to make explicit. Parry's son, the late Adam Parry (1971, pp. ix–lxii), has beautifully traced the fascinating development of his father's thought, from his MA thesis at the University of California at Berkeley in the early 1920s till his untimely death in 1935.

Not every element in Parry's plenary vision was entirely new. The fundamental axiom governing his thought from the early 1920s on, 'the dependence of the choice of words and word-forms on the shape of the [orally composed] hexameter line' in the Homeric poems (Adam Parry 1971, p. xix), had been anticipated in the work of J. E. Ellendt and H. Düntzer. Other elements in Parry's germinal insight had also been anticipated. Arnold van Gennep had noted formulary structuring in poetry of oral cultures of the present age, and M. Murko had recognized the absence of exact verbatim memory in oral poetry of such cultures. More importantly, Marcel Jousse, the Jesuit priest and scholar, who had been reared in a residually oral peasant milieu in France and who spent most of his adult life in the Middle East soaking up its oral culture, had sharply differentiated the oral composition in such cultures from all written composition. Jousse (1925) had styled oral cultures and the personality structures they produced *verbomoteur* ('verbomotor' – regrettably, Jousse's work has not been translated into English; see Ong 1967b, pp. 30, 147–8, 335–6). Milman Parry's vision included and fused all these insights and others to provide a provable account of what Homeric poetry was and of how the conditions under which it was produced made it what it was.

Parry's vision, however, even where partly anticipated by these earlier scholars, was his own, for when it initially presented itself to him in the early 1920s, he apparently did not even know of the existence of any of these scholars just mentioned (Adam Parry 1971, p. xxii). Doubtless, of course, subtle influences in the air at the time that had influenced earlier scholars were also influencing him.

As matured and demonstrated in his Paris doctoral dissertation (Milman Parry 1928), Parry's discovery might be put this way: virtually every distinctive feature of Homeric poetry is due to the economy enforced on it by oral methods of composition. These can be reconstructed by careful study of the verse itself, once one puts aside the assumptions about expression and thought processes engrained in the psyche by generations of literate culture. This discovery was revolutionary in literary circles and would have tremendous repercussions elsewhere in cultural and psychic history.

What are some of the deeper implications of this discovery, and particularly of Parry's use of the axiom earlier noted, 'the dependence of the choice of words and word-forms on the shape of the hexameter line'? Düntzer had noted that the Homeric epithets used for wine are all metrically different and that the use of a given epithet was determined not by its precise meaning so much as by the metrical needs of the passage in which it turned up (Adam Parry 1971, p. xx). The appositeness of the Homeric epithet had been piously and grossly exaggerated. The oral poet had an abundant repertoire of epithets diversified enough to provide an epithet for any metrical exigency that might arise as he stitched his story together – differently at each telling, for, as will be seen, oral poets do not normally work from verbatim memorization of their verse.

Now, it is obvious that metrical needs in one way or another determine the selection of words by any poet composing in meter. But the general presumption had been that proper metrical terms somehow suggested themselves to the poetic imagination in a fluid and largely unpredictable way, correlated only with 'genius' (that is, with an ability essentially inexplicable). Poets, as idealized by chirographic cultures and even more by typographic cultures, were not expected to use prefabricated materials. If a poet did echo bits of earlier poems, he was expected to modulate these into his own 'kind of thing'. Certain practices, it is true, went against this presumption, notably the use of phrase books providing standard ways of saying things for those writing post-classical Latin poetry. Latin phrase books flourished, particularly after the invention of printing made compilations easily multipliable, and they continued to flourish far through the nineteenth century, when the *Gradus ad Parnassum* was much in use by schoolboys (Ong 1967b, pp.

85–6; 1971, pp. 77, 261–3; 1977, pp. 166, 178). The *Gradus* provided epithetic and other phrases from classical Latin poets, with the long and short syllables all conveniently marked for metrical fit, so that the aspirant poet could assemble a poem from the *Gradus* as boys might assemble a structure from an old Erector set or Meccano set or from a set of Tinker Toys. The over-all structure could be of his own making but the pieces were all there before he came along.

This kind of procedure, however, was viewed as tolerable only in beginners. The competent poet was supposed to generate his own metrically fitted phrases. Commonplace thought might be tolerated, but not commonplace language. In An *Essay on Criticism* (1711) Alexander Pope expected the poet's 'wit' to guarantee that when he treated 'what oft was thought' he did it in such a way that readers found it 'ne'er so well expressed'. The way of putting the accepted truth had to be original. Shortly after Pope, the Romantic Age demanded still more originality. For the extreme Romantic, the perfect poet should ideally be like God Himself, creating *ex nihilo*: the better he or she was, the less predictable was anything and everything in the poem. Only beginners or permanently poor poets used prefabricated stuff.

Homer, by the consensus of centuries, was no beginner poet, nor was he a poor poet. Perhaps he was even a congenital 'genius', who had never been through a fledgling stage at all but could fly the moment he was hatched – like the precocious Mwindo, the Nyanga epic hero, the 'Little-One-just-Born-He-Walked'. In any case, in the *Iliad* and the *Odyssey* Homer was normally taken to be fully accomplished, consummately skilled. Yet it now began to appear that he had had some kind of phrase book in his head. Careful study of the sort Milman Parry was doing showed that he repeated formula after formula. The meaning of the Greek term 'rhapsodize', *rhapsōidein*, 'to stitch song together' (*rhaptein*, to stitch; *ōide*, song), became ominous: Homer stitched together prefabricated parts. Instead of a creator, you had an assembly-line worker.

This idea was particularly threatening to far-gone literates. For literates are educated never to use clichés, in principle. How to live with the fact that the Homeric poems, more and more, appeared to be made up of clichés, or elements very like clichés? By and large, as Parry's work had proceeded and was carried forward by later scholars, it became evident that only a tiny fraction of the words in the *Iliad* and the *Odyssey* were not parts of formulas, and to a degree devastatingly predictable formulas.

Moreover, the standardized formulas were grouped around equally standardized themes, such as the council, the gathering of the army, the challenge, the despoiling of the vanquished, the hero's shield, and so on and on (Lord 1960, pp. 68–98). A repertoire of similar themes is found in oral narrative and other oral discourse around the world. (Written narrative and other written discourses use themes, too, of necessity, but the themes are infinitely more varied and less obtrusive.)

The entire language of the Homeric poems, with its curious mix of early and late Aeolic and Ionic peculiarities, was best explained not as an overlaying of several texts but as a language generated over the years by epic poets using old set expressions which they preserved and/or reworked largely for metrical purposes. After being shaped and reshaped centuries earlier, the two epics were set down in the new Greek alphabet around 700–650 BC, the first lengthy compositions to be put into this alphabet (Havelock 1963, p. 115). Their language was not a Greek that anyone had ever spoken in day-to-day life, but a Greek specially contoured through use of poets learning from one another generation after generation. (Traces of a comparable special language are familiar even today, for example, in the peculiar formulas still found in the English used for fairy tales.)

How could any poetry that was so unabashedly formulary, so constituted of prefabricated parts, still be so good? Milman Parry faced up squarely to this question. There was no use denying the now known fact that the Homeric poems valued and somehow made capital of what later readers had been trained in principle to disvalue, namely, the set phrase, the formula, the expected qualifier – to put it more bluntly, the cliché.

Certain of these wider implications remained to be worked out later in great detail by Eric A. Havelock (1963). Homeric Greeks valued clichés because not only the poets but the entire oral noetic world or thought world relied upon the formulaic constitution of thought. In an oral culture, knowledge, once acquired, had to be constantly repeated or it would be lost: fixed, formulaic thought patterns were essential for wisdom and effective administration. But, by Plato's day (427?–347

BC) a change had set in: the Greeks had at long last effectively interior-ized writing – something which took several centuries after the development of the Greek alphabet around 720–700 BC (Havelock 1963, p. 49, citing Rhys Carpenter). The new way to store knowledge was not in mnemonic formulas but in the written text. This freed the mind for more original, more abstract thought. Havelock shows that Plato excluded poets from his ideal republic essentially (if not quite consciously) because he found himself in a new chirographically styled noetic world in which the formula or cliché, beloved of all traditional poets, was outmoded and counterproductive.

All these are disturbing conclusions for a western culture that has identified closely with Homer as part of an idealized Greek antiquity. They show Homeric Greece cultivating as a poetic and noetic virtue what we have regarded as a vice, and they show that the relationship between Homeric Greece and everything that philosophy after Plato stood for was, however superficially cordial and continuous, in fact deeply antagonistic, if often at the unconscious rather than the conscious level. The conflict wracked Plato's own unconscious. For Plato expresses serious reservations in the *Phaedrus* and his *Seventh Letter* about writing, as a mechanical, inhuman way of processing knowledge, unresponsive to questions and destructive of memory, although, as we now know, the philosophical thinking Plato fought for depended entirely on writing. No wonder the implications here resisted surfacing for so long. The importance of ancient Greek civilization to all the world was beginning to show in an entirely new light: it marked the point in human history when deeply interiorized alphabetic literacy first clashed head-on with orality. And, despite Plato's uneasiness, at the time neither Plato nor anyone else was or could be explicitly aware that this was what was going on.

Parry's concept of the formula was worked out in the study of Greek hexameter verse. As others have dealt with the concept and developed it, various disputes have inevitably arisen as to how to contain or extend or adapt the definition (see Adam Parry 1971, p. xxviii, n. 1). One reason for this is that in Parry's concept there is a deeper stratum of meaning not immediately apparent from his definition of the formula, 'a group of words which is regularly employed under the same metrical conditions to express a given essential idea' (Adam Parry

1971, p. 272). This stratum has been explored most intensively by David E. Bynum in *The Daemon in the Wood* (1978, pp. 11–18, and *passim*). Bynum notes that 'Parry's "essential ideas" are seldom altogether so simple as the shortness of Parry's definition or the usual brevity of formulas themselves, the conventionality of the epic style, or the banality of most formulas' lexical reference may suggest' (1978, p. 13). Bynum distinguishes between 'formulaic' elements and 'strictly formulary (exactly repeated) phrases' (cf. Adam Parry 1971, p. xxxiii, n. 1). Although these latter mark oral poetry (Lord 1960, pp. 33–65), in such poetry they occur and recur in clusters (in one of Bynum's instances, for example, *high trees* attend the *commotion of a terrific warrior's approach* – 1978, p. 18). The clusters constitute the organizing principles of the formulas, so that the 'essential idea' is not subject to clear, straightforward formulation but is rather a kind of fictional complex held together largely in the unconscious.

Bynum's impressive book focuses in great part around the elemental fiction which he styles the Two Tree pattern and which he identifies in oral narrative and associated iconography around the world from Mesopotamian and Mediterranean antiquity through oral narrative in modern Yugoslavia, Central Africa, and elsewhere. Throughout, 'the notions of separation, gratuity, and an unpredictable danger' cluster around one tree (the green tree) and 'the ideas of unification, recompense, reciprocity' cluster about the other (the dry tree, hewn wood) – 1978, p. 145. Bynum's attention to this and other distinctively oral 'elemental fiction' helps us to make some clearer distinctions between oral narrative organization and chirographic-typographic narrative organization than have previously been possible.

Such distinctions will be attended to in this book on grounds different from but neighboring on Bynum's. Foley (1980a) has shown that exactly what an oral formula is and how it works depends on the tradition in which it is used, but that there is ample common ground in all traditions to make the concept valid. Unless it is clearly indicated otherwise, I shall understand formula and formulary and formulaic here as referring quite generically to more or less exactly repeated set phrases or set expressions (such as proverbs) in verse or prose, which, as will be seen, do have a function in oral culture more crucial and pervasive than any they may have in a writing or print or electronic culture. (Cf. Adam Parry 1971, p. xxxiii, n. 1.)

Oral formulaic thought and expression ride deep in consciousness and the unconscious, and they do not vanish as soon as one used to them takes pen in hand. Finnegan (1977, p. 70) reports, with apparently some surprise, Opland's observation that when Xhosa poets learn to write, their written poetry is also characterized by a formulaic style. It would in fact be utterly surprising if they could manage any other style, especially since formulaic style marks not poetry alone but, more or less, all thought and expression in primary oral culture. Early written poetry everywhere, it seems, is at first necessarily a mimicking in script of oral performance. The mind has initially no properly chirographic resources. You scratch out on a surface words you imagine yourself saying aloud in some realizable oral setting. Only very gradually does writing become composition in writing, a kind of discourse – poetic or otherwise – that is put together without a feeling that the one writing is actually speaking aloud (as early writers may well have done in composing). As noted later here, Clanchy reports how even the eleventh-century Eadmer of Canterbury seems to think of composing in writing as 'dictating to himself' (1979, p. 218). Oral habits of thought and expression, including massive use of formulaic elements, sustained in use largely by the teaching of the old classical rhetoric, still marked prose style of almost every sort in Tudor England some two thousand years after Plato's campaign against oral poets (Ong 1971, pp. 23–47). They were effectively obliterated in English, for the most part, only with the Romantic Movement two centuries later. Many modern cultures that have known writing for centuries but have never fully interiorized it, such as Arabic culture and certain other Mediterranean cultures (e.g. Greek – Tannen 1980a), rely heavily on formulaic thought and expression still. Kahlil Gibran has made a career of providing oral formulary products in print to literate Americans who find novel the proverb-like utterances that, according to a Lebanese friend of mine, citizens of Beirut regard as commonplace.

## CONSEQUENT AND RELATED WORK

Many of Milman Parry's conclusions and emphases have of course been somewhat modified by subsequent scholarship (see, for example, Stoltz and Shannon 1976), but his central message about orality and its implications for poetic structures and for aesthetics has revolutionized for good Homeric studies and other studies as well, from anthropology to literary history. Adam Parry (1971, pp. xliv-lxxx) has described some of the immediate effects of the revolution which his father wrought. Holoka (1973) and Haymes (1973) have recorded many others in their invaluable bibliographical surveys. Although Parry's work has been attacked and revised in some of its details, the few totally unreceptive reactions to his work have mostly by now simply been put aside as products of the unreflective chirographic-typographic mentality which at first blocked any real comprehension of what Parry was saying and which his work itself has now rendered obsolete.

Scholars are still elaborating and qualifying the fuller implications of Parry's discoveries and insights. Whitman (1958) early supplemented it with his ambitious outline of the *Iliad* as structured by the formulaic tendency to repeat at the end of an episode elements from the episode's beginning; the epic is built like a Chinese puzzle, boxes within boxes, according to Whitman's analysis. For understanding orality as contrasted with literacy, however, the most significant developments following upon Parry have been worked out by Albert B. Lord and Eric A. Havelock. In *The Singer of Tales* (1960), Lord carried through and extended Parry's work with convincing finesse, reporting on lengthy field trips and massive taping of oral performances by Serbo-Croatian epic singers and of lengthy interviews with these singers. Earlier, Francis Magoun and those who studied with him and Lord at Harvard, notably Robert Creed and Jess Bessinger, were already applying Parry's ideas to the study of Old English poetry (Foley 1980b, p. 490).

Havelock's *Preface to Plato* (1963) has extended Parry's and Lord's findings about orality in oral epic narrative out into the whole of ancient oral Greek culture and has shown convincingly how the beginnings of Greek philosophy were tied in with the restructuring of thought brought about by writing. Plato's exclusion of poets from his

Republic was in fact Plato's rejection of the pristine aggregative, para-
tactic, oral-style thinking perpetuated in Homer in favor of the keen
analysis or dissection of the world and of thought itself made possible
by the interiorization of the alphabet in the Greek psyche. In a subsequent work, Origins of Western Literacy (1976), Havelock attributes the
ascendency of Greek analytic thought to the Greeks' introduction of
vowels into the alphabet. The original alphabet, invented by Semitic
peoples, had consisted only of consonants and some semivowels. In
introducing vowels, the Greeks reached a new level of abstract, analytic,
visual coding of the elusive world of sound. This achievement presaged
and implemented their later abstract intellectual achievements.

The line of work initiated by Parry has yet to be joined to work in
the many fields with which it can readily connect. But a few important
connections have already been made. For example, in his magisterial
and judicious work on The Epic in Africa (1979), Isidore Okpewho brings
Parry's insights and analyses (in this case as elaborated in Lord's work)
to bear on the oral art forms of cultures quite different from the European, so that the African epic and the ancient Greek epic throw reciprocal light on one another. Joseph C. Miller (1980) treats African oral
tradition and history. Eugene Eoyang (1977) has shown how neglect
of the psychodynamics of orality has led to misconceptions about early
Chinese narrative, and other authors collected by Plaks (1977) have
examined formulary antecedents to literary Chinese narrative. Zwettler
has dealt with Classical Arabic poetry (1977). Bruce Rosenberg (1970)
has studied the survival of the old orality in American folk preachers. In
a festschrift in honor of Lord, John Miles Foley (1981) has collected
new studies on orality from the Balkans to Nigeria and New Mexico
and from antiquity to the present. And other specialized work is now
appearing.

Anthropologists have gone more directly into the matter of orality.
Drawing not only on Parry and Lord and Havelock but also on others'
work, including early work of my own on the effect of print on
sixteenth-century thought processes (Ong 1958b – cited by Goody
from a 1974 reprinting), Jack Goody (1977) has convincingly shown
how shifts hitherto labeled as shifts from magic to science, or from the
so-called 'prelogical' to the more and more 'rational' state of consciousness, or from Lévi-Strauss's 'savage' mind to domesticated

thought, can be more economically and cogently explained as shifts from orality to various stages of literacy. I had earlier suggested (1967b, p. 189) that many of the contrasts often made between 'western' and other views seem reducible to contrasts between deeply interiorized literacy and more or less residually oral states of consciousness. The late Marshall McLuhan's well-known work (1962, 1964) has also made much of ear-eye, oral-textual contrasts, calling attention to James Joyce's precociously acute awareness of ear-eye polarities and relating to such polarities a great amount of otherwise quite disparate scholarly work brought together by McLuhan's vast eclectic learning and his startling insights. McLuhan attracted the attention not only of scholars (Eisenstein 1979, pp. x–xi, xvii) but also of people working in the mass media, of business leaders, and of the generally informed public, largely because of fascination with his many gnomic or oracular pronouncements, too glib for some readers but often deeply perceptive. These he called 'probes'. He generally moved rapidly from one 'probe' to another, seldom if ever undertaking any thorough explanation of a 'linear' (that is, analytic) sort. His cardinal gnomic saying, 'The medium is the message', registered his acute awareness of the importance of the shift from orality through literacy and print to electronic media. Few people have had so stimulating an effect as Marshall McLuhan on so many diverse minds, including those who disagreed with him or believed they did.

However, if attention to sophisticated orality-literacy contrasts is growing in some circles, it is still relatively rare in many fields where it could be helpful. For example, the early and late stages of consciousness which Julian Jaynes (1977) describes and relates to neurophysiological changes in the bicameral mind would also appear to lend themselves largely to much simpler and more verifiable description in terms of a shift from orality to literacy. Jaynes discerns a primitive stage of consciousness in which the brain was strongly 'bicameral', with the right hemisphere producing uncontrollable 'voices' attributed to the gods which the left hemisphere processed into speech. The 'voices' began to lose their effectiveness between 2000 and 1000 BC. This period, it will be noted, is neatly bisected by the invention of the alphabet around 1500 BC, and Jaynes indeed believes that writing helped bring about the breakdown of the original bicamerality. The

*Iliad* provides him with examples of bicamerality in its unselfconscious characters. Jaynes dates the *Odyssey* a hundred years later than the *Iliad* and believes that wily Odysseus marks a breakthrough into the modern self-conscious mind, no longer under the rule of the 'voices'. Whatever one makes of Jaynes's theories, one cannot but be struck by the resemblance between the characteristics of the early or 'bicameral' psyche as Jaynes describes it − lack of introspectivity, of analytic prowess, of concern with the will as such, of a sense of difference between past and future − and the characteristics of the psyche in oral cultures not only in the past but even today. The effects of oral states of consciousness are bizarre to the literate mind, and they can invite elaborate explanations which may turn out to be needless. Bicamerality may mean simply orality. The question of orality and bicamerality perhaps needs further investigation.

# 3

## SOME PSYCHODYNAMICS OF ORALITY

### SOUNDED WORD AS POWER AND ACTION

As a result of the work just reviewed, and of other work which will be cited, it is possible to generalize somewhat about the psychodynamics of primary oral cultures, that is, of oral cultures untouched by writing. For brevity, when the context keeps the meaning clear, I shall refer to primary oral cultures simply as oral cultures.

Fully literate persons can only with great difficulty imagine what a primary oral culture is like, that is, a culture with no knowledge whatsoever of writing or even of the possibility of writing. Try to imagine a culture where no one has ever 'looked up' anything. In a primary oral culture, the expression 'to look up something' is an empty phrase: it would have no conceivable meaning. Without writing, words as such have no visual presence, even when the objects they represent are visual. They are sounds. You might 'call' them back – 'recall' them. But there is nowhere to 'look' for them. They have no focus and no trace (a visual metaphor, showing dependency on writing), not even a trajectory. They are occurrences, events.

To learn what a primary oral culture is and what the nature of our problem is regarding such a culture, it helps first to reflect on the nature of sound itself as sound (Ong 1967b, pp. 111–38). All sensation takes place in time, but sound has a special relationship to time unlike that of the other fields that register in human sensation. Sound exists only when it is going out of existence. It is not simply perishable but essentially evanescent, and it is sensed as evanescent. When I pronounce the word 'permanence', by the time I get to the '-pence', the 'perma-' is gone, and has to be gone.

There is no way to stop sound and have sound. I can stop a moving picture camera and hold one frame fixed on the screen. If I stop the movement of sound, I have nothing – only silence, no sound at all. All sensation takes place in time, but no other sensory field totally resists a holding action, stabilization, in quite this way. Vision can register motion, but it can also register immobility. Indeed, it favors immobility, for to examine something closely by vision, we prefer to have it quiet. We often reduce motion to a series of still shots the better to see what motion is. There is no equivalent of a still shot for sound. An oscillogram is silent. It lies outside the sound world.

For anyone who has a sense of what words are in a primary oral culture, or a culture not far removed from primary orality, it is not surprising that the Hebrew term *dabar* means 'word' and 'event'. Malinowski (1923, pp. 45 1, 470-81) has made the point that among 'primitive' (oral) peoples generally language is a mode of action and not simply a countersign of thought, though he had trouble explaining what he was getting at (Sampson 1980, pp. 223–6), since understanding of the psychodynamics of orality was virtually nonexistent in 1923. Neither is it surprising that oral peoples commonly, and probably universally, consider words to have great power. Sound cannot be sounding without the use of power. A hunter can see a buffalo, smell, taste, and touch a buffalo when the buffalo is completely inert, even dead, but if he hears a buffalo, he had better watch out: something is going on. In this sense, all sound, and especially oral utterance, which comes from inside living organisms, is 'dynamic'.

The fact that oral peoples commonly and in all likelihood universally consider words to have magical potency is clearly tied in, at least unconsciously, with their sense of the word as necessarily spoken, sounded, and hence power-driven. Deeply typographic folk forget to think of words as primarily oral, as events, and hence as necessarily powered: for them, words tend rather to be assimilated to things, 'out there' on a flat surface. Such 'things' are not so readily associated with magic, for they are not actions, but are in a radical sense dead, though subject to dynamic resurrection (Ong 1977, pp. 230–71).

Oral peoples commonly think of names (one kind of words) as conveying power over things. Explanations of Adam's naming of the animals in Genesis 2:20 usually call condescending attention to this presumably quaint archaic belief. Such a belief is in fact far less quaint than it seems to unreflective chirographic and typographic folk. First of all, names do give human beings power over what they name: without learning a vast store of names, one is simply powerless to understand, for example, chemistry and to practice chemical engineering. And so with all other intellectual knowledge. Secondly, chirographic and typographic folk tend to think of names as labels, written or printed tags imaginatively affixed to an object named. Oral folk have no sense of a name as a tag, for they have no idea of a name as something that can be seen. Written or printed representations of words can be labels; real, spoken words cannot be.

## YOU KNOW WHAT YOU CAN RECALL: MNEMONICS AND FORMULAS

In an oral culture, restriction of words to sound determines not only modes of expression but also thought processes.

You know what you can recall. When we say we know Euclidean geometry, we mean not that we have in mind at the moment every one of its propositions and proofs but rather that we can bring them to mind readily. We can recall them. The theorem 'You know what you can recall' applies also to an oral culture. But how do persons in an oral culture recall? The organized knowledge that literates today study so that they 'know' it, that is, can recall it, has, with very few if any exceptions, been assembled and made available to them in writing. This is the case not only with Euclidean geometry but also with American Revolutionary history, or even baseball batting averages or traffic regulations.

An oral culture has no texts. How does it get together organized material for recall? This is the same as asking, 'What does it or can it know in an organized fashion?'

Suppose a person in an oral culture would undertake to think through a particular complex problem and would finally manage to articulate a solution which itself is relatively complex, consisting, let us say, of a few hundred words. How does he or she retain for later recall the verbalization so painstakingly elaborated? In the total absence of any writing, there is nothing outside the thinker, no text, to enable him or her to produce the same line of thought again or even to verify whether he or she has done so or not. *Aides-mémoire* such as notched sticks or a series of carefully arranged objects will not of themselves retrieve a complicated series of assertions. How, in fact, could a lengthy, analytic solution ever be assembled in the first place? An inter-locutor is virtually essential: it is hard to talk to yourself for hours on end. Sustained thought in an oral culture is tied to communication.

But even with a listener to stimulate and ground your thought, the bits and pieces of your thought cannot be preserved in jotted notes. How could you ever call back to mind what you had so laboriously worked out? The only answer is: Think memorable thoughts. In a primary oral culture, to solve effectively the problem of retaining and retrieving carefully articulated thought, you have to do your thinking in mnemonic patterns, shaped for ready oral recurrence. Your thought must come into being in heavily rhythmic, balanced patterns, in repeti-tions or antitheses, in alliterations and assonances, in epithetic and other formulary expressions, in standard thematic settings (the assembly, the meal, the duel, the hero's 'helper', and so on), in prov-erbs which are constantly heard by everyone so that they come to mind readily and which themselves are patterned for retention and ready recall, or in other mnemonic form. Serious thought is intertwined with memory systems. Mnemonic needs determine even syntax (Havelock 1963, pp. 87–96, 131–2, 294–6).

Protracted orally based thought, even when not in formal verse, tends to be highly rhythmic, for rhythm aids recall, even physiologic-ally. Jousse (1978) has shown the intimate linkage between rhythmic oral patterns, the breathing process, gesture, and the bilateral sym-metry of the human body in ancient Aramaic and Hellenic targums, and thus also in ancient Hebrew. Among the ancient Greeks, Hesiod, who was intermediate between oral Homeric Greece and fully developed Greek literacy, delivered quasi-philosophic material in the formulaic verse forms that structured it into the oral culture from which he had emerged (Havelock 1963, pp. 97–8, 294–301).

Formulas help implement rhythmic discourse and also act as mnemonic aids in their own right, as set expressions circulating through the mouths and ears of all. 'Red in the morning, the sailor's warning; red in the night, the sailor's delight.' 'Divide and conquer.' 'To err is human, to forgive is divine.' 'Sorrow is better than laughter, because when the face is sad the heart grows wiser' (Ecclesiastes 7:3). 'The clinging vine.' 'The sturdy oak.' 'Chase off nature and she returns at a gallop.' Fixed, often rhythmically balanced, expressions of this sort and of other sorts can be found occasionally in print, indeed can be 'looked up' in books of sayings, but in oral cultures they are not occasional. They are incessant. They form the substance of thought itself. Thought in any extended form is impossible without them, for it consists in them.

The more sophisticated orally patterned thought is, the more it is likely to be marked by set expressions skillfully used. This is true of oral cultures generally from those of Homeric Greece to those of the present day across the globe. Havelock's *Preface to Plato* (1963) and fictional works such as Chinua Achebe's novel *No Longer at Ease* (1961), which draws directly on Ibo oral tradition in West Africa, alike provide abundant instances of thought patterns of orally educated characters who move in these oral, mnemonically tooled grooves, as the speakers reflect, with high intelligence and sophistication, on the situations in which they find themselves involved. The law itself in oral cultures is enshrined in formulaic sayings, proverbs, which are not mere jurisprudential decorations, but themselves constitute the law. A judge in an oral culture is often called on to articulate sets of relevant proverbs out of which he can produce equitable decisions in the cases under formal litigation before him (Ong 1978, p. 5)

In an oral culture, to think through something in nonformulaic, non-patterned, non-mnemonic terms, even if it were possible, would be a waste of time, for such thought, once worked through, could never be recovered with any effectiveness, as it could be with the aid of writing. It would not be abiding knowledge but simply a passing thought, however complex. Heavy patterning and communal fixed formulas in oral cultures serve some of the purposes of writing in chirographic cultures, but in doing so they of course determine the kind of thinking that can be done, the way experience is intellectually organized. In an oral culture, experience is intellectualized mnemonically. This is one reason why, for a St Augustine of Hippo (AD 354–430), as for other savants living in a culture that knew some literacy but still carried an overwhelmingly massive oral residue, memory bulks so large when he treats of the powers of the mind.

Of course, all expression and all thought is to a degree formulaic in the sense that every word and every concept conveyed in a word is a kind of formula, a fixed way of processing the data of experience, determining the way experience and reflection are intellectually organized, and acting as a mnemonic device of sorts. Putting experience into any words (which means transforming it at least a little bit – not the same as falsifying it) can implement its recall. The formulas characterizing orality are more elaborate, however, than are individual words, though some may be relatively simple: the *Beowulf*-poet's 'whale-road' is a formula (metaphorical) for the sea in a sense in which the term 'sea' is not.

## FURTHER CHARACTERISTICS OF ORALLY BASED THOUGHT AND EXPRESSION

Awareness of the mnemonic base of the thought and expression in primary oral cultures opens the way to understanding some further characteristics of orally based thought and expression in addition to their formulaic styling. The characteristics treated here are some of those which set off orally based thought and expression from chirographically and typographically based thought and expression, the characteristics, that is, which are most likely to strike those reared in writing and print cultures as surprising. This inventory of characteristics is not presented as exclusive or conclusive but as suggestive, for much more work and reflection are needed to deepen understanding of orally based thought (and thereby understanding of chirographically based, typographically based, and electronically based thought).

In a primary oral culture, thought and expression tend to be of the following sorts.

## (i)  Additive rather than subordinative

A familiar instance of additive oral style is the creation narrative in Genesis 1:1–5, which is indeed a text but one preserving recognizable oral patterning. The Douay version (1610), produced in a culture with a still massive oral residue, keeps close in many ways to the additive Hebrew original (as mediated through the Latin from which the Douay version was made):

> In the beginning God created heaven and earth. And the earth was void and empty, and darkness was upon the face of the deep; and the spirit of God moved over the waters. And God said: Be light made. And light was made. And God saw the light that it was good; and he divided the light from the darkness. And he called the light Day, and the darkness Night; and there was evening and morning one day.

Nine introductory 'ands'. Adjusted to sensibilities shaped more by writing and print, the New American Bible (1970) translates:

> In the beginning, when God created the heavens and the earth, the earth was a formless wasteland, and darkness covered the abyss, while a mighty wind swept over the waters. Then God said, 'Let there be light', and there was light. God saw how good the light was. God then separated the light from the darkness. God called the light 'day' and the darkness he called 'night'. Thus evening came, and morning followed – the first day.

Two introductory 'ands', each submerged in a compound sentence. The Douay renders the Hebrew we or wa ('and') simply as 'and'. The New American renders it 'and', 'when', 'then', 'thus', or 'while', to provide a flow of narration with the analytic, reasoned subordination that characterizes writing (Chafe 1982) and that appears more natural in twentieth-century texts. Oral structures often look to pragmatics (the convenience of the speaker – Sherzer, 1974, reports lengthy public oral performances among the Cuna incomprehensible to their hearers). Chirographic structures look more to syntactics (organization of the discourse itself), as Givón has suggested (1979). Written discourse develops more elaborate and fixed grammar than oral discourse does because to provide meaning it is more dependent simply upon linguistic structure, since it lacks the normal full existential contexts which surround oral discourse and help determine meaning in oral discourse somewhat independently of grammar.

It would be a mistake to think that the Douay is simply 'closer' to the original today than the New American is. It is closer in that it renders *we* or *wa* always by the same word, but it strikes the present-day sensibility as remote, archaic, and even quaint. Peoples in oral cultures or cultures with high oral residue, including the culture that produced the Bible, do not savor this sort of expression as so archaic or quaint. It feels natural and normal to them somewhat as the New American version feels natural and normal to us.

Other instances of additive structure can be found across the world in primary oral narrative, of which we now have a massive supply on tape (see Foley, 1980b, for listing of some tapes).

## (ii) Aggregative rather than analytic

This characteristic is closely tied to reliance on formulas to implement memory. The elements of orally based thought and expression tend to be not so much simple integers as clusters of integers, such as parallel terms or phrases or clauses, antithetical terms or phrases or clauses, epithets. Oral folk prefer, especially in formal discourse, not the soldier, but the brave soldier; not the princess, but the beautiful princess; not the oak, but the sturdy oak. Oral expression thus carries a load of epithets and other formulary baggage which high literacy rejects as cumbersome and tiresomely redundant because of its aggregative weight (Ong 1977, pp. 188–212).

The clichés in political denunciations in many low-technology, developing cultures – enemy of the people, capitalist war-mongers – that strike high literates as mindless are residual formulary essentials of oral thought processes. One of the many indications of a high, if subsiding, oral residue in the culture of the Soviet Union is (or was a few years ago, when I encountered it) the insistence on speaking there always of 'the Glorious Revolution of October 26' – the epithetic formula here is obligatory stabilization, as were Homeric epithetic formulas 'wise Nestor' or 'clever Odysseus', or as 'the glorious Fourth of July' used to be in the pockets of oral residue common even in the early twentieth-century United States. The former Soviet Union still announced each year the official epithets for various *loci classici* in Soviet history.

An oral culture may well ask in a riddle why oaks are sturdy, but it does so to assure you that they are, to keep the aggregate intact, not really to question or cast doubt on the attribution. (For examples directly from the oral culture of the Luba in Zaire, see Faik-Nzuji 1970.) Traditional expressions in oral cultures must not be dismantled: it has been hard work getting them together over the generations, and there is nowhere outside the mind to store them. So soldiers are brave and princesses beautiful and oaks sturdy forever. This is not to say that there may not be other epithets for soldiers or princesses or oaks, even contrary epithets, but these are standard, too: the braggart soldier, the unhappy princess, can also be part of the equipment. What obtains for epithets obtains for other formulas. Once a formulary expression has crystallized, it had best be kept intact. Without a writing system, breaking up thought – that is, analysis – is a high-risk procedure. As Lévi-Strauss has well put it in a summary statement 'the savage [i.e. oral] mind totalizes' (1966, p. 245).

### (iii) Redundant or 'copious'

Thought requires some sort of continuity. Writing establishes in the text a 'line' of continuity outside the mind. If distraction confuses or obliterates from the mind the context out of which emerges the material I am now reading, the context can be retrieved by glancing back over the text selectively. Backlooping can be entirely occasional, purely *ad hoc*. The mind concentrates its own energies on moving ahead because what it backloops into lies quiescent outside itself, always available piecemeal on the inscribed page. In oral discourse, the situation is different. There is nothing to backloop into outside the mind, for the oral utterance has vanished as soon as it is uttered. Hence the mind must move ahead more slowly, keeping close to the focus of attention much of what it has already dealt with. Redundancy, repetition of the just-said, keeps both speaker and hearer surely on the track.

Since redundancy characterizes oral thought and speech, it is in a profound sense more natural to thought and speech than is sparse linearity. Sparsely linear or analytic thought and speech are artificial creations, structured by the technology of writing. Eliminating redundancy on a significant scale demands a time-obviating technology, writing, which imposes some kind of strain on the psyche in preventing expression from falling into its more natural patterns. The psyche can manage the strain in part because handwriting is physically such a slow process – typically about one-tenth of the speed of oral speech (Chafe 1982). With writing, the mind is forced into a slowed-down pattern that affords it the opportunity to interfere with and reorganize its more normal, redundant processes.

Redundancy is also favored by the physical conditions of oral expression before a large audience, where redundancy is in fact more marked than in most face-to-face conversation. Not everyone in a large audience understands every word a speaker utters, if only because of acoustical problems. It is advantageous for the speaker to say the same thing, or equivalently the same thing, two or three times. If you miss the 'not only . . . 'you can supply it by inference from the 'but also . . .'. Until electronic amplification reduced acoustical problems to a minimum, public speakers as late as, for example, William Jennings Bryan (1860–1925) continued the old redundancy in their public addresses and by force of habit let them spill over into their writing. In some kinds of acoustic surrogates for oral verbal communication, redundancy reaches fantastic dimensions, as in African drum talk. It takes on the average around eight times as many words to say something on the drums as in the spoken language (Ong 1977, p. 101).

The public speaker's need to keep going while he is running through his mind what to say next also encourages redundancy. In oral delivery, though a pause may be effective, hesitation is always disabling. Hence it is better to repeat something, artfully if possible, rather than simply to stop speaking while fishing for the next idea. Oral cultures encourage fluency, fulsomeness, volubility. Rhetoricians were to call this *copia*. They continued to encourage it, by a kind of oversight, when they had modulated rhetoric from an art of public speaking to an art of writing. Early written texts, through the Middle Ages and the Renaissance, are often bloated with 'amplification', annoyingly redundant by modern standards. Concern with *copia* remains intense in western culture so long as the culture sustains massive oral residue – which is roughly until the age of Romanticism or even beyond. Thomas Babington Macaulay (1800–59) is one of the many fulsome early Victorians whose pleonastic written compositions still read much as an exuberant, orally composed oration would sound, as do also, very often, the writings of Winston Churchill (1874–1965).

## (iv) Conservative or traditionalist

Since in a primary oral culture conceptualized knowledge that is not repeated aloud soon vanishes, oral societies must invest great energy in saying over and over again what has been learned arduously over the ages. This need establishes a highly traditionalist or conservative set of mind that with good reason inhibits intellectual experimentation. Knowledge is hard to come by and precious, and society regards highly those wise old men and women who specialize in conserving it, who know and can tell the stories of the days of old. By storing knowledge outside the mind, writing and, even more, print downgrade the figures of the wise old man and the wise old woman, repeaters of the past, in favor of younger discoverers of something new.

Writing is of course conservative in its own ways. Shortly after it first appeared, it served to freeze legal codes in early Sumeria (Oppenheim 1964, p. 232). But by taking conservative functions on itself, the text frees the mind of conservative tasks, that is, of its memory work, and thus enables the mind to turn itself to new speculation (Havelock 1963, pp. 254–305).Indeed, the residual orality of a given chirographic culture can be calculated to a degree from the mnemonic load it leaves on the mind, that is, from the amount of memorization the culture's educational procedures require (Goody 1968a, pp. 13–14).

Of course oral cultures do not lack originality of their own kind. Narrative originality lodges not in making up new stories but in managing a particular interaction with this audience at this time – at every telling the story has to be introduced uniquely into a unique situation, for in oral cultures an audience must be brought to respond, often vigorously. But narrators also introduce new elements into old stories (Goody 1977, pp.29–30). In oral tradition, there will be as many minor variants of a myth as there are repetitions of it, and the number of repetitions can be increased indefinitely. Praise poems of chiefs invite entrepreneurship, as the old formulas and themes have to be made to interact with new and often complicated political situations. But the formulas and themes are reshuffled rather than supplanted with new materials.

Religious practices, and with them cosmologies and deepseated beliefs, also change in oral cultures. Disappointed with the practical results of the cult at a given shrine when cures there are infrequent, vigorous leaders – the 'intellectuals' in oral society, Goody styles them (1977, p. 30) – invent new shrines and with these new conceptual universes. Yet these new universes and the other changes that show a certain originality come into being in an essentially formulaic and thematic noetic economy. They are seldom if ever explicitly touted for their novelty but are presented as fitting the traditions of the ancestors.

### (v) Close to the human lifeworld

In the absence of elaborate analytic categories that depend on writing to structure knowledge at a distance from lived experience, oral cultures must conceptualize and verbalize all their knowledge with more or less close reference to the human lifeworld, assimilating the alien, objective world to the more immediate, familiar interaction of human beings. A chirographic (writing) culture and even more a typographic (print) culture can distance and in a way denature even the human, itemizing such things as the names of leaders and political divisions in an abstract, neutral list entirely devoid of a human action context. An oral culture has no vehicle so neutral as a list. In the latter half of the second book, the *Iliad* presents the famous catalogue of the ships – over four hundred lines – which compiles the names of Grecian leaders and the regions they ruled, but in a total context of human action: the names of persons and places occur as involved in doings (Havelock 1963, pp. 176–80). The normal and very likely the only place in Homeric Greece where this sort of political information could be found in verbalized form was in a narrative or a genealogy, which is not a neutral list but an account describing personal relations (cf. Goody and Watt 1968, p. 32). Oral cultures know few statistics or facts divorced from human or quasi-human activity.

An oral culture likewise has nothing corresponding to how-to-do-it manuals for the trades (such manuals in fact are extremely rare and always crude even in chirographic cultures, coming into effective existence only after print has been considerably interiorized – Ong 1967b, pp. 28–9, 234, 258). Trades were learned by apprenticeship (as they still largely are even in high-technology cultures), which means from observation and practice with only minimal verbalized explanation. The maximum verbal articulation of such things as navigation procedures, which were crucial to Homeric culture, would have been encountered not in any abstract manual-style description at all but in such things as the following passage from the *Iliad* i. 141–4, where the abstract description is embedded in a narrative presenting specific commands for human action or accounts of specific acts:

> As for now a black ship let us draw to the great salt sea
> And therein oarsmen let us advisedly gather and thereupon a
>     hecatomb
> Let us set and upon the deck Chryseis of fair cheeks
> Let us embark. And one man as captain, a man of counsel, there must
>     be.

(quoted in Havelock 1963, p. 81; see also ibid., pp. 174–5). Primary oral culture is little concerned with preserving knowledge of skills as an abstract, self-subsistent corpus.

## (vi) Agonistically toned

Many, if not all, oral or residually oral cultures strike literates as extraordinarily agonistic in their verbal performance and indeed in their lifestyle. Writing fosters abstractions that disengage knowledge from the arena where human beings struggle with one another. It separates the knower from the known. By keeping knowledge embedded in the human lifeworld, orality situates knowledge within a context of struggle. Proverbs and riddles are not used simply to store knowledge but to engage others in verbal and intellectual combat: utterance of one proverb or riddle challenges hearers to top it with a more apposite or a contradictory one (Abrahams 1968; 1972). Bragging about one's own prowess and/or verbal tongue-lashings of an opponent figure regularly in encounters between characters in narrative: in the Iliad, in Beowulf, throughout medieval European romance, in The Mwindo Epic and countless other African stories (Okpewho 1979; Obiechina 1975), in the Bible, as between David and Goliath (1 Samuel 17:43–7). Standard in oral societies across the world, reciprocal name-calling has been fitted with a specific name in linguistics: flyting (or fliting). Growing up in a still dominantly oral culture, certain young black males in the United States, the Caribbean, and elsewhere, engage in what is known variously as the 'dozens' or 'joning' or 'sounding' or by other names, in which one opponent tries to outdo the other in vilifying the other's mother. The dozens is not a real fight but an art form, as are the other stylized verbal tongue lashings in other cultures.

Not only in the use to which knowledge is put, but also in the celebration of physical behavior, oral cultures reveal themselves as agonistically programmed. Enthusiastic description of physical violence often marks oral narrative. In the Iliad, for example, Books viii and x would at least rival the most sensational television and cinema shows today in outright violence and far surpass them in exquisitely gory detail, which can be less repulsive when described verbally than when presented visually. Portrayal of gross physical violence, central to much oral epic and other oral genres and residual through much early literacy, gradually wanes or becomes peripheral in later literary narrative. It survives in medieval ballads but is already being spoofed by Thomas Nashe in The Unfortunate Traveller (1594). As literary narrative moves toward the serious novel, it eventually pulls the focus of action more and more to interior crises and away from purely exterior crises.

The common and persistent physical hardships of life in many early societies of course explain in part the high evidence of violence in early verbal art forms. Ignorance of physical causes of disease and disaster can also foster personal tensions. Since the disease or disaster is caused by something, in lieu of physical causes the personal malevolence of another human being – a magician, a witch – can be assumed and personal hostilities thereby increased. But violence in oral art forms is also connected with the structure of orality itself. When all verbal communication must be by direct word of mouth, involved in the give-and-take dynamics of sound, interpersonal relations are kept high – both attractions and, even more, antagonisms.

The other side of agonistic name-calling or vituperation in oral or residually oral cultures is the fulsome expression of praise which is found everywhere in connection with orality. It is well known in the much-studied present-day African oral praise poems (Finnegan 1970; Opland 1975) as all through the residually oral western rhetorical tradition stretching from classical antiquity through the eighteenth century. 'I come to bury Caesar, not to praise him', Marcus Antonius cries in his funeral oration in Shakespeare's *Julius Caesar* (v. ii. 79), and then proceeds to praise Caesar in rhetorical patterns of encomium which were drilled into the heads of all Renaissance schoolboys and which Erasmus used so wittily in his *Praise of Folly*. The fulsome praise in the old, residually oral, rhetoric tradition strikes persons from a high-literacy culture as insincere, flatulent, and comically pretentious. But praise goes with the highly polarized, agonistic, oral world of good and evil, virtue and vice, villains and heroes.

The agonistic dynamics of oral thought processes and expression have been central to the development of western culture, where they were institutionalized by the 'art' of rhetoric, and by the related dialectic of Socrates and Plato, which furnished agonistic oral verbalization with a scientific base worked out with the help of writing. More will be said about this later.

### (vii) Empathetic and participatory rather than objectively distanced

For an oral culture learning or knowing means achieving close, empathetic, communal identification with the known (Havelock 1963, pp. 145–6), 'getting with it'. Writing separates the knower from the known and thus sets up conditions for 'objectivity', in the sense of personal disengagement or distancing. The 'objectivity' which Homer and other oral performers do have is that enforced by formulaic expression: the individual's reaction is not expressed as simply individual or 'subjective' but rather as encased in the communal reaction, the communal 'soul'. Under the influence of writing, despite his protest against it, Plato had excluded the poets from his Republic, for studying them was essentially learning to react with 'soul', to feel oneself identified with Achilles or Odysseus (Havelock 1963, pp. 197–233). Treating another primary oral setting over two thousand years later, the editors of The Mwindo Epic (1971, p. 37) call attention to a similar strong identification of Candi Rureke, the performer of the epic, and through him of his listeners, with the hero Mwindo, an identification which actually affects the grammar of the narration, so that on occasion the narrator slips into the first person when describing the actions of the hero. So bound together are narrator, audience, and character that Rureke has the epic character Mwindo himself address the scribes taking down Rureke's performance: 'Scribe, march!' or 'O scribe you, you see that I am already going.' In the sensibility of the narrator and his audience the hero of the oral performance assimilates into the oral world even the transcribers who are de-oralizing it into text.

## (viii)  Homeostatic

By contrast with literate societies, oral societies can be characterized as homeostatic (Goody and Watt 1968, pp. 31–4). That is to say, oral societies live very much in a present which keeps itself in equilibrium or homeostasis by sloughing off memories which no longer have present relevance.

The forces governing homeostasis can be sensed by reflection on the condition of words in a primary oral setting. Print cultures have invented dictionaries in which the various meanings of a word as it occurs in datable texts can be recorded in formal definitions. Words thus are known to have layers of meaning, many of them quite irrelevant to ordinary present meanings. Dictionaries advertise semantic discrepancies.

Oral cultures of course have no dictionaries and few semantic discrepancies. The meaning of each word is controlled by what Goody and Watt (1968, p. 29) call 'direct semantic ratification', that is, by the real-life situations in which the word is used here and now. The oral mind is uninterested in definitions (Laura 1976, pp. 48–99). Words acquire their meanings only from their always insistent actual habitat, which is not, as in a dictionary, simply other words, but includes also gestures, vocal inflections, facial expression, and the entire human, existential setting in which the real, spoken word always occurs. Word meanings come continuously out of the present, though past meanings of course have shaped the present meaning in many and varied ways, no longer recognized.

It is true that oral art forms, such as epic, retain some words in archaic forms and senses. But they retain such words, too, through current use – not the current use of ordinary village discourse but the current use of ordinary epic poets, who preserve archaic forms in their special vocabulary. These performances are part of ordinary social life and so the archaic forms are current, though limited to poetic activity. Memory of the old meaning of old terms thus has some durability, but not unlimited durability.

When generations pass and the object or institution referred to by the archaic word is no longer part of present, lived experience, though the word has been retained, its meaning is commonly altered or simply vanishes. African talking drums, as used for example among the Lokele in eastern Zaire, speak in elaborate formulas that preserve certain archaic words which the Lokele drummers can vocalize but whose meaning they no longer know (Carrington 1974, pp. 41–2; Ong 1977, pp. 94–5) Whatever these words referred to has dropped out of Lokele daily experience, and the term that remains has become empty. Rhymes and games transmitted orally from one generation of small children to the next even in high-technology culture have similar words which have lost their original referential meanings and are in effect nonsense syllables. Many instances of such survival of empty terms can be found in Opie and Opie (1952), who, as literates, of course manage to recover and report the original meanings of the terms lost to their present oral users.

Goody and Watt (1968, pp. 31–3) cite Laura Bohannan, Emrys Peters, and Godfrey and Monica Wilson for striking instances of the homeostasis of oral cultures in the handing on of genealogies. Some decades ago among the Tiv people of Nigeria the genealogies actually used orally in settling court disputes have been found to diverge considerably from the genealogies carefully recorded in writing by the British forty years earlier (because of their importance then, too, in court disputes). The later Tiv have maintained that they were using the same genealogies as forty years earlier and that the earlier written record was wrong. What had happened was that the later genealogies had been adjusted to the changed social relations among the Tiv: they were the same in that they functioned in the same way to regulate the real world. The integrity of the past was subordinate to the integrity of the present.

Goody and Watt (1968, p. 33) report an even more strikingly detailed case of 'structural amnesia' among the Gonja in Ghana. Written records made by the British at the turn of the twentieth century show that Gonja oral tradition then presented Ndewura Jakpa, the founder of the state of Gonja, as having had seven sons, each of whom was ruler of one of the seven territorial divisions of the state. By the time sixty years later when the myths of state were again recorded, two of the seven divisions had disappeared, one by assimilation to another division and the other by reason of a boundary shift. In these later myths, Ndewura Jakpa had five sons, and no mention was made of the two extinct divisions. The Gonja were still in contact with their past, tenacious about this contact in their myths, but the part of the past with no immediately discernible relevance to the present had simply fallen away. The present imposed its own economy on past remembrances. Packard (1980, p. 157) has noted that Claude Lévi-Strauss, T. O. Beidelman, Edmund Leach and others have suggested that oral traditions reflect a society's present cultural values rather than idle curiosity about the past. He finds this is true of the Bashu, as Harms (1980, p. 178) finds it also true of the Bobangi.

The implications here for oral genealogies need to be noted. A West African griot or other oral genealogist will recite those genealogies which his hearers listen to. If he knows genealogies which are no longer called for, they drop from his repertoire and eventually disappear. The genealogies of political winners are of course more likely to survive than those of losers. Henige (1980, p. 255), reporting on Ganda and Myoro kinglists, notes that the 'oral mode . . . allows for inconvenient parts of the past to be forgotten' because of 'the exigencies of the continuing present'. Moreover, skilled oral narrators deliberately vary their traditional narratives because part of their skill is their ability to adjust to new audiences and new situations or simply to be coquettish. A West African griot employed by a princely family

(Okpewho 1979, pp. 25–6, 247, n. 33; p. 248, n. 36) will adjust his recitation to compliment his employers. Oral cultures encourage triumphalism, which in modern times has regularly tended somewhat to disappear as once-oral societies become more and more literate.

## (ix)  Situational rather than abstract

All conceptual thinking is to a degree abstract. So 'concrete' a term as 'tree' does not refer simply to a singular 'concrete' tree but is an abstraction, drawn out of, away from, individual, sensible actuality; it refers to a concept which is neither this tree nor that tree but can apply to any tree. Each individual object that we style a tree is truly 'concrete', simply itself, not 'abstract' at all, but the term we apply to the individual object is in itself abstract. Nevertheless, if all conceptual thinking is thus to some degree abstract, some uses of concepts are more abstract than other uses.

Oral cultures tend to use concepts in situational, operational frames of reference that are minimally abstract in the sense that they remain close to the living human lifeworld. There is a considerable literature bearing on this phenomenon. Havelock (1978a) has shown that pre-Socratic Greeks thought of justice in operational rather than formally conceptualized ways and the late Anne Amory Parry (1973) made much the same point about the epithet *amymōn* applied by Homer to Aegisthus: the epithet means not 'blameless', a tidy abstraction with which literates have translated the term, but 'beautiful-in-the-way-a-warrior-ready-to-fight-is-beautiful'.

No work on operational thinking is richer for the present purpose than A. R. Luria's *Cognitive Development: Its Cultural and Social Foundations* (1976). At the suggestion of the distinguished Soviet psychologist Lev Vygotsky, Luria did extensive fieldwork with illiterate (that is, oral) persons and somewhat literate persons in the remoter areas of Uzbekistan (the homeland of Avicenna) and Kirghizia in the Soviet Union during the years 1931–2. Luria's book was published in its original Russian edition only in 1974, forty-two years after his research was completed, and appeared in English translation two years later.

Luria's work provides more adequate insights into the operation of orally based thought than had the theories of Lucien Lévy-Bruhl (1923), who concluded that 'primitive' (in fact, orally based) thought was 'prelogical' and magical in the sense that it was based on belief systems rather than on practical actuality, or than had the proposals of Lévy-Bruhl's opponents such as Franz Boas (not George Boas, as erroneously in Luria 1976, p. 8), who maintained that primitive peoples thought as we do but used a different set of categories.

In an elaborate framework of Marxist theory, Luria attends to some degree to matters other than the immediate consequences of literacy, such as 'the unregulated individualistic economy centered on agriculture' and 'the beginnings of collectivization' (1976, p. 14), and he does not systematically encode his findings expressly in terms of oral-literacy differences. But despite the elaborate Marxist scaffolding, Luria's report clearly turns in fact on the differences between orality and literacy. He identifies the persons he interviews on a scale ranging from illiteracy to various levels of moderate literacy and his data fall clearly into the classes of orally based versus chirographically based noetic processes. The contrasts that show between illiterates (by far the larger number of his subjects) and literates as such are marked and certainly significant (often Luria notes this fact explicitly) and they show what work reported on and cited by Carothers (1959) also shows: it takes only a moderate degree of literacy to make a tremendous difference in thought processes.

Luria and his associates gathered data in the course of long conversations with subjects in the relaxed atmosphere of a tea house, introducing the questions for the survey itself informally, as something like riddles, with which the subjects were familiar. Thus every effort was made to adapt the questions to the subjects in their own milieu. The subjects were not leaders in their societies, but there is every reason to suppose that they had a normal range of intelligence and were quite representative of the culture. Among Luria's findings the following may be noted as of special interest here.

(1) Illiterate (oral) subjects identified geometrical figures by assigning them the names of objects, never abstractly as circles, squares, etc. A circle would be called a plate, sieve, bucket, watch, or moon; a square would be called a mirror, door, house, apricot drying-board. Luria's subjects identified the designs as representations of real things they

knew. They never dealt with abstract circles or squares but rather with concrete objects. Teachers' school students on the other hand, moderately literate, identified geometrical figures by categorical geometric names: circles, squares, triangles, and so on (1976, pp. 32–9). They had been trained to give school-room answers, not real-life responses.

(2) Subjects were presented with drawings of four objects, three belonging to one category and the fourth to another, and were asked to group together those that were similar or could be placed in one group or designated by one word. One series consisted of drawings of the objects *hammer, saw, log, hatchet*. Illiterate subjects consistently thought of the group not in categorical terms (three tools, the log not a tool) but in terms of practical situations – 'situational thinking' – without adverting at all to the classification 'tool' as applying to all but the log. If you are a workman with tools and see a log, you think of applying the tool to it, not of keeping the tool away from what it was made for – in some weird intellectual game. A 25-year-old illiterate peasant: 'They're all alike. The saw will saw the log and the hatchet will chop it into small pieces. If one of these has to go, I'd throw out the hatchet. It doesn't do as good a job as a saw' (1976, p. 56). Told that the hammer, saw, and hatchet are all tools, he discounts the categorical class and persists in situational thinking: 'Yes, but even if we have tools, we still need wood – otherwise we can't build anything' (ibid.). Asked why another person had rejected one item in another series of four that he felt all belonged together, he replied, 'Probably that kind of thinking runs in his blood'.

By contrast an 18-year-old who had studied at a village school for only two years, not only classified a similar series in categorical terms but insisted on the correctness of the classification under attack (1976, p. 74). A barely literate worker, aged 56, mingled situational grouping and categorical grouping, though the latter predominated. Given the series *axe, hatchet, sickle* to complete from the series *saw, ear of grain, log*, he completed the series with the saw – 'They are all farming tools' – but then reconsidered and added about the grain, 'You could reap it with the sickle' (1976, p. 72). Abstract classification was not entirely satisfying.

At points in his discussions Luria undertook to teach illiterate subjects some principles of abstract classification. But their grasp was never firm, and when they actually returned to working out a problem for themselves, they would revert to situational rather than categorical thinking (1976, p. 67). They were convinced that thinking other than operational thinking, that is, categorical thinking, was not important, uninteresting, trivializing (1976, pp. 54–5). One recalls Malinowski's account (1923, p. 502) of how 'primitives' (oral peoples) have names for the fauna and flora that are useful in their lives but treat other things in the forest as unimportant generalized background: 'That is just "bush".' 'Merely a flying animal.'

(3) We know that formal logic is the invention of Greek culture after it had interiorized the technology of alphabetic writing, and so made a permanent part of its noetic resources the kind of thinking that alphabetic writing made possible. In the light of this knowledge, Luria's experiments with illiterates' reactions to formally syllogistic and inferential reasoning are particularly revealing. In brief, his illiterate subjects seemed not to operate with formal deductive procedures at all – which is not the same as to say that they could not think or that their thinking was not governed by logic, but only that they would not fit their thinking into pure logical forms, which they seem to have found uninteresting. Why should they be interesting? Syllogisms relate to thought, but in practical matters no one operates in formally stated syllogisms.

*Precious metals do not rust. Gold is a precious metal. Does it rust or not?* Typical responses to this query included: 'Do precious metals rust or not? Does gold rust or not?' (peasant, 18 years of age); 'Precious metal rusts. Precious gold rusts' (34-year-old illiterate peasant) (1976, p. 104). *In the Far North, where there is snow, all bears are white. Novaya Zembla is in the Far North and there is always snow there. What color are the bears?* Here is a typical response, 'I don't know. I've seen a black bear. I've never seen any others. . . . Each locality has its own animals' (1976, pp. 108–9). You find what color bears are by looking at them. Who ever heard of reasoning out in practical life the color of a polar bear? Besides, how am I sure that you know for sure that all bears are white in a snowy country? When the syllogism is given to him a second time, a barely literate 45-year-old chairman of a collective farm manages 'To go by your words, they should all be white' (1976, p. 114) . 'To go by your words' appears to indicate awareness of the formal intellectual structures. A little literacy goes a long way. On the other hand, the chairman's limited literacy leaves him more comfortable in the person-to-person human lifeworld than in a world of pure abstractions: 'To go by your words. . . .' It is your responsibility, not mine, if the answer comes out in such a fashion.

Referring to work by Michael Cole and Sylvia Scribner in Liberia (1973), James Fernandez (1980) pointed out that a syllogism is self-contained: its conclusions are derived from its premises only. He notes that persons not academically educated are not acquainted with this special ground rule but tend rather in their interpretation of given statements, in a syllogism as elsewhere, to go beyond the statements themselves, as one does normally in real-life situations or in riddles (common in all oral cultures). I would add the observation that the syllogism is thus like a text, fixed, boxed-off, isolated. This fact dramatizes the chirographic base of logic. The riddle belongs in the oral world. To solve a riddle, canniness is needed: one draws on knowledge, often deeply subconscious, beyond the words themselves in the riddle.

(4) In Luria's field work, requests for definitions of even the most concrete objects met with resistance. 'Try to explain to me what a tree is.' 'Why should I? Everyone knows what a tree is, they don't need me telling them', replied one illiterate peasant, aged 22 (1976, p. 86). Why define, when a real-life setting is infinitely more satisfactory than a definition? Basically, the peasant was right. There is no way to refute the world of primary orality. All you can do is walk away from it into literacy.

'How would you define a tree in two words?' 'In two words? Apple tree, elm, poplar.' 'Say you go to a place where there are no cars. What will you tell people [a car is]?' 'If I go, I'll tell them that buses have four legs, chairs in front for people to sit on, a roof for shade and an engine. But when you get right down to it, I'd say: "If you get in a car and go for a drive, you'll find out."' The respondent enumerates some features but turns back ultimately to personal, situational experience (1976, p. 87).

By contrast, a literate collective-farm worker, aged 30: 'It's made in a factory. In one trip it can cover the distance it would take a horse ten days to make – it moves that fast. It uses fire and steam. We first have to set the fire going so the water gets steaming hot – the steam gives the machine its power. . . . I don't know whether there is water in a car, must be. But water isn't enough, it also needs fire' (1976, p. 90). Although he was not well informed, he did make an attempt to define a car. His definition, however, is not a sharp-focused description of visual appearance – this kind of description is beyond the capacity of the oral mind – but a definition in terms of its operations.

(5) Luria's illiterates had difficulty in articulate self-analysis. Self-analysis requires a certain demolition of situational thinking. It calls for isolation of the self, around which the entire lived world swirls for each individual person, removal of the center of every situation from that situation enough to allow the center, the self, to be examined and described. Luria put his questions only after protracted conversation about people's characteristics and their individual differences (1976, p. 148). A 38-year-old man, illiterate, from a mountain pasture camp was asked (1976, p. 150), 'What sort of person are you, what's your character like, what are your good qualities and shortcomings? How would you describe yourself?' 'I came here from Uch-Kurgan, I was very poor, and now I'm married and have children.' 'Are you satisfied with yourself or would you like to be different?' 'It would be good if I had a little more land and could sow some wheat.' Externals command attention. 'And what are your shortcomings?' 'This year I sowed one pood of wheat, and we're gradually fixing the shortcomings.' More external situations. 'Well, people are different – calm, hot-tempered, or sometimes their memory is poor. What do you think of yourself?' 'We behave well – if we were bad people, no one would respect us' (1976, p. 15). Self-evaluation modulated into group evaluation ('we') and then handled in terms of expected reactions from others. Another man, a peasant aged 36, asked what sort of person he was, responded with touching and humane directness: 'What can I say about my own heart? How can I talk about my character? Ask others; they can tell you about me. I myself can't say anything.' Judgement bears in on the individual from outside, not from within.

These are a few samples from Luria's many, but they are typical. One could argue that responses were not optimal because the respondents were not used to being asked these kinds of questions, no matter how cleverly Luria could work them into riddle-like settings. But lack of familiarity is precisely the point: an oral culture simply does not deal in such items as geometrical figures, abstract categorization, formally logical reasoning processes, definitions, or even comprehensive descriptions, or articulated self-analysis, all of which derive not simply from thought itself but from text-formed thought. Luria's questions are schoolroom questions associated with the use of texts, and indeed closely resemble or are identical with standard intelligence test questions got up by literates. They are legitimate, but they come from a world the oral respondent does not share.

The subject's reactions suggest that it is perhaps impossible to devise a test in writing or even an oral test shaped in a literate setting that would assess accurately the native intellectual abilities of persons from a highly oral culture. Gladwin (1970, p. 219) notes that the Pulawat Islanders in the South Pacific respect their navigators, who have to be highly intelligent for their complex and demanding skill, not because they consider them 'intelligent' but quite simply because they are good navigators. Asked what he thought of a new village school principal, a Central African responded to Carrington (1974, p. 61), 'Let's watch a little how he dances'. Oral folk assess intelligence not as extrapolated from contrived textbook quizzes but as situated in operational contexts.

Plying students or anyone else with analytic questions of this sort appears at a very late stage of textuality. Such questions are in fact missing not only from oral cultures, but also from writing cultures. Written examination questions came into general use (in the West) only well after print had worked its effects on consciousness, thousands of years after the invention of writing. Classical Latin has no word for an 'examination' such as we 'take' today and try to 'pass' in school. Until the past few generations in the West, and still in perhaps most of the world today, academic practice has demanded that students in class, 'recite', that is, feed back orally to the teacher statements (formulas – the oral heritage) that they had memorized from classroom instruction or from textbooks (Ong 1967b, pp. 53–76).

Proponents of intelligence tests need to recognize that our ordinary intelligence test questions are tailored to a special kind of consciousness, one deeply conditioned by literacy and print, 'modern consciousness' (Berger 1978). A highly intelligent person from an oral or residually oral culture might be expected normally to react to Luria's type of question, as many of his respondents clearly did, not by answering the seemingly mindless question itself but by trying to assess the total puzzling context (the oral mind totalizes): What is he asking me this stupid question for? What is he trying to do? (See also Ong 1978, p. 4). 'What is a tree?' Does he really expect me to respond to that when he and everyone else has seen thousands of trees? Riddles I can work with. But this is no riddle. Is it a game? Of course it is a game, but the oral person is unfamiliar with the rules. The people who ask such questions have been living in a barrage of such questions from infancy and are not aware that they are using special rules.

In a society with some literacy, such as that of Luria's subjects, illiterates can and often do of course have experience of literately organized thinking on the part of others. They will, for example, have heard someone read written compositions or have heard conversations such as only literates can engage in. One value of Luria's work is that it shows that such passing acquaintanceship with literate organization of knowledge has, at least so far as his cases show, no discernible effect on illiterates. Writing has to be personally interiorized to affect thinking processes.

Persons who have interiorized writing not only write but also speak literately, which is to say that they organize, to varying degrees, even their oral expression in thought patterns and verbal patterns that they would not know of unless they could write. Because it does not follow these patterns, literates have considered oral organization of thought naive. Oral thinking, however, can be quite sophisticated and in its own way reflective. Navaho narrators of Navaho folkloric animal stories can provide elaborate explanations of the various implications of the stories for an understanding of complex matters in human life from the physiological to the psychological and moral, and are perfectly aware of such things as physical inconsistencies (for example, coyotes with amber balls for eyes) and the need to interpret elements in the stories symbolically (Toelken 1976, p. 156). To assume that oral peoples are essentially unintelligent, that their mental processes are 'crude', is the kind of thinking that for centuries brought scholars to assume falsely that because the Homeric poems are so skillful, they must be basically written compositions.

Nor must we imagine that orally based thought is 'prelogical' or 'illogical' in any simplistic sense – such as, for example, in the sense that oral folk do not understand causal relationships. They know very well that if you push hard on a mobile object, the push causes it to move. What is true is that they cannot organize elaborate concatenations of causes in the analytic kind of linear sequences which can only be set up with the help of texts. The lengthy sequences they produce, such as genealogies, are not analytic but aggregative. But oral cultures can produce amazingly complex and intelligent and beautiful organizations of thought and experience. To understand how they do so, it will be necessary to discuss some of the operations of oral memory.

## ORAL MEMORIZATION

Verbal memory skill is understandably a valued asset in oral cultures. But the way verbal memory works in oral art forms is quite different from what literates in the past commonly imagined. In a literate culture verbatim memorization is commonly done from a text, to which the memorizer returns as often as necessary to perfect and test verbatim mastery. In the past, literates have commonly assumed that oral memorization in an oral culture, normally achieved the same goal of absolutely verbatim repetition. How such repetition could be verified before sound recordings were known was unclear, since in the absence of writing the only way to test for verbatim repetition of lengthy passages would be the simultaneous recitation of the passages by two or more persons together. Successive recitations could not be checked against each other. But instances of simultaneous recitation in oral cultures were hardly sought for. Literates were happy simply to assume that the prodigious oral memory functioned somehow according to their own verbatim textual model.

In assessing more realistically the nature of verbal memory in primary oral cultures, the work of Milman Parry and Albert Lord again proved revolutionary. Parry's work with the Homeric poems focused the issue. Parry demonstrated that the Iliad and the Odyssey were basically oral creations, whatever circumstances governed their commitment to writing. At first blush, this discovery would seem to have confirmed the assumption of verbatim memorization. The Iliad and the Odyssey were strictly metrical. How could a singer produce on demand a narrative consisting of thousands of dactylic hexameter lines unless he had them memorized word for word? Literates who can recite lengthy metrical works on demand have memorized them verbatim from texts. Parry (1928, in Parry 1971), however, laid the grounds for a new approach that could account for such production very well without verbatim memorization. As has been seen in Chapter 2, he showed that the hexameters were made up not simply of word-units but of formulas, groups of words for dealing with traditional materials, each formula shaped to fit into a hexameter line. The poet had a massive vocabulary of hexameterized phrases. With his hexameterized vocabulary, he could fabricate correct metrical lines without end, so long as he was dealing with traditional materials.

Thus in the Homeric poems, for Odysseus and Hector and Athena and Apollo and the other characters the poet had epithets and verbs which would fit them into the meter neatly when, for example, any one of them had to be announced as saying something. *Metephē polymētis Odysseus* (there spoke up clever Odysseus) or *prosephē polymētis Odysseus* (there spoke out clever Odysseus) occurs 72 times in the poems (Milman Parry 1971, p. 51). Odysseus is *polymētis* (clever) not just because he is this kind of character but also because without the epithet *polymētis* he could not be readily worked into the meter. As earlier noted, the appositeness of these and other Homeric epithets has been piously exaggerated. The poet had thousands of other similarly functioning metrical formulas that could fit into his varying metrical needs almost any situation, person, thing, or action. Indeed, most words in the *Iliad* and the *Odyssey* occur as parts of identifiable formulas.

Parry's work showed that metrically tailored formulas controlled the composition of the ancient Greek epic and that the formulas could be shifted around quite handily without interfering with the story line or the tone of the epic. Did oral singers actually shift the formulas, so that individual metrically regular renditions of the same story differed in wording? Or was the story mastered verbatim, so that it was rendered the same way at every performance? Since pretextual Homeric poets had all been dead for well over two thousand years, they could not be taped for direct evidence. But direct evidence was available from living narrative poets in modern (former) Yugoslavia, a country adjacent to and in part overlapping ancient Greece. Parry found such poets composing oral epic narrative, for which there was no text. Their narrative poems, like Homer's, were metric and formulaic, although their verse meter happened to be a different one from the ancient Greek dactylic hexameter. Lord continued and extended Parry's work, building up the massive collection of oral recordings of modern Yugoslav narrative poets now in the Parry Collection at Harvard University.

Most of these living South Slavic narrative poets – and indeed all of the better ones – are illiterate. Learning to read and write disables the oral poet, Lord found: it introduces into his mind the concept of a text as controlling the narrative and thereby interferes with the oral composing processes, which have nothing to do with texts but are 'the remembrance of songs sung' (Peabody 1975, p. 216).

Oral poets' memory of songs sung is agile: it was 'not unusual' to find a Yugoslav bard singing 'from ten to twenty ten-syllable lines a minute' (Lord 1960, p. 17). Comparison of the recorded songs, however, reveals that, though metrically regular, they were never sung the same way twice. Basically the same formulas and themes recurred, but they were stitched together or 'rhapsodized' differently in each rendition even by the same poet, depending on audience reaction, the mood of the poet or of the occasion, and other social and psychological factors.

Orally recorded interviews with the twentieth-century bards supplemented records of their performances. From these interviews, and from direct observation, we know how the bards learn: by listening for months and years to other bards who never sing a narrative the same way twice but who use over and over again the standard formulas in connection with the standard themes. Formulas are of course somewhat variable, as are themes, and a given poet's rhapsodizing or 'stitching together' of narratives will differ recognizably from another's. Certain turns of phrases will be idiosyncratic. But essentially, the materials, themes and formulas, and their use belong in a clearly identifiable tradition. Originality consists not in the introduction of new materials but in fitting the traditional materials effectively into each individual, unique situation and/or audience.

The memory feats of these oral bards are remarkable, but they are unlike those associated with memorization of texts. Literates are usually surprised to learn that the bard planning to retell the story he has heard only once wants often to wait a day or so after he had heard the story before he himself repeats it. In memorizing a written text, postponing its recitation generally weakens recall. An oral poet is not working with texts or in a textual framework. He needs time to let the story sink into his own store of themes and formulas, time to 'get with' the story. In recalling and retelling the story, he has not in any literate sense 'memorized' its metrical rendition from the version of the other singer – a version long gone forever when the new singer is mulling over the story for his own rendition (Lord 1960, pp. 20–9). The fixed materials in the bard's memory are a float of themes and formulas out of which all stories are variously built.

One of the most telling discoveries in Lord's work has been that, although singers are aware that two different singers never sing the same song exactly alike, nevertheless a singer will protest that he can do his own version of a song line for line and word for word any time, and indeed, 'just the same twenty years from now' (Lord 1960, p. 27). When, however, their purported verbatim renditions are recorded and compared, they turn out to be never the same, though the songs are recognizable versions of the same story. 'Word for word and line for line', as Lord interprets (1960, p. 28), is simply an emphatic way of saying 'like'. 'Line' is obviously a text-based concept, and even the concept of a 'word' as a discrete entity apart from a flow of speech seems somewhat text-based. Goody (1977, p. 115) has pointed out that an entirely oral language which has a term for speech in general, or for a rhythmic unit of a song, or for an utterance, or for a theme, may have no ready term for a 'word' as an isolated item, a 'bit' of speech, as in, 'The last sentence here consists of twenty-six words'. Or does it? Maybe there are twenty-eight. If you cannot write, is 'text-based' one word or two? The sense of individual words as significantly discrete items is fostered by writing, which, here as elsewhere, is diaeretic, separative. (Early manuscripts tend not to separate words clearly from each other, but to run them together.)

Significantly, illiterate singers in the widely literate culture of modern former Yugoslavia develop and express attitudes toward writing (Lord 1960, p. 28). They admire literacy and believe that a literate person can do even better what they do, namely, recreate a lengthy song after hearing it only once. This is precisely what literates cannot do, or can do only with difficulty. As literates attribute literate kinds of achievement to oral performers, so oral performers attribute oral kinds of achievement to literates.

Lord early showed (1960) the applicability of oral-formulaic analysis to Old English (*Beowulf*) and others have shown various ways in which oral-formulaic methods help explain oral or residually oral composition in the European Middle Ages, in German, French, Portuguese, and other languages (see Foley 1980b). Fieldwork across the globe has corroborated and extended the work done by Parry and, far more extensively, by Lord in Yugoslavia. For example, Goody (1977, pp. 118–19) reports how, among the LoDagaa of northern Ghana, where the Invocation to the Bagre, like the Lord's Prayer among Christians, is 'something everyone "knows"', the renditions of the invocation are nevertheless by no means stable. The Invocation consists of only 'a dozen lines or so', and, if you know the language, as Goody does, and pronounce the opening phrase of the Invocation, your hearer may take up the refrain, correcting any mistakes he or she finds you making. However, taping shows that the wording of the Invocation can vary significantly from one recitation to the other, even in the case of recitations by the same individual, and even in individuals who will correct you when your version does not correspond to their (current) version.

Goody's findings here, and the findings of others (Opland 1975; 1976), make it clear that oral peoples at times do try for verbatim repetition of poems or other oral art forms. What is their success? Most often it is minimal by literate standards. From South Africa Opland (1976, p. 114) reports earnest efforts at verbatim repetition and the results: 'Any poet in the community will repeat the poem which is in my limited testing at least sixty per cent in correlation with other versions.' Success hardly matches ambition here. Sixty per cent accuracy in memorization would earn a pretty low mark in schoolroom recitation of a text or in an actor's rendition of a play's script.

Many instances of 'memorization' of oral poetry adduced as evidence of 'prior composition' by the poet, such as the instances in Finnegan (1977, pp. 76–82), seem to be of no greater verbatim accuracy. In fact, Finnegan claims only 'close similarity, in places amounting to word-for-word repetition' (1977, p. 76) and 'much more verbal and line-for-line repetition than one might expect from the Yugoslav analogy' (1977, p. 78; on the value of these comparisons and the ambiguous significance of 'oral poetry' in Finnegan, see Foley 1979).

More recent work, however, has brought to light some instances of more exact verbatim memorization among oral peoples. One is an instance of ritual verbalization among the Curia, off the Panama coast, reported by Joel Sherzer (1982). In 1970 Sherzer had taped a lengthy magic puberty rite formula being taught by a man who was a girls' puberty rite specialist to other such specialists. He returned in 1979 with a transcription he had made of the formula and found that the same man could match the transcription verbatim, phoneme for phoneme. Although Sherzer does not state how widespread or durable the exact verbatim formula in question was within any given group of formula experts over a period of time, the instance he gives is a clear-cut one of success with verbatim reproduction. (The instances referred to by Sherzer 1982, n. 3, from Finnegan 1977, as already indicated here above, all appear ambiguous, at best, and thus not equatable with his own instance.)

Two other instances comparable to Sherzer's show verbatim reproduction of oral materials fostered not by a ritualized setting but by special linguistic or musical constraints. One is from Somali classical poetry, which has a scansion pattern seemingly more complex and rigid than that of ancient Greek epic, so that the language cannot be varied so readily. John William Johnson notes that the Somali oral poets 'learn the rules of prosody in a manner very similar, if not identical to the way they learn grammar itself' (1979b, p. 118; see also Johnson 1979a). They can no more state what the metrical rules are than they can state the rules of Somali grammar. The Somali poets do not normally compose and perform at the same time, but work out a composition in private, word-for-word, which they afterwards recite in public themselves or pass on to another to recite. This again is a clear instance of oral verbatim memorization. How stable the verbalization is over any period of time (several years, a decade or so) apparently remains to be investigated.

The second instance shows how music may act as a constraint to fix a verbatim oral narrative. Drawing on his own intensive fieldwork in Japan, Eric Rutledge (1981) reports on a still extant, but vestigial,

Japanese tradition, in which an oral narrative, *The Tale of the Heike*, is chanted to music, with some few 'white voice' sections unaccompanied instrumentally and some purely instrumental interludes. The narrative and musical accompaniment are memorized by apprentices, who begin as young children working with an oral master. The masters (there are not many left) undertake to train their apprentices in verbatim recitation of the chant through rigorous drill over several years, and succeed remarkably, though they themselves make changes in their own recitations of which they are unaware. Certain movements in the narrative are more errorprone than others. At some points the music stabilizes the text completely, but at others it generates errors of the same sorts found in manuscript copying, such as those produced by *homoioteleuton* – a copyist (or oral performer) skips from one occurrence of a concluding phrase to a later occurrence of the same concluding phrase, leaving out the intervening material. Again, we have here cultivated verbatim rendition of a sort, less than totally invariable, but noteworthy.

Although in these instances the production of oral poetry or other oral verbalization by consciously cultivated memorization is not the same as the oral-formulaic practice in Homeric Greece or the modern former Yugoslavia or in countless other traditions, verbatim memorization apparently does not at all free the oral noetic processes from dependence on formulas, but if anything increases the dependence. In the case of Somali oral poetry, Francesco Antinucci has shown that this poetry has not merely phonological, metrical constraints, but also syntactic constraints. That is to say, only certain specific syntactic structures occur in the lines of the poems: in instances Antinucci presents, only two types of syntactic structures out of the hundreds possible (1979, p. 148). This is certainly formulaic composition with a vengeance, for formulas are nothing if not 'constraints' and here we are dealing with syntactic formulas (which are also found in the economy of the poems that Parry and Lord worked with). Rutledge (1981) notes the formulaic character of the material in the Heike chants, which indeed are so formulary as to contain many archaic words the meanings of which the masters do not even know. Sherzer (1982) also calls specific attention to the fact that the utterances he finds recited verbatim are made up of formulaic elements similar to those in oral performances of the ordinary, rhapsodic, nonverbatim type. He suggests that we think of a continuum between the 'fixed' and the 'flexible' use of formulaic elements. Sometimes formulaic elements are managed in an effort to establish verbatim sameness, sometimes they work to implement a certain adaptability or variation (though users of the formulaic elements, as Lord has shown, may generally think of what is in fact 'flexible' or variable use as being 'fixed' use). Sherzer's suggestion certainly is a wise suggestion.

Oral memorization deserves more and closer study, especially in ritual. Sherzer's verbatim instances are from ritual, and Rutledge hints in his paper and states explicitly in a letter to me (22 January 1982) that the Heike chants are ritualistic in setting. Chafe (1982), treating specifically the Seneca language, suggests that ritual language as compared to colloquial language is like writing in that it 'has a permanence which colloquial language does not. The same oral ritual is presented again and again: not verbatim, to be sure, but with a content, style, and formulaic structure which remain constant from performance to performance'. There can be little doubt, all in all, that in oral cultures generally, by far most of the oral recitation falls toward the flexible end of the continuum, and even in ritual. Even in cultures which know and depend on writing but retain a living contact with pristine orality, that is, retain a high oral residue, ritual utterance itself is often not typically verbatim. 'Do this in memory of me' Jesus said at the Last Supper (Luke 22:19). Christians celebrate the Eucharist as their central act of worship because of Jesus' directive. But the crucial words that Christians repeat as Jesus' words in fulfilling this directive (that is, the words 'This is my body . . . ; this is the cup of my blood . . .') do not appear in exactly the same way in any two places where they are cited in the New Testament. The early Christian Church remembered, in pretextual, oral form, even in her textualized rituals, and even at those very points where she was commanded to remember most assiduously.

Statements are often made about verbatim oral memorization of the Vedic hymns in India, presumably in complete independence of any texts. Such statements, so far as I know, have never been assessed in view of the findings of Parry and Lord and related findings concerning oral 'memorization'. The Vedas are lengthy collections and old, probably composed between 1500 and 900 or 500 BC – the variance that must be allowed in possible dates shows how vague are present-day contacts with the original settings in which grew the hymns, prayers, and liturgical formulas that make up these collections. Typical references still cited today to attest to verbatim memorization of the Vedas are from 1906 or 1927 (Kiparsky 1976, pp. 99–100), before any of Parry's work was completed, or from 1954 (Bright 1981), before Lord's (1960) and Havelock's work (1963). In *The Destiny of the Veda in India* (1965) the distinguished French Indologist and translator of the Rig-Veda Louis Renou does not even advert to the kinds of questions that arise in the wake of Parry's work.

There is no doubt that oral transmission was important in the history of the Vedas (Renou 1965, pp. 25–6 – #26 – and notes, pp. 83–4). Brahman teachers or gurus and their students devoted intensive effort to verbatim memorization, even crisscrossing the words in various patterns to ensure oral mastery of their positions in relation to one another (Basham 1963, p. 164), though whether this latter pattern was used before a text had been developed appears an insoluble problem. In the wake of the recent studies of oral memory, however, questions arise as to the ways in which memory of the Vedas actually worked in a purely oral setting – if there ever was such a setting for the Vedas totally independent of texts. Without a text, how could a given hymn – not to mention the totality of hymns in the collections – be stabilized word for word, and that over many generations? Statements, made in good conscience by oral persons, that renditions are word for word the same, as we have seen, can be quite contrary to fact. Mere assertions, frequently made by literates, that such lengthy texts were retained verbatim over generations in a totally oral society can no longer be taken at face value without verification. What was retained? The first recitation of a poem by its originator? How could the originator ever repeat it word for word the second time and be sure he had done so? A version which a powerful teacher worked up? This appears a possibility. But his working it up in his own version shows variability in the tradition, and suggests that in the mouth of another powerful teacher more variations might well come wittingly or unwittingly.

In point of fact, the Vedic texts – on which we base knowledge of the Vedas today – have a complex history and many variants, facts which seem to suggest that they hardly originated from an absolutely verbatim oral tradition. Indeed, the formulaic and thematic structure of the Vedas, conspicuous even in translations, relates them to other oral performances we know, and indicates that they warrant further study in connection with what has been discovered recently about formulaic elements, thematic elements, and oral mnemonics. Peabody's work (1975) already directly encourages such study in his examination of relations between the older Indo-European tradition and Greek versification. For example, the incidence of high redundancy or its lack in the Vedas could itself be an indication of the degree to which they are of more or less oral provenance (see Peabody 1975, p. 173).

In all cases, verbatim or not, oral memorization is subject to variation from direct social pressures. Narrators narrate what audiences call for or will tolerate. When the market for a printed book declines, the presses stop rolling but thousands of copies may remain. When the market for an oral genealogy disappears, so does the genealogy itself, utterly. As noted above (pp. 48–9), the genealogies of winners tend to survive (and to be improved), those of losers tend to vanish (or to be recast). Interaction with living audiences can actively interfere with verbal stability: audience expectations can help fix themes and formulas. I had such expectations enforced on me a few years ago by a niece of mine, still a tiny child young enough to preserve a clearly oral mindset (though one infiltrated by the literacy around her). I was telling her the story of 'The Three Little Pigs': 'He huffed and he puffed, and he huffed and he puffed, and he huffed and he puffed'. Cathy bridled at the formula I used. She knew the story, and my formula was not what she expected. 'He huffed and he puffed, and he puffed and he huffed, and he huffed and he puffed', she pouted. I reworded the narrative, complying to audience demand for what had been said before, as other oral narrators have often done.

Finally, it should be noted that oral memory differs significantly from textual memory in that oral memory has a high somatic component. Peabody (1975, p. 197) has observed that 'From all over the world and from all periods of time . . . traditional composition has been associated with hand activity. The aborigines of Australia and other areas often make string figures together with their songs. Other peoples manipulate beads on strings. Most descriptions of bards include stringed instruments or drums'. (See also Lord 1960; Havelock

1978a, pp. 220–2; Biebuyck and Mateene 1971, frontispiece.) To these instances one can add other examples of hand activity, such as gesturing, often elaborate and stylized (Scheub 1977), and other bodily activities such as rocking back and forth or dancing. The Talmud, though a text, is still vocalized by highly oral Orthodox Jews in Israel with a forward-and-backward rocking of the torso, as I myself have witnessed.

The oral word, as we have noted, never exists in a simply verbal context, as a written word does. Spoken words are always modifications of a total, existential situation, which always engages the body. Bodily activity beyond mere vocalization is not adventitious or contrived in oral communication, but is natural and even inevitable. In oral verbalization, particularly public verbalization, absolute motionlessness is itself a powerful gesture.

## VERBOMOTOR LIFESTYLE

Much in the foregoing account of orality can be used to identify what can be called 'verbomotor' cultures, that is, cultures in which, by contrast with high-technology cultures, courses of action and attitudes toward issues depend significantly more on effective use of words, and thus on human interaction, and significantly less on non-verbal, often largely visual input from the 'objective' world of things. Jousse (1925) used his term *verbomoteur* to refer chiefly to ancient Hebrew and Aramaic cultures and surrounding cultures, which knew some writing but remained basically oral and word-oriented in lifestyle rather than object-oriented. We are expanding its use here to include all cultures that retain enough oral residue to remain significantly word-attentive in a person-interactive context (the oral type of context) rather than object-attentive. It should, of course, be noted that words and objects are never totally disjunct: words represent objects, and perception of objects is in part conditioned by the store of words into which perceptions are nested. Nature states no 'facts': these come only within statements devised by human beings to refer to the seamless web of actuality around them.

The cultures which we are here styling verbomotor are likely to strike technological man as making all too much of speech itself, as overvaluing and certainly overpracticing rhetoric. In primary oral cultures, even business is not business: it is fundamentally rhetoric. Purchasing something at a Middle East souk or bazaar is not a simple economic transaction, as it would be at Woolworth's and as a high-technology culture is likely to presume it would be in the nature of things. Rather, it is a series of verbal (and somatic) maneuvers, a polite duel, a contest of wits, an operation in oral agonistic.

In oral cultures a request for information is commonly interpreted interactively (Malinowski 1923, pp. 451, 470–81), as agonistic, and, instead of being really answered, is frequently parried. An illuminating story is told of a visitor in County Cork, Ireland, an especially oral region in a country which in every region preserves massive residual orality. The visitor saw a Corkman leaning against the post office. He went up to him, pounded with his hand on the post office wall next to the Corkman's shoulder, and asked, 'Is this the post office?' The Corkman was not taken in. He looked at his questioner quietly and with great concern: ' 'Twouldn't be a postage stamp you were lookin' for, would it?' He treated the enquiry not as a request for information but as something the enquirer was doing to him. So he did something in turn to the enquirer to see what would happen. All natives of Cork, according to the mythology, treat all questions this way. Always answer a question by asking another. Never let down your oral guard.

Primary orality fosters personality structures that in certain ways are more communal and externalized, and less introspective than those common among literates. Oral communication unites people in groups. Writing and reading are solitary activities that throw the psyche back on itself. A teacher speaking to a class which he feels and which feels itself as a close-knit group, finds that if the class is asked to pick up its textbooks and read a given passage, the unity of the group vanishes as each person enters into his or her private lifeworld. An example of the contrast between orality and literacy on these grounds is found in Carother's report (1959) of evidence that oral peoples commonly externalize schizoid behavior where literates interiorize it. Literates often manifest tendencies (loss of contact with environment) by psychic withdrawal into a dreamworld of their own (schizophrenic delusional systematization), oral folk commonly manifest their schizoid tendencies by extreme external confusion, leading often to violent action, including mutilation of the self and of others. This behavior is frequent enough to have given rise to special terms to designate it: the old-time Scandinavian warrior going 'berserk', the Southeast Asian person running 'amok'.

## THE NOETIC ROLE OF HEROIC 'HEAVY' FIGURES AND OF THE BIZARRE

The heroic tradition of primary oral culture and of early literate culture, with its massive oral residue, relates to the agonistic lifestyle, but it is best and most radically explained in terms of the needs of oral noetic processes. Oral memory works effectively with 'heavy' characters, persons whose deeds are monumental, memorable and commonly public. Thus the noetic economy of its nature generates outsize figures, that is, heroic figures, not for romantic reasons or reflectively didactic reasons but for much more basic reasons: to organize experience in some sort of permanently memorable form. Colorless personalities cannot survive oral mnemonics. To assure weight and memorability, heroic figures tend to be type figures: wise Nestor, furious Achilles, clever Odysseus, omnicompetent Mwindo ('Little-One-Just-Born-He-Walked', Kábútwa-kénda, his common epithet). The same mnemonic or noetic economy enforces itself still where oral settings persist in literate cultures, as in the telling of fairy stories to children: the overpoweringly innocent Little Red Riding Hood, the unfathomably wicked wolf, the incredibly tall beanstalk that Jack has to climb – for non-human figures acquire heroic dimensions, too. Bizarre figures here add another mnemonic aid: it is easier to remember the Cyclops than a two-eyed monster, or Cerberus than an ordinary one-headed dog (see Yates 1966, pp. 9–11, 65–7). Formulary number groupings are likewise mnemonically helpful: the Seven Against Thebes, the Three Graces, the Three Fates, and so on. All this is not to deny that other forces besides mere mnemonic serviceability produce heroic figures and groupings. Psychoanalytic theory can explain a great many of these forces. But in an oral noetic economy, mnemonic serviceability is a *sine qua non*, and, no matter what the other forces, without proper mnemonic shaping of verbalization the figures will not survive.

As writing and eventually print gradually alter the old oral noetic structures, narrative builds less and less on 'heavy' figures until, some three centuries after print, it can move comfortably in the ordinary human lifeworld typical of the novel. Here, in place of the hero, one eventually encounters even the antihero, who, instead of facing up to the foe, constantly turns tail and runs away, as the protagonist in John Updike's *Rabbit Run*. The heroic and marvelous had served a specific function in organizing knowledge in an oral world. With the control of information and memory brought about by writing and, more intensely, by print, you do not need a hero in the old sense to mobilize knowledge in story form. The situation has nothing to do with a putative 'loss of ideals'.

## THE INTERIORITY OF SOUND

In treating some psychodynamics of orality, we have thus far attended chiefly to one characteristic of sound itself, its evanescence, its relationship to time. Sound exists only when it is going out of existence. Other characteristics of sound also determine or influence oral psychodynamics. The principal one of these other characteristics is the unique relationship of sound to interiority when sound is compared to the rest of the senses. This relationship is important because of the interiority of human consciousness and of human communication itself. It can be discussed only summarily here. I have treated the matter in greater fullness and depth in *The Presence of the Word*, to which the interested reader is referred (1967b, Index).

To test the physical interior of an object as interior, no sense works so directly as sound. The human sense of sight is adapted best to light diffusely reflected from surfaces. (Diffuse reflection, as from a printed page or a landscape, contrasts with specular reflection, as from a mirror.) A source of light, such as a fire, may be intriguing but it is optically baffling: the eye cannot get a 'fix' on anything within the fire. Similarly, a translucent object, such as alabaster, is intriguing because, although it is not a source of light, the eye cannot get a 'fix' on it either. Depth can be perceived by the eye, but most satisfactorily as a series of surfaces: the trunks of trees in a grove, for example, or chairs in an auditorium. The eye does not perceive an interior strictly as an interior: inside a room, the walls it perceives are still surfaces, outsides.

Taste and smell are not much help in registering interiority or exteriority. Touch is. But touch partially destroys interiority in the process of perceiving it. If I wish to discover by touch whether a box is empty or full, I have to make a hole in the box to insert a hand or finger: this means that the box is to that extent open, to that extent less an interior.

Hearing can register interiority without violating it. I can rap a box to find whether it is empty or full or a wall to find whether it is hollow or solid inside. Or I can ring a coin to learn whether it is silver or lead.

Sounds all register the interior structures of whatever it is that produces them. A violin filled with concrete will not sound like a normal violin. A saxophone sounds differently from a flute: it is structured differently inside. And above all, the human voice comes from inside the human organism which provides the voice's resonances.

Sight isolates, sound incorporates. Whereas sight situates the observer outside what he views, at a distance, sound pours into the hearer. Vision dissects, as Merleau-Ponty has observed (1961). Vision comes to a human being from one direction at a time: to look at a room or a landscape, I must move my eyes around from one part to another. When I hear, however, I gather sound simultaneously from every direction at once: I am at the center of my auditory world, which envelopes me, establishing me at a kind of core of sensation and existence. This centering effect of sound is what high-fidelity sound reproduction exploits with intense sophistication. You can immerse yourself in hearing, in sound. There is no way to immerse yourself similarly in sight.

By contrast with vision, the dissecting sense, sound is thus a unifying sense. A typical visual ideal is clarity and distinctness, a taking apart (Descartes' campaigning for clarity and distinctness registered an intensification of vision in the human sensorium – Ong 1967b, pp. 63, 221). The auditory ideal, by contrast, is harmony, a putting together.

Interiority and harmony are characteristics of human consciousness. The consciousness of each human person is totally interiorized, known to the person from the inside and inaccessible to any other person directly from the inside. Everyone who says 'I' means something different by it from what every other person means. What is 'I' to me is only 'you' to you. And this 'I' incorporates experience into itself by 'getting it all together'. Knowledge is ultimately not a fractioning but a unifying phenomenon, a striving for harmony. Without harmony, an interior condition, the psyche is in bad health.

It should be noted that the concepts interior and exterior are not mathematical concepts and cannot be differentiated mathematically. They are existentially grounded concepts, based on experience of one's own body, which is both inside me (I do not ask you to stop kicking my body but to stop kicking *me*) and outside me (I feel myself as in some sense inside my body). The body is a frontier between myself and everything else. What we mean by 'interior' and 'exterior' can be conveyed only by reference to experience of bodiliness. Attempted definitions of 'interior' and 'exterior' are inevitably tautological: 'interior' is defined by 'in', which is defined by 'between', which is defined by 'inside', and so on round and round the tautological circle. The same is true with 'exterior'. When we speak of interior and exterior, even in the case of physical objects, we are referring to our own sense of ourselves: I am *inside* here and everything else is *outside*. By interior and exterior we point to our own experience of bodiliness (Ong 1967b, pp. 117–22, 176–9, 228, 231) and analyze other objects by reference to this experience.

In a primary oral culture, where the word has its existence only in sound, with no reference whatsoever to any visually perceptible text, and no awareness of even the possibility of such a text, the phenomenology of sound enters deeply into human beings' feel for existence, as processed by the spoken word. For the way in which the word is experienced is always momentous in psychic life. The centering action of sound (the field of sound is not spread out before me but is all around me) affects man's sense of the cosmos. For oral cultures, the cosmos is an ongoing event with man at its center. Man is the *umbilicus mundi*, the navel of the world (Eliade 1958, pp. 231–5, etc.). Only after print and the extensive experience with maps that print implemented would human beings, when they thought about the cosmos or universe or 'world', think primarily of something laid out before their eyes, as in a modern printed atlas, a vast surface or assemblage of surfaces (vision presents surfaces) ready to be 'explored'. The ancient oral world knew few 'explorers', though it did know many itinerants, travelers, voyagers, adventurers, and pilgrims.

It will be seen that most of the characteristics of orally based thought and expression discussed earlier in this chapter relate intimately to the unifying, centralizing, interiorizing economy of sound as perceived by human beings. A sound-dominated verbal economy is consonant with aggregative (harmonizing) tendencies rather than with analytic, dissecting tendencies (which would come with the inscribed, visualized word: vision is a dissecting sense). It is consonant also with the conservative holism (the homeostatic present that must be kept intact, the formulary expressions that must be kept intact), with situational thinking (again holistic, with human action at the center) rather than abstract thinking, with a certain humanistic organization of knowledge around the actions of human and anthropomorphic beings, interiorized persons, rather than around impersonal things.

The denominators used here to describe the primary oral world will be useful again later to describe what happened to human consciousness when writing and print reduced the oral-aural world to a world of visualized pages.

## ORALITY, COMMUNITY AND THE SACRAL

Because in its physical constitution as sound, the spoken word proceeds from the human interior and manifests human beings to one another as conscious interiors, as persons, the spoken word forms human beings into close-knit groups. When a speaker is addressing an audience, the members of the audience normally become a unity, with themselves and with the speaker. If the speaker asks the audience to read a handout provided for them, as each reader enters into his or her own private reading world, the unity of the audience is shattered, to be re-established only when oral speech begins again. Writing and print isolate. There is no collective noun or concept for readers corresponding to 'audience'. The collective 'readership' – this magazine has a readership of two million – is a far-gone abstraction. To think of readers as a united group, we have to fall back on calling them an 'audience', as though they were in fact listeners. The spoken word forms unities on a large scale, too: countries with two or more different spoken languages are likely to have major problems in establishing or maintaining national unity, as today in Canada or Belgium or many developing countries.

The interiorizing force of the oral word relates in a special way to the sacral, to the ultimate concerns of existence. In most religions the spoken word functions integrally in ceremonial and devotional life. Eventually in the larger world religions sacred texts develop, too, in which the sense of the sacral is attached also to the written word. Still, a textually supported religious tradition can continue to authenticate the primacy of the oral in many ways. In Christianity, for example, the Bible is read aloud at liturgical services. For God is thought of always as 'speaking' to human beings, not as writing to them. The orality of the mindset in the Biblical text, even in its epistolary sections, is over-whelming (Ong 1967b, pp. 176–91). The Hebrew *dabar*, which means word, means also event and thus refers directly to the spoken word. The spoken word is always an event, a movement in time, completely lacking in the thing-like repose of the written or printed word. In Trinitarian theology, the Second Person of the Godhead is the Word, and the human analogue for the Word here is not the human written word, but the human spoken word. God the Father 'speaks' to his Son: he does not inscribe him. Jesus, the Word of God, left nothing in writing, though he could read and write (Luke 4:16). 'Faith comes through hearing', we read in the Letter to the Romans (10:17). 'The letter kills, the spirit [breath, on which rides the spoken word] gives life' (2 Corinthians 3:6).

## WORDS ARE NOT SIGNS

Jacques Derrida has made the point that 'there is no linguistic sign before writing' (1976, p. 14). But neither is there a linguistic 'sign' after writing if the oral reference of the written text is adverted to. Though it releases unheard-of potentials of the word, a textual, visual representation of a word is not a real word, but a 'secondary model-ing system' (cf. Lotman 1977). Thought is nested in speech, not in texts, all of which have their meanings through reference of the vis-ible symbol to the world of sound. What the reader is seeing on this page are not real words but coded symbols whereby a properly informed human being can evoke in his or her consciousness real words, in actual or imagined sound. It is impossible for script to be more than marks on a surface unless it is used by a conscious human being as a cue to sounded words, real or imagined, directly or indirectly.

Chirographic and typographic folk find it convincing to think of the word, essentially a sound, as a 'sign' because 'sign' refers primarily to something visually apprehended. *Signum*, which furnished us with the word 'sign', meant the standard that a unit of the Roman army carried aloft for visual identification – etymologically, the 'object one follows' (Proto-Indo-European root, *sekw-*, to follow). Though the Romans knew the alphabet, this *signum* was not a lettered word but some kind of pictorial design or image, such as an eagle, for example.

The feeling for letter names as labels or tags was long in establishing itself, for primary orality lingered in residue, as will be seen, centuries after the invention of writing and even of print. As late as the European Renaissance, quite literate alchemists using labels for their vials and boxes tended to put on the labels not a written name, but iconographic signs, such as various signs of the zodiac, and shopkeepers identified their shops not with lettered words but with iconographic symbols such as the ivy bush for a tavern, the barber's pole, the pawnbroker's three spheres. (On iconographic labeling, see Yates 1966.) These tags or labels do not at all name what they refer to: the words 'ivy bush' are not the word 'tavern', the word 'pole' is not the word 'barber'. Names were still words that moved through time: these quiescent, unspoken, symbols were something else again. They were 'signs', as words are not.

Our complacency in thinking of words as signs is due to the tendency, perhaps incipient in oral cultures but clearly marked in chirographic cultures and far more marked in typographic and electronic cultures, to reduce all sensation and indeed all human experience to visual analogues. Sound is an event in time, and 'time marches on', relentlessly, with no stop or division. Time is seemingly tamed if we treat it spatially on a calendar or the face of a clock, where we can make it appear as divided into separate units next to each other. But this also falsifies time. Real time has no divisions at all, but is uninterruptedly continuous: at midnight yesterday did not click over into today. No one can find the exact point of midnight, and if it is not exact, how can it be midnight? And we have no experience of today as being next to yesterday, as it is represented on a calendar. Reduced to space, time seems more under control – but only seems to be, for real, indivisible time carries us to real death. (This is not to deny that spatial reductionism is immeasurably useful and technologically necessary, but only to say that its accomplishments are intellectually limited, and can be deceiving.) Similarly, we reduce sound to oscillograph patterns and to waves of certain 'lengths', which can be worked with by a deaf person who can have no knowledge of what the experience of sound is. Or we reduce sound to script and to the most radical of all scripts, the alphabet.

Oral man is not so likely to think of words as 'signs', quiescent visual phenomena. Homer refers to them with the standard epithet 'winged words' – which suggests evanescence, power, and freedom: words are constantly moving, but by flight, which is a powerful form of movement, and one lifting the flier free of the ordinary, gross, heavy, 'objective' world.

In contending with Jean Jacques Rousseau, Derrida is of course quite correct in rejecting the persuasion that writing is no more than incidental to the spoken word (Derrida 1976, p. 7). But to try to construct a logic of writing without investigation in depth of the orality out of which writing emerged and in which writing is permanently and ineluctably grounded is to limit one's understanding, although it does produce at the same time effects that are brilliantly intriguing but also at times psychedelic, that is, due to sensory distortions. Freeing ourselves of chirographic and typographic bias in our understanding of language is probably more difficult than any of us can imagine, far more difficult, it would seem, than the 'deconstruction' of literature, for this 'deconstruction' remains a literary activity. More will be said about this problem in treating the internalizing of technology in the next chapter.

# 4

## WRITING RESTRUCTURES CONSCIOUSNESS

### THE NEW WORLD OF AUTONOMOUS DISCOURSE

A deeper understanding of pristine or primary orality enables us better to understand the new world of writing, what it truly is, and what functionally literate human beings really are: beings whose thought processes do not grow out of simply natural powers but out of these powers as structured, directly or indirectly, by the technology of writing. Without writing, the literate mind would not and could not think as it does, not only when engaged in writing but normally even when it is composing its thoughts in oral form. More than any other single invention, writing has transformed human consciousness.

Writing establishes what has been called 'context-free' language (Hirsch 1977, pp. 21–3, 26) or 'autonomous' discourse (Olson 1980a), discourse which cannot be directly questioned or contested as oral speech can be because written discourse has been detached from its author.

Oral cultures know a kind of autonomous discourse in fixed ritual formulas (Olson 1980a, pp. 187–94; Chafe 1982), as well as in vatic sayings or prophesies, for which the utterer himself or herself is considered only the channel, not the source. The Delphic oracle was not responsible for her oracular utterances, for they were held to be the voice of the god. Writing, and even more print, has some of this vatic quality. Like the oracle or the prophet, the book relays an utterance from a source, the one who really 'said' or wrote the book. The author might be challenged if only he or she could be reached, but the author cannot be reached in any book. There is no way directly to refute a text. After absolutely total and devastating refutation, it says exactly the same thing as before. This is one reason why 'the book says' is popularly tantamount to 'it is true'. It is also one reason why books have been burnt. A text stating what the whole world knows is false will state falsehood forever, so long as the text exists. Texts are inherently contumacious.

## PLATO, WRITING AND COMPUTERS

Most persons are surprised, and many distressed, to learn that essentially the same objections commonly urged today against computers were urged by Plato in the *Phaedrus* (274–7) and in the *Seventh Letter* against writing. Writing, Plato has Socrates say in the *Phaedrus*, is inhuman, pretending to establish outside the mind what in reality can be only in the mind. It is a thing, a manufactured product. The same of course is said of computers. Secondly, Plato's Socrates urges, writing destroys memory. Those who use writing will become forgetful, relying on an external resource for what they lack in internal resources. Writing weakens the mind. Today, parents and others fear that pocket calculators provide an external resource for what ought to be the internal resource of memorized multiplication tables. Calculators weaken the mind, relieve it of the work that keeps it strong. Thirdly, a written text is basically unresponsive. If you ask a person to explain his or her statement, you can get an explanation; if you ask a text, you get back nothing except the same, often stupid, words which called for your question in the first place. In the modern critique of the computer, the same objection is put, 'Garbage in, garbage out'. Fourthly, in keeping with the agonistic mentality of oral cultures, Plato's Socrates also holds it against writing that the written word cannot defend itself as the natural spoken word can: real speech and thought always exist essentially in a context of give-and-take between real persons.

Writing is passive, out of it, in an unreal, unnatural world. So are computers.

A fortiori, print is vulnerable to these same charges. Those who are disturbed by Plato's misgivings about writing will be even more disturbed to find that print created similar misgivings when it was first introduced. Hieronimo Squarciafico, who in fact promoted the printing of the Latin classics, also argued in 1477 that already 'abundance of books makes men less studious' (quoted in Lowry 1979, pp. 29–31): it destroys memory and enfeebles the mind by relieving it of too much work (the pocket-computer complaint once more), downgrading the wise man and wise woman in favor of the pocket compendium. Of course, others saw print as a welcome leveler: everyone becomes a wise man or woman (Lowry 1979, pp. 31–2).

One weakness in Plato's position was that, to make his objections effective, he put them into writing, just as one weakness in anti-print positions is that their proponents, to make their objections more effective, put the objections into print. The same weakness in anti-computer positions is that, to make them effective, their proponents articulate them in articles or books printed from tapes composed on computer terminals. Writing and print and the computer are all ways of technologizing the word. Once the word is technologized, there is no effective way to criticize what technology has done with it without the aid of the highest technology available. Moreover, the new technology is not merely used to convey the critique: in fact, it brought the critique into existence. Plato's philosophically analytic thought, as has been seen (Havelock 1963), including his critique of writing, was possible only because of the effects that writing was beginning to have on mental processes.

In fact, as Havelock has beautifully shown (1963), Plato's entire epistemology was unwittingly a programmed rejection of the old oral, mobile, warm, personally interactive lifeworld of oral culture (represented by the poets, whom he would not allow in his Republic). The term idea, form, is visually based, coming from the same root as the Latin video, to see, and such English derivatives as vision, visible, or videotape. Platonic form was form conceived of by analogy with visible form. The Platonic ideas are voiceless, immobile, devoid of all warmth, not interactive but isolated, not part of the human lifeworld at all but utterly above and beyond it. Plato of course was not at all fully aware of the unconscious forces at work in his psyche to produce this reaction, or overreaction, of the literate person to lingering, retardant orality.

Such considerations alert us to the paradoxes that beset the relationships between the original spoken word and all its technological transformations. The reason for the tantalizing involutions here is obviously that intelligence is relentlessly reflexive, so that even the external tools that it uses to implement its workings become 'internalized', that is, part of its own reflexive process.

One of the most startling paradoxes inherent in writing is its close association with death. This association is suggested in Plato's charge that writing is inhuman, thing-like, and that it destroys memory. It is also abundantly evident in countless references to writing (and/or print) traceable in printed dictionaries of quotations, from 2 Corinthians 3:6, 'The letter kills but the spirit gives life' and Horace's reference to his three books of Odes as a 'monument' (Odes iii.30. 1), presaging his own death, on to and beyond Henry Vaughan's assurance to Sir Thomas Bodley that in the Bodleian Library at Oxford 'every book is thy epitaph'. In Pippa Passes, Robert Browning calls attention to the still widespread practice of pressing living flowers to death between the pages of printed books, 'faded yellow blossoms/twixt page and page'. The dead flower, once alive, is the psychic equivalent of the verbal text. The paradox lies in the fact that the deadness of the text, its removal from the living human lifeworld, its rigid visual fixity, assures its endurance and its potential for being resurrected into limitless living contexts by a potentially infinite number of living readers (Ong 1977, pp. 230–71).

## WRITING IS A TECHNOLOGY

Plato was thinking of writing as an external, alien technology, as many people today think of the computer. Because we have by today so deeply interiorized writing, made it so much a part of ourselves, as Plato's age had not yet made it fully a part of itself (Havelock 1963), we find it difficult to consider writing to be a technology as we commonly assume printing and the computer to be. Yet writing (and especially alphabetic writing) is a technology, calling for the use of tools and other equipment: styli or brushes or pens, carefully prepared surfaces such as paper, animal skins, strips of wood, as well as inks or paints, and much more. Clanchy (1979, pp. 88–115) discusses the matter circumstantially, in its western medieval context, in his chapter entitled 'The technology of writing'. Writing is in a way the most drastic of the three technologies. It initiated what print and computers only continue, the reduction of dynamic sound to quiescent space, the separation of the word from the living present, where alone spoken words can exist.

By contrast with natural, oral speech, writing is completely artificial. There is no way to write 'naturally'. Oral speech is fully natural to human beings in the sense that every human being in every culture who is not physiologically or psychologically impaired learns to talk. Talk implements conscious life but it wells up into consciousness out of unconscious depths, though of course with the conscious as well as unconscious co-operation of society. Grammar rules live in the unconscious in the sense that you can know how to use the rules and even how to set up new rules without being able to state what they are.

Writing or script differs as such from speech in that it does not inevitably well up out of the unconscious. The process of putting spoken language into writing is governed by consciously contrived, articulable rules: for example, a certain pictogram will stand for a certain specific word, or *a* will represent a certain phoneme, *b* another, and so on. (This is not to deny that the writer–reader situation created by writing deeply affects unconscious processes involved in composing in writing, once one has learned the explicit, conscious rules. More about this later.)

To say writing is artificial is not to condemn it but to praise it. Like other artificial creations and indeed more than any other, it is utterly invaluable and indeed essential for the realization of fuller, interior, human potentials. Technologies are not mere exterior aids but also interior transformations of consciousness, and never more than when they affect the word. Such transformations can be uplifting. Writing heightens consciousness. Alienation from a natural milieu can be good for us and indeed is in many ways essential for full human life. To live and to understand fully, we need not only proximity but also distance. This writing provides for consciousness as nothing else does.

Technologies are artificial, but – paradox again – artificiality is natural to human beings. Technology, properly interiorized, does not degrade human life but on the contrary enhances it. The modern orchestra, for example, is the result of high technology. A violin is an instrument, which is to say a tool. An organ is a huge machine, with sources of power – pumps, bellows, electric generators – totally outside its operator. Beethoven's score for his Fifth Symphony consists of very careful directions to highly trained technicians, specifying exactly how to use their tools. *Legato*: do not take your finger off one key until you have hit the next. *Staccato*: hit the key and take your finger off immediately. And so on. As musicologists well know, it is pointless to object to electronic compositions such as Morton Subotnik's *The Wild Bull* on the grounds that the sounds come out of a mechanical contrivance. What do you think the sounds of an organ come out of? Or the sounds of a violin or even of a whistle? The fact is that by using a mechanical contrivance, a violinist or an organist can express something poignantly human that cannot be expressed without the mechanical contrivance. To achieve such expression of course the violinist or organist has to have interiorized the technology, made the tool or machine a second nature, a psychological part of himself or herself. This calls for years of 'practice', learning how to make the tool do what it can do. Such shaping of a tool to oneself, learning a technological skill, is hardly dehumanizing. The use of a technology can enrich the human psyche, enlarge the human spirit, intensify its interior life. Writing is an even more deeply interiorized technology than instrumental musical performance is. But to understand what it is, which means to understand it in relation to its past, to orality, the fact that it is a technology must be honestly faced.

## WHAT IS 'WRITING' OR 'SCRIPT'?

Writing, in the strict sense of the word, the technology which has shaped and powered the intellectual activity of modern man, was a very late development in human history. *Homo sapiens* has been on earth perhaps some 50,000 years (Leakey and Lewin 1979, pp. 141 and 168). The first script, or true writing, that we know, was developed among the Sumerians in Mesopotamia only around the year 3500 BC (Diringer 1953; Gelb 1963).

Human beings had been drawing pictures for countless millennia before this. And various recording devices or *aides-mémoire* had been used by various societies: a notched stick, rows of pebbles, other tallying devices such as the quipu of the Incas (a stick with suspended cords onto which other cords were tied), the 'winter count' calendars of the Native American Plains Indians, and so on. But a script is more than a mere memory aid. Even when it is pictographic, a script is more than pictures. Pictures represent objects. A picture of a man and a house and a tree of itself *says* nothing. (If a proper code or set of conventions is supplied, it might: but a code is not picturable, unless with the help of another unpicturable code. Codes ultimately have to be explained by something more than pictures; that is, either in words or in a total human context, humanly understood.) A script in the sense of true writing, as understood here, does not consist of mere pictures, of representations of things, but is a representation of an *utterance*, of words that someone says or is imagined to say.

It is of course possible to count as 'writing' any semiotic mark, that is, any visible or sensible mark which an individual makes and assigns a meaning to. Thus a simple scratch on a rock or a notch on a stick interpretable only by the one who makes it would be 'writing'. If this is what is meant by writing, the antiquity of writing is perhaps comparable to the antiquity of speech. However, investigations of writing which take 'writing' to mean any visible or sensible mark with an assigned meaning merge writing with purely biological behavior. When does a footprint or a deposit of feces or urine (used by many species of animals for communication – Wilson 1975, pp. 228–9) become 'writing'? Using the term 'writing' in this extended sense to include any semiotic marking trivializes its meaning. The critical and unique breakthrough into new worlds of knowledge was achieved within human consciousness not when simple semiotic marking was devised but when a coded system of visible marks was invented whereby a writer could determine the exact words that the reader would generate from the text. This is what we usually mean today by writing in its sharply focused sense.

With writing or script in this full sense, encoded visible markings engage words fully so that the exquisitely intricate structures and references evolved in sound can be visibly recorded exactly in their specific complexity and, because visibly recorded, can implement production of still more exquisite structures and references, far surpassing the potentials of oral utterance. Writing, in this ordinary sense, was and is the most momentous of all human technological inventions. It is not a mere appendage to speech. Because it moves speech from the oral–aural to a new sensory world, that of vision, it transforms speech and thought as well. Notches on sticks and other *aides-mémoire* lead up to writing, but they do not restructure the human lifeworld as true writing does.

True writing systems can and usually do develop gradually from a cruder use of mere memory aides. Intermediate stages exist. In some coded systems the writer can predict only approximately what the reader will read off, as in the system developed by the Vai in Liberia (Scribner and Cole 1978) or even in ancient Egyptian hieroglyphics. The tightest control of all is achieved by the alphabet, although even this is never quite perfect in all instances. If I mark a document 'read', this might be a past participle (pronounced to rhyme with 'red') indicating that the document has been gone over, or it might be an imperative (pronounced to rhyme with 'reed') indicating that it is to be gone over. Even with the alphabet, extra-textual context is sometimes needed, but only in exceptional cases – how exceptional will depend on how well the alphabet has been tailored to a given language.

## MANY SCRIPTS BUT ONLY ONE ALPHABET

Many scripts across the world have been developed independently of one another (Diringer 1953; Diringer 1960; Gelb 1963): Mesopotamian cuneiform 3500 BC (approximate dates here from Diringer 1962), Egyptian hieroglyphics 3000 BC (with perhaps some influence from cuneiform), Minoan or Mycenean 'Linear B' 1200 BC, Indus Valley script 3000–2400 BC, Chinese script 1500 BC, Mayan script AD 50, Aztec script AD 1400.

Scripts have complex antecedents. Most if not all scripts trace back directly or indirectly to some sort of picture writing, or, sometimes perhaps, at an even more elemental level, to the use of tokens. It has been suggested that the cuneiform script of the Sumerians, the first of all known scripts (c. 3500 BC), grew at least in part out of a system of recording economic transactions by using clay tokens encased in small, hollow but totally closed pod-like containers or bullae, with indentations on the outside representing the tokens inside (Schmandt-Besserat 1978). Thus the symbols on the outside of the bulla – say, seven indentations – carried with them, inside the bulla, evidence of what they represented – say, seven little clay artefacts distinctively shaped, to represent cows, or ewes or other things not yet decipherable – as though words were always proffered with their concrete significations attached. The economic setting of such prechirographic use of tokens could help associate them with writing, for the first cuneiform script, from the same region as the bullae, whatever its exact antecedents, served mostly workaday economic and administrative purposes in urban societies. Urbanization provided the incentive to develop record keeping. Using writing for imaginative creations, as spoken words have been used in tales or lyric, that is, using writing to produce literature in the more specific sense of this term, comes quite late in the history of script.

Pictures can serve simply as *aides-mémoire*, or they can be equipped with a code enabling them to represent more or less exactly specific words in various grammatical relation to each other. Chinese character writing is still today basically made up of pictures, but pictures stylized and codified in intricate ways which make it certainly the most complex writing system the world has ever known. Pictographic communication such as found among early Native American Indians and many others (Mackay 1978, p. 32) did not develop into a true script because the code remained too unfixed. Pictographic representations of several objects served as a kind of allegorical memorandum for parties who were dealing with certain restricted subjects which helped determine in advance how these particular pictures related to each other. But often, even then, the meaning intended did not come entirely clear.

Out of pictographs (a picture of a tree represents the word for a tree), scripts develop other kinds of symbols. One kind is the ideograph, in which the meaning is a concept not directly represented by the picture but established by code: for example, in the Chinese pictograph a stylized picture of two trees does not represent the words 'two trees' but the word 'woods'; stylized pictures of a woman and child side-by-side represent the word 'good', and so on. The spoken word for woman is [ny], for child [dzə], for good [hau]: the pictorial etymology, as here, need have no relationship to the phonemic etymology. Writers of Chinese relate to their language quite differently from Chinese speakers who cannot write. In a special sense, numerals such as 1, 2, 3 are interlinguistic ideographs (though not pictographs): they represent the same concept but not the same sound in languages which have entirely different words for 1, 2, 3. And even within the lexicon of a given language, the signs 1, 2, 3 and so on are in a way connected directly with the concept rather than the word: the words for 1 ('one') and 2 ('two') relate to the concepts '1st' and '2nd' but not to the words 'first' and 'second'.

Another kind of pictograph is rebus writing (the picture of the sole of a foot could represent in English also the fish called a sole, sole in the sense of only, or soul as paired with body; pictures of a mill, a walk, and a key in that order could represent the word 'Milwaukee'). Since at this point the symbol represents primarily a sound, a rebus is a kind of phonogram (sound-symbol), but only mediately: the sound is designated not by an abstract coded sign, as a letter of the alphabet, but by a picture of one of the several things the sound signifies.

All pictographic systems, even with ideographs and rebuses, require a dismaying number of symbols. Chinese is the largest, most complex, and richest: the K'anghsi dictionary of Chinese in AD 1716 lists 40,545 characters. No Chinese or Sinologist knows them all, or ever did. Few Chinese who write can write all of the spoken Chinese words that they can understand. To become significantly learned in the Chinese writing system normally takes some twenty years. Such a script is basically time-consuming and élitist. There can be no doubt that the characters will be replaced by the roman alphabet as soon as all the people in the People's Republic of China master the same Chinese language ('dialect'), the Mandarin now being taught everywhere. The loss to literature will be enormous, but not so enormous as a Chinese typewriter using over 40,000 characters.

One advantage of a basically pictographic system is that persons speaking different Chinese 'dialects' (really different Chinese languages, mutually incomprehensible, though basically of the same structure) who are unable to understand one another's speech can understand one another's writing. They read off different sounds for the same character (picture), somewhat as a Frenchman and a Luba and a Vietnamese and an Englishman will know what each other means by the Arabic numerals 1, 2, 3, and so on, but will not recognize the numeral if pronounced by one of the others. (However, the Chinese characters are basically pictures, though exquisitely stylized, as 1, 2, 3 are not.)

Some languages are written in syllabaries, in which each sign represents a consonant and a following vowel sound. Thus the Japanese Katakana syllabary has five separate symbols respectively for *ka, ke, ki, ko, ku,* five others for *ma, me, mi, mo, mu,* and so on. The Japanese language happens to be so constituted that it can utilize a syllabary script: its words are made up of parts always consisting of a consonantal sound followed by a vowel sound (*n* functions as a quasi-syllable), with no consonant clusters (as in 'pitchfork', 'equipment'). With its many different kinds of syllables, and its frequent consonant clusters, English could not be effectively managed in a syllabary. Some syllabaries are less developed than Japanese. In that of the Vai in Liberia, for example, there is not a full one-to-one correspondence between the visual symbols and the units of sound. The writing provides only a kind of map to the utterance it registers, and it is very difficult to read, even for a skilled scribe (Scribner and Cole 1978, p. 456).

Many writing systems are in fact hybrid systems, mixing two or more principles. The Japanese system is hybrid (besides a syllabary, it uses Chinese characters, pronounced in its own non-Chinese way); the Korean system is hybrid (besides *hangul*, a true alphabet, perhaps the most efficient of all alphabets, it uses Chinese characters pronounced its own way); the ancient Egyptian hieroglyphic system was hybrid (some symbols were pictographs, some ideographs, some rebuses); Chinese character writing itself is hybrid (mixed pictographs, ideographs, rebuses, and various combinations, often of extreme complexity, cultural richness and poetic beauty). Indeed, because of the tendency of scripts to start with pictographs and move to ideographs and rebuses, perhaps most writing systems other than the alphabet are to some degree hybrid. And even alphabetic writing becomes hybrid when it writes 1 instead of *one*.

The most remarkable fact about the alphabet no doubt is that it was invented only once. It was worked up by a Semitic people or Semitic peoples around the year 1500 BC, in the same general geographic area where the first of all scripts appeared, the cuneiform, but two millennia later than the cuneiform. (Diringer 1962, pp. 121–2, discusses the two variants of the original alphabet, the North Semitic and the South Semitic.) Every alphabet in the world – Hebrew, Ugaritic, Greek, Roman, Cyrillic, Arabic, Tamil, Malayalam, Korean – derives in one way or another from the original Semitic development, though, as in Ugaritic and Korean script, the physical design of the letters may not always be related to the Semitic design.

Hebrew and other Semitic languages, such as Arabic, do not to this day have letters for vowels. A Hebrew newspaper or book still today prints only consonants (and so-called semi–vowels [j] and [w], which are in effect the consonantal forms of [i] and [u]): if we were to follow Hebrew usage in English we would write and print 'cnsnts' for 'consonants'. The letter aleph, adapted by the ancient Greeks to indicate the vowel alpha, which became our roman 'a', is not a vowel but a consonant in Hebrew and other Semitic alphabets, representing a glottal stop (the sound between the two vowel sounds in the English 'huh-uh', meaning 'no'). Late in the history of the Hebrew alphabet, vowel 'points', little dots and dashes below or above the letters to indicate the proper vowel, were added to many texts, often for the benefit of those who did not know the language very well, and today in Israel these 'points' are added to words for very young children learning to read – up to the third grade or so. Languages are organized in many different ways, and the Semitic languages are so constituted that they are easy to read when words are written only with consonants.

This way of writing only with consonants and semi-consonants (y as in 'you', w) has led some linguists (Gelb 1963; Havelock 1963, p. 129) to call what other linguists call the Hebrew alphabet a syllabary, or perhaps an unvocalized or 'reduced' syllabary. However, it appears somewhat awkward to think of the Hebrew letter beth (b) as a syllable when it in fact simply represents the phoneme [b], to which the reader has to add whatever vowel sound the word and context call for. Besides, when vowel points are used, they are added to the letters (above or below the line) just as vowels are added to our consonants. And modern Israelis and Arabs, who agree on so little else, both generally agree that both are writing letters in an alphabet. For an understanding of the development of writing out of orality, it appears at least unobjectionable to think of the Semitic script simply as an alphabet of consonants (and semivowels) for which readers, as they read, simply and easily supply the appropriate vowels.

When this is all said, however, about the Semitic alphabet, it does appear that the Greeks did something of major psychological importance when they developed the first alphabet complete with vowels. Havelock (1976) believes that this crucial, more nearly total transformation of the word from sound to sight gave ancient Greek culture its intellectual ascendancy over other ancient cultures. The reader of Semitic writing had to draw on non-textual as well as textual data: he had to know the language he was reading in order to know what vowels to supply between the consonants. Semitic writing was still very much immersed in the non-textual human lifeworld. The vocalic Greek alphabet was more remote from that world (as Plato's ideas were to be). It analyzed sound more abstractly into purely spatial components. It could be used to write or read words even from languages one did not know (allowing for some inaccuracies due to phonemic differences between languages). Little children could acquire the Greek alphabet when they were very young and their vocabulary limited. (It has just been noted that for Israeli schoolchildren to about the third grade vowel 'points' have to be added to the ordinary consonantal Hebrew script.) The Greek alphabet was democratizing in the sense that it was easy for everyone to learn. It was also internationalizing in that it provided a way of processing even foreign tongues. This Greek achievement in abstractly analyzing the elusive world of sound into visual equivalents (not perfectly, of course, but in effect fully) both presaged and implemented their further analytic exploits.

It appears that the structure of the Greek language, the fact that it was not based on a system like the Semitic that was hospitable to omission of vowels from writing, turned out to be a perhaps accidental but crucial intellectual advantage. Kerckhove (1981) has suggested that, more than other writing systems, the completely phonetic alphabet favors left-hemisphere activity in the brain, and thus on neurophysiological grounds fosters abstract, analytic thought.

The reason why the alphabet was invented so late and why it was invented only once can be sensed if we reflect on the nature of sound. For the alphabet operates more directly on sound as sound than the other scripts, reducing sound directly to spatial equivalents, and in smaller, more analytic, more manageable units than a syllabary: instead of one symbol for the sound *ba*, you have two, *b* plus *a*.

Sound, as has earlier been explained, exists only when it is going out of existence. I cannot have all of a word present at once: when I say 'existence', by the time I get to the '-tence', the 'exis-' is gone. The alphabet implies that matters are otherwise, that a word is a thing, not an event, that it is present all at once, and that it can be cut up into little pieces, which can even be written forwards and pronounced backwards: 'p-a-r-t' can be pronounced 'trap'. If you put the word 'part' on a sound tape and reverse the tape, you do not get 'trap', but a completely different sound, neither 'part' nor 'trap'. A picture, say, of a bird does not reduce sound to space, for it represents an object, not a word. It will be the equivalent of any number of words, depending on the language used to interpret it: *oiseau, uccello, pájaro, Vogel, sae, tori,* 'bird'.

All script represents words as in some way things, quiescent objects, immobile marks for assimilation by vision. Rebuses or phonograms, which occur irregularly in some pictographic writing, represent the sound of one word by the picture of another (the 'sole' of a foot representing the 'soul' as paired with body, in the fictitious example used above). But the rebus (phonogram), though it may represent several things, is still a picture of one of the things it represents. The alphabet, though it probably derives from pictograms, has lost all connection with things as things. It represents sound itself as a thing, transforming the evanescent world of sound to the quiescent, quasi-permanent world of space.

The phonetic alphabet invented by ancient Semites and perfected by ancient Greeks, is by far the most adaptable of all writing systems in reducing sound to visible form. It is perhaps also the least aesthetic of all major writing systems: it can be beautifully designed, but never so exquisitely as Chinese characters. It is a democratizing script, easy for everybody to learn. Chinese character writing, like many other writing systems, is intrinsically élitist: to master it thoroughly requires protracted leisure. The democratizing quality of the alphabet can be seen in South Korea. In Korean books and newspapers the text is a mixture of alphabetically spelt words and hundreds of different Chinese characters. But all public signs are always written in the alphabet alone, which virtually everyone can read since it is completely mastered in the lower grades of elementary school, whereas the 1800 *han*, or Chinese characters, minimally needed besides the alphabet for reading most literature in Korean, are not commonly all mastered before the end of secondary school.

Perhaps the most remarkable single achievement in the history of the alphabet was in Korea, where in AD 1443 King Sejong of the Yi Dynasty decreed that an alphabet should be devised for Korean. Up to that time Korean had been written only with Chinese characters, laboriously adapted to fit (and interact with) the vocabulary of Korean, a language not at all related to Chinese (though it has many Chinese loan words, mostly so Koreanized as to be incomprehensible to any Chinese). Thousands upon thousands of Koreans — all Koreans who could write — had spent or were spending the better part of their lives mastering the complicated Sino-Korean chirography. They were hardly likely to welcome a new writing system which would render their laboriously acquired skills obsolete. But the Yi Dynasty was powerful and Sejong's decree in the face of massive anticipated resistance suggests that he had comparably powerful ego structures. The accommodation of the alphabet to a given language has generally taken many years, or generations. Sejong's assembly of scholars had the Korean alphabet ready in three years, a masterful achievement, virtually perfect in its accommodation to Korean phonemics and aesthetically designed to produce an alphabetic script with something of the appearance of a text in Chinese characters. But the reception of this remarkable achievement was predictable. The alphabet was used only for unscholarly, practical, vulgarian purposes. 'Serious' writers continued to use the Chinese character writing in which they had so laboriously trained themselves. Serious literature was élitist and wanted to be known as élitist. Only in the twentieth century, with the greater democratization of Korea, did the alphabet achieve its present (still less than total) ascendancy.

## THE ONSET OF LITERACY

When a fully formed script of any sort, alphabetic or other, first makes its way from outside into a particular society, it does so necessarily at first in restricted sectors and with varying effects and implications. Writing is often regarded at first as an instrument of secret and magic power (Goody 1968b, p. 236). Traces of this early attitude toward writing can still show etymologically: the Middle English 'grammarye' or grammar, referring to book-learning, came to mean occult or magical lore, and through one Scottish dialectical form has emerged in our present English vocabulary as 'glamor' (spell-casting power). 'Glamor girls' are really grammar girls. The futhark or runic alphabet of medieval Northern Europe was commonly associated with magic. Scraps of writing are used as magic amulets (Goody 1968b, pp. 201–3), but they also can be valued simply because of the wonderful permanence they confer on words. The Nigerian novelist Chinua Achebe describes how in an Ibo village the one man who knew how to read hoarded in his house every bit of printed material that came his way – newspapers, cartons, receipts (Achebe 1961, pp. 120–1). It all seemed too remarkable to throw away.

Some societies of limited literacy have regarded writing as dangerous to the unwary reader, demanding a guru-like figure to mediate between reader and text (Goody and Watt 1968, p. 13). Literacy can be restricted to special groups such as the clergy (Tambiah 1968, pp. 113–14). Texts can be felt to have intrinsic religious value: illiterates profit from rubbing the book on their foreheads, or from whirling prayer-wheels bearing texts they cannot read (Goody 1968a, pp. 15–16). Tibetan monks used to sit on the banks of streams 'printing pages of charms and formulas on the surface of the water with woodcut blocks' (Goody 1968a, p. 16, quoting R. B. Eckvall). The still flourishing 'cargo cults' of some South Pacific islands are well known: illiterates or semi-literates think that the commercial papers – orders, bills of lading, receipts, and the like – that they know figure in shipping operations are magical instruments to make ships and cargo come in from across the sea, and they elaborate various rituals manipulating written texts in the hope that cargo will turn up for their own possession and use (Meggitt 1968, pp. 300–9). In ancient Greek culture Havelock discovers a general pattern of restricted literacy applicable to many other cultures: shortly after the introduction of writing a 'craft literacy' develops (Havelock 1963; cf. Havelock and Herschell 1978). At this stage writing is a trade practiced by craftsmen, whom others hire to write a letter or document as they might hire a stone-mason to build a house, or a shipwright to build a boat. Such was the state of affairs in West African kingdoms, such as Mali, from the Middle Ages into the twentieth century (Wilks 1968; Goody 1968b). At such a craft-literacy stage, there is no need for an individual to know reading and writing any more than any other trade. Only around Plato's time in ancient Greece, more than three centuries after the introduction of the Greek alphabet, was this stage transcended when writing was finally diffused through the Greek population and interiorized enough to affect thought processes generally (Havelock 1963).

The physical properties of early writing materials encouraged the continuance of scribal culture (see Clanchy 1979, pp. 88–115, on 'The technology of writing'). Instead of evenly surfaced machine-made paper and relatively durable ball-point pens, the early writer had more recalcitrant technological equipment. For writing surfaces, he had wet clay bricks, animal skins (parchment, vellum) scraped free of fat and hair, often smoothed with pumice and whitened with chalk, frequently reprocessed by scraping off an earlier text (palimpsests). Or he had the bark of trees, papyrus (better than most surfaces but still rough by high-technology standards), dried leaves or other vegetation, wax layered onto wooden tablets often hinged to form a diptych worn on a belt (these wax tablets were used for notes, the wax being smoothed over again for re-use), wooden rods (Clanchy 1979, p. 95) and other wooden and stone surfaces of various sorts. There were no corner stationery stores selling pads of paper. There was no paper. As inscribing tools the scribes had various kinds of styli, goose quills which had to be slit and sharpened over and over again with what we still call a 'pen knife', brushes (particularly in East Asia), or various other instruments for incising surfaces and/or spreading inks or paints. Fluid inks were mixed in various ways and readied for use into hollow bovine horns (inkhorns) or in other acid resistant containers, or, commonly in East Asia, brushes were wetted and dabbed on dry ink blocks, as in watercolor painting.

Special mechanical skills were required for working with such writing materials, and not all 'writers' had such skills suitably developed for protracted composition. Paper made writing physically easier. But paper, manufactured in China probably by the second century BC and diffused by Arabs to the Middle East by the eighth century of the Christian era, was first manufactured in Europe only in the twelfth century.

Longstanding oral mental habits of thinking through one's thoughts aloud encourage dictation, but so did the state of writing technology. In the physical act of writing, the medieval Englishman Orderic Vitalis says, 'the whole body labors' (Clanchy 1979, p. 90). Through the Middle Ages in Europe authors often employed scribes. Composition in writing, working out one's thought pen-in-hand, particularly in briefer compositions, was, of course, practiced to some extent from antiquity, but it became widespread for literary and other prolonged composition at different times in different cultures. It was still rare in eleventh-century England, and, when it occurred, even this late, could be done in a psychological setting so oral that we find it hard to imagine. The eleventh-century Eadmer of St Albans says that, when he composed in writing, he felt he was dictating to himself (Clanchy 1979, p. 218). St Thomas Aquinas, who wrote his own manuscripts, organizes his *Summa theologiae* in quasi-oral format: each section or 'question' begins with a recitation of objections against the position Thomas will take, then Thomas states his position, and finally answers the objections in order. Similarly, an early poet would write down a poem by imagining himself declaiming it to an audience. Few if any novelists today write a novel by imagining themselves declaiming it aloud, though they might be exquisitely aware of the sound effects of the words. High literacy fosters truly written composition, in which the author composes a text which is precisely a text, puts his or her words together on paper. This gives thought different contours from those of orally sustained thought. More will be said (that is, written) here later about the effects of literacy on thought processes.

## FROM MEMORY TO WRITTEN RECORDS

Long after a culture has begun to use writing, it may still not give writing high ratings. A present-day literate usually assumes that written records have more force than spoken words as evidence of a long-past state of affairs, especially in court. Earlier cultures that knew literacy but had not so fully interiorized it, have often assumed quite the opposite. The amount of credence accorded to written records undoubtedly varied from culture to culture, but Clanchy's careful case history of the use of literacy for practical administrative purposes in eleventh- and twelfth-century England (1979) gives an informative sample of how much orality could linger in the presence of writing, even in an administrative milieu.

In the period he studies, Clanchy finds that 'documents did not immediately inspire trust' (Clanchy 1979, p. 230). People had to be persuaded that writing improved the old oral methods sufficiently to warrant all the expense and troublesome techniques it involved. Before the use of documents, collective oral testimony was commonly used to establish, for example, the age of feudal heirs. To settle a dispute in 1127 as to whether the customs dues at the port of Sandwich went to St Augustine's Abbey at Canterbury or to Christ Church, a jury was chosen consisting of twelve men from Dover and twelve from Sandwich, 'mature, wise seniors of many years, having good testimony'. Each juror then swore that, as 'I have received from my ancestors, and I have seen and heard from my youth', the tolls belong to Christ Church (Clanchy 1979, pp. 232–3). They were publicly remembering what others before them had remembered.

Witnesses were *prima facie* more credible than texts because they could be challenged and made to defend their statements, whereas texts could not (this, it will be recalled, was exactly one of Plato's objections to writing). Notarial methods of authenticating documents undertake to build authenticating mechanisms into written texts, but notarial methods developed late in literate cultures, and much later in England than in Italy (Clanchy 1979, pp. 235–6). Written documents themselves were often authenticated not in writing but by symbolic objects (such as a knife, attached to the document by a parchment thong – Clanchy 1979, p. 24). Indeed symbolic objects alone could serve as instruments transferring property. In c. 1130, Thomas de Muschamps conveyed his estate of Hetherslaw to the monks at Durham by offering his sword on an altar (Clanchy 1979, p. 25). Even after the Domesday Book (1085–6) and the accompanying increase in written documentation, the story of the Earle Warrenne shows how the old oral state of mind still persisted: before the judges in quo warranto procedures under Edward I (reigned 1272–1306), the Earle Warrenne exhibited not a charter but 'an ancient and rusty sword', protesting that his ancestors had come with William the Conqueror to take England by the sword and that he would defend his lands with the sword. Clanchy points out (1979, pp. 21–2) that the story is somewhat questionable because of certain inconsistencies, but notes also that its persistence attests to an earlier state of mind familiar with the witness value of symbolic gifts.

Early charters conveying land in England were originally not even dated (1979, pp. 231, 236–41), probably for a variety of reasons. Clanchy suggests that the most profound reason was probably that 'dating required the scribe to express an opinion about his place in time' (1979, p. 238), which demanded that he choose a point of reference. What point? Was he to locate this document by reference to the creation of the world? To the Crucifixion? To the birth of Christ? Popes dated documents this way, from Christ's birth, but was it presumptuous to date a secular document as popes dated theirs? In high technology cultures today, everyone lives each day in a frame of abstract computed time enforced by millions of printed calendars, clocks, and watches. In twelfth-century England there were no clocks or watches or wall or desk calendars.

Before writing was deeply interiorized by print, people did not feel themselves situated every moment of their lives in abstract computed time of any sort. It appears unlikely that most persons in medieval or even Renaissance western Europe would ordinarily have been aware of the number of the current calendar year – from the birth of Christ or any other point in the past. Why should they be? Indecision concerning what point to compute from attested the trivialities of the issue. In a culture with no newspapers or other currently dated material to impinge on consciousness, what would be the point for most people in knowing the current calendar year? The abstract calendar number would relate to nothing in real life. Most persons did not know and never even tried to discover in what calendar year they had been born.

Moreover, charters were undoubtedly assimilated somewhat to symbolic gifts, such as knives or swords. These were identifiable by their looks. And indeed, charters were quite regularly forged to make them look like what a court (however erroneously) felt a charter should look like (Clanchy 1979, p. 249, citing P. H. Sawyer). 'Forgers', Clanchy points out, were not 'occasional deviants on the peripheries of legal practice' but 'experts entrenched at the centre of literary and intellectual culture in the twelfth century.' Of the 164 now extant charters of Edward the Confessor, 44 are certainly forged, only 64 certainly authentic, and the rest uncertainly one or the other.

The verifiable errors resulting from the still radically oral economic and juridical procedures that Clanchy reports were minimal because the fuller past was mostly inaccessible to consciousness. 'Remembered truth was . . . flexible and up to date' (Clanchy 1979, p. 233). As has been seen in instances from modern Nigeria and Ghana (Goody and Watt 1968, pp. 31–4), in an oral economy of thought, matters from the past without any sort of present relevance commonly dropped into oblivion. Customary law, trimmed of material no longer of use, was automatically always up to date and thus youthful – a fact which, paradoxically, makes customary law seem inevitable and thus very old (cf. Clanchy 1979, p. 233). Persons whose world view has been formed by high literacy need to remind themselves that in functionally oral cultures the past is not felt as an itemized terrain, peppered with verifiable and disputed 'facts' or bits of information. It is the domain of the ancestors, a resonant source for renewing awareness of present existence, which itself is not an itemized terrain either. Orality knows no lists or charts or figures.

Goody (1977, pp. 52–111) has examined in detail the noetic significance of tables and lists, of which the calendar is one example. Writing makes such apparatus possible. Indeed, writing was in a sense invented largely to make something like lists: by far most of the earliest writing we know, that in the cuneiform script of the Sumerians beginning around 3500 BC, is account-keeping. Primary oral cultures commonly situate their equivalent of lists in narrative, as in the catalogue of the ships and captains in the *Iliad* (ii. 461–879) – not an objective tally but an operational display in a story about a war. In the text of the Torah, which set down in writing thought forms still basically oral, the equivalent of geography (establishing the relationship of one place to another) is put into a formulary action narrative (Numbers 33:16 ff): 'Setting out from the desert of Sinai, they camped at Kibroth-hattaavah. Setting out from Kibroth-hattaavah, they camped at Hazeroth. Setting out from Hazeroth, they camped at Rithmah . . .', and so on for many more verses. Even genealogies out of such orally framed tradition are in effect commonly narrative. Instead of a recitation of names, we find a sequence of 'begats', of statements of what someone did: 'Irad begat Mehajael, Mehajael begat Methusael, Methusael begat Lamech' (Genesis 4:18). This sort of aggregation derives partly from the oral drive to use formulas, partly from the oral mnemonic drive to exploit balance (recurrence of subject-predicate-object produces a swing which aids recall and which a mere sequence of names would lack), partly from the oral drive to redundancy (each person is mentioned twice, as begetter and begotten), and partly from the oral drive to narrate rather than simply to juxtapose (the persons are not immobilized as in a police line-up, but are doing something – namely, begetting).

These biblical passages obviously are written records, but they come from an orally constituted sensibility and tradition. They are not felt as thing-like, but as reconstitutions of events in time. Orally presented sequences are always occurrences in time, impossible to 'examine', because they are not presented visually but rather are utterances which are heard. In a primary oral culture or a culture with heavy oral residue, even genealogies are not 'lists' of data but rather 'memory of songs sung'. Texts are thing-like, immobilized in visual space, subject to what Goody calls 'backward scanning' (1977, pp. 49–50). Goody shows in detail how, when anthropologists display on a written or printed surface lists of various items found in oral myths (clans, regions of the earth, kinds of winds, and so on), they actually deform the mental world in which the myths have their own existence. The satisfaction that myths provide is essentially not 'coherent' in a tabular way.

Lists of the sort Goody discusses are of course useful if we are reflectively aware of the distortion they inevitably introduce. Visual presentation of verbalized material in space has its own particular economy, its own laws of motion and structure. Texts in various scripts around the world are read variously from right to left, or left to right, or top to bottom, or all these ways at once as in boustrophedon writing, but never anywhere, so far as is known, from bottom to top. Texts assimilate utterance to the human body. They introduce a feeling for 'headings' in accumulations of knowledge: 'chapter' derives from the Latin *caput*, meaning head (as of the human body). Pages have not only 'heads' but also 'feet', for footnotes. References are given to what is 'above' and 'below' in a text when what is meant is several pages back or farther on. The significance of the vertical and the horizontal in texts deserves serious study. Kerckhove (1981) suggests that growth in left-hemisphere dominance governed the drift in early Greek writing from right-to-left movement, to boustrophedon movement ('ox-plowing' pattern, one line going right, then a turn around a corner into the next line going left, the letters inverted according to the direction of the line), to *stoichedon* style (vertical lines), and finally to definitive left-to-right movement on a horizontal line. All this is quite a different world of order from anything in the oral sensibility, which has no way of operating with 'headings' or verbal linearity. Across the world the alphabet, the ruthlessly efficient reducer of sound to space, is pressed into direct service for setting up the new space-defined sequences: items are marked *a, b, c*, and so on to indicate their sequences, and even poems in the early days of literacy are composed with the first letter of the first word of successive lines following the order of the alphabet. The alphabet as a simple sequence of letters is a major bridge between oral mnemonic and literate mnemonics: generally the sequence of the letters of the alphabet is memorized orally and then used for largely visual retrieval of materials, as in indexes.

Charts, which range elements of thought not simply in one line of rank but simultaneously in horizontal and various cross-cross orders, represent a frame of thought even farther removed than lists are from the oral noetic processes which such charts are supposed to represent. The extensive use of lists and particularly of charts so commonplace in our high-technology cultures is a result not simply of writing, but of the deep interiorization of print (Ong 1958b, pp. 307–18, and *passim*), which implements the use of fixed diagrammatic word-charts and other informational uses of neutral space far beyond anything feasible in any writing culture.

## SOME DYNAMICS OF TEXTUALITY

The condition of words in a text is quite different from their condition in spoken discourse. Although they refer to sounds and are meaning-less unless they can be related – externally or in the imagination – to the sounds or, more precisely, the phonemes they encode, written words are isolated from the fuller context in which spoken words come into being. The word in its natural, oral habitat is a part of a real, existential present. Spoken utterance is addressed by a real, living per-son to another real, living person or real, living persons, at a specific time in a real setting which includes always much more than mere words. Spoken words are always modifications of a total situation which is more than verbal. They never occur alone, in a context simply of words.

Yet words are alone in a text. Moreover, in composing a text, in 'writing' something, the one producing the written utterance is also alone. Writing is a solipsistic operation. I am writing a book which I hope will be read by hundreds of thousands of people, so I must be isolated from everyone. While writing the present book, I have left word that I am 'out' for hours and days – so that no one, including persons who will presumably read the book, can interrupt my solitude.

In a text even the words that are there lack their full phonetic qual-ities. In oral speech, a word must have one or another intonation or tone of voice – lively, excited, quiet, incensed, resigned, or whatever. It is impossible to speak a word orally without any intonation. In a text punctuation can signal tone minimally: a question mark or a comma, for example, generally calls for the voice to be raised a bit. Literate tradition, adopted and adapted by skilled critics, can also supply some extratextual clues for intonations, but not complete ones. Actors spend hours determining how actually to utter the words in the text before them. A given passage might be delivered by one actor in a shout, by another in a whisper.

Extratextual context is missing not only for readers but also for the writer. Lack of verifiable context is what makes writing normally so much more agonizing an activity than oral presentation to a real audi-ence. 'The writer's audience is always a fiction' (Ong 1977, pp. 53–81). The writer must set up a role in which absent and often unknown readers can cast themselves. Even in writing to a close friend I have to fictionalize a mood for him, to which he is expected to conform. The reader must also fictionalize the writer. When my friend reads my letter, I may be in an entirely different frame of mind from when I wrote it. Indeed, I may very well be dead. For a text to convey its message, it does not matter whether the author is dead or alive. Most books extant today were written by persons now dead. Spoken utterance comes only from the living.

Even in a personal diary addressed to myself I must fictionalize the addressee. Indeed, the diary demands, in a way, the maximum fictionalizing of the utterer and the addressee. Writing is always a kind of imitation talking, and in a diary I therefore am pretending that I am talking to myself. But I never really talk this way to myself. Nor could I without writing or indeed without print. The personal diary is a very late literary form, in effect unknown until the seventeenth century (Boerner 1969). The kind of verbalized solipsistic reveries it implies are a product of consciousness as shaped by print culture. And for which self am I writing? Myself today? As I think I will be ten years from now? As I hope I will be? For myself as I imagine myself or hope others may imagine me? Questions such as this can and do fill diary writers with anxieties and often enough lead to discontinuation of diaries. The diarist can no longer live with his or her fiction.

The ways in which readers are fictionalized is the underside of literary history, of which the topside is the history of genres and the handling of character and plot. Early writing provides the reader with conspicuous help for situating himself imaginatively. It presents philosophical material in dialogues, such as those of Plato's Socrates, which the reader can imagine himself overhearing. Or episodes are to be imagined as told to a live audience on successive days. Later, in the Middle Ages, writing will present philosophical and theological texts in objection-and-response form, so that the reader can imagine an oral disputation. Boccaccio and Chaucer will provide the reader with fictional groups of men and women telling stories to one another, that is, a 'frame story', so that the reader can pretend to be one of the listening company. But who is talking to whom in *Pride and Prejudice* or in *Le Rouge et le noir*, or in *Adam Bede*? Nineteenth-century novelists self-consciously intone, 'dear reader', over and over again to remind themselves that they are not telling a story but writing one in which both author and reader are having difficulty situating themselves. The psychodynamics of writing matured very slowly in narrative.

And what is the reader supposed to make himself out to be in *Finnegans Wake*? Only a reader. But of a special fictional sort. Most readers of English cannot or will not make themselves into the special kind of reader Joyce demands. Some take courses in universities to learn how to fictionalize themselves à la Joyce. Although Joyce's text is very oral in the sense that it reads well aloud, the voice and its hearer do not fit into any imaginable real-life setting, but only the imaginative setting of *Finnegans Wake*, which is imaginable only because of the writing and print that has gone before it. *Finnegans Wake* was composed in writing, but for print: with its idiosyncratic spelling and usages, it would be virtually impossible to multiply it accurately in handwritten copies. There is no mimesis here in Aristotle's sense, except ironically. Writing is indeed the seedbed of irony, and the longer the writing (and print) tradition endures, the heavier the ironic growth becomes (Ong 1977, pp. 272–302).

## DISTANCE, PRECISION, GRAPHOLECTS AND MAGNAVOCABULARIES

The distancing which writing effects develops a new kind of precision in verbalization by removing it from the rich but chaotic existential context of much oral utterance. Oral performances can be impressive in their magniloquence and communal wisdom, whether they are lengthy, as in formal narrative, or brief and apophthegmatic, as in proverbs. Yet wisdom has to do with a total and relatively infrangible social context. Orally managed language and thought are not noted for analytic precision.

Of course, all language and thought are to some degree analytic: they break down the dense continuum of experience, William James's 'big, blooming, buzzing confusion', into more or less separate parts, meaningful segments. But written words sharpen analysis, for the individual words are called on to do more. To make yourself clear without gesture, without facial expression, without intonation, without a real hearer, you have to foresee circumspectly all possible meanings a statement may have for any possible reader in any possible situation, and you have to make your language work so as to come clear all by itself, with no existential context. The need for this exquisite circumspection makes writing the agonizing work it commonly is.

What Goody (1977, p. 128) calls 'backward scanning' makes it possible in writing to eliminate inconsistencies (Goody 1977, pp. 49–50), to choose between words with a reflective selectivity that invests thought and words with new discriminatory powers. In an oral culture, the flow of words, the corresponding flood of thought, the *copia* advocated in Europe by rhetoricians from classical antiquity through the Renaissance, tends to manage discrepancies by glossing them over – the etymology here is telling, *glossa*, tongue, by 'tonguing' them over. With writing, words once 'uttered', outered, put down on the surface, can be eliminated, erased, changed. There is no equivalent for this in an oral performance, no way to erase a spoken word: corrections do not remove an infelicity or an error, they merely supplement it with denial and patchwork. The *bricolage* or patchwork that Lévi-Strauss (1966, 1970) finds characteristic of 'primitive' or 'savage' thought patterns can be seen here to be due to the oral noetic situation. Corrections in oral performance tend to be counterproductive, to render the speaker unconvincing. So you keep them to a minimum or avoid them altogether. In writing, corrections can be tremendously productive, for how can the reader know they have even been made?

Of course, once the chirographically initiated feel for precision and analytic exactitude is interiorized, it can feed back into speech, and does. Although Plato's thought is couched in dialogue form, its exquisite precision is due to the effects of writing on the noetic processes, for the dialogues are in fact written texts. Through a chirographically managed text couched in dialogue form, they move dialectically toward the analytic clarification of issues which Socrates and Plato had inherited in more 'totalized', non-analytic, narratized, oral form.

In *The Greek Concept of Justice: From Its Shadow in Homer to Its Substance in Plato* (1978a), Havelock has treated the movement which Plato's work brought to a head. Nothing of Plato's analytic targeting on an abstract concept of justice is to be found in any known purely oral cultures. Similarly, the deadly targeting on issues and on adversaries' weaknesses in Cicero's orations is the work of a literate mind, although we know that Cicero did not compose his orations in script before he gave them but wrote down afterwards the texts that we now have (Ong 1967b, pp. 56–7). The exquisitely analytic oral disputations in medieval universities and in later scholastic tradition into the present century (Ong 1981, pp. 137–8) were the work of minds honed by writing texts and by reading and commenting on texts, orally and in writing.

By separating the knower from the known (Havelock 1963), writing makes possible increasingly articulate introspectivity, opening the psyche as never before not only to the external objective world quite distinct from itself but also to the interior self against whom the objective world is set. Writing makes possible the great introspective religious traditions such as Buddhism, Judaism, Christianity, and Islam. All these have sacred texts. The ancient Greeks and Romans knew writing and used it, particularly the Greeks, to elaborate philosophical and scientific knowledge. But they developed no sacred texts comparable to the Vedas or the Bible or the Koran, and their religion failed to establish itself in the recesses of the psyche which writing had opened for them. It became only a genteel, archaic literary resource for writers such as Ovid and a framework of external observances, lacking urgent personal meaning.

Writing develops codes in a language different from oral codes in the same language. Basil Bernstein (1974, pp. 134–5, 176, 181, 197–8) distinguishes the 'restricted linguistic code' or 'public language' of the lower-class English dialects in Britain and the 'elaborated linguistic code' or 'private language' of the middle- and upper-class dialects. Walt Wolfram (1972) had earlier noted distinctions like Bernstein's between Black American English and standard American English. The restricted linguistic code can be at least as expressive and precise as the elaborated code in contexts which are familiar and shared by speaker and hearer. For dealing with the unfamiliar expressively and precisely, however, the restricted linguistic code will not do; an elaborated linguistic code is absolutely needed. The restricted linguistic code is evidently largely oral in origin and use and, like oral thought and expression generally, operates contextually, close to the human lifeworld: the group whom Bernstein found using this code were messenger boys with no grammar school education. Their expression has a formula-like quality and strings thoughts together not in careful subordination but 'like beads on a frame' (1974, p. 134) – recognizably the formulaic and aggregative mode of oral culture. The elaborated code is one which is formed with the necessary aid of writing, and, for full elaboration, of print. The group Bernstein found using this code were from the six major public schools that provided the most intensive education in reading and writing in Britain (1974, p. 83). Bernstein's 'restricted' and 'elaborated' linguistic codes could be relabeled 'oral-based' and 'text-based' codes respectively. Olson (1977) has shown how orality relegates meaning largely to context whereas writing concentrates meaning in language itself.

Writing and print develop special kinds of dialects. Most languages have never been committed to writing at all, as has been seen (p. 7 above). But certain languages, or more properly dialects, have invested massively in writing. Often, as in England or Germany or Italy, where a cluster of dialects is found, one regional dialectic has developed chirographically beyond all others, for economic, political, religious, or other reasons, and has eventually become a national language. In England this happened to the upper-class London English dialect, in Germany, to Hochdeutsch (the German of the highlands to the south), in Italy to Tuscan. While it is true that these were all at root regional and/ or class dialects, their status as chirographically controlled national languages has made them different kinds of dialects or language from those which are not written on a large scale. As Guxman has pointed out (1970, pp. 773–6), a national written language has had to be isolated from its original dialect base, has discarded certain dialectal forms, has developed various layers of vocabulary from sources not dialectal at all, and has developed also certain syntactical peculiarities. This kind of established written language Haugen (1966, pp. 50–71) has aptly styled a 'grapholect'.

A modern grapholect such as 'English', to use the simple term which is commonly used to refer to this grapholect, has been worked over for centuries, first and most intensively, it seems, by the chancery of Henry V (Richardson 1980), then by normative theorists, grammarians, lexicographers, and others. It has been recorded massively in writing and print and now on computers so that those competent in the grapholect today can establish easy contact not only with millions of other persons but also with the thought of centuries past, for the other dialects of English as well as thousands of foreign languages are interpreted in the grapholect. In this sense, the grapholect includes all the other dialects: it explains them as they cannot explain themselves. The grapholect bears the marks of the millions of minds which have used it to share their consciousnesses with one another. Into it has been hammered a massive vocabulary of an order of magnitude impossible for an oral tongue. *Webster's Third New International Dictionary* (1971) states in its Preface that it could have included 'many times' more than the 450,000 words it does include. Assuming that 'many times' must mean at least three times, and rounding out the figures, we can understand that the editors have on hand a record of some million and a half words used in print in English. Oral languages and oral dialects can get along with a small fraction of this number.

The lexical richness of grapholects begins with writing, but its fullness is due to print. For the resources of a modern grapholect are available largely through dictionaries. There are limited word lists of various sorts from very early in the history of writing (Goody 1977, pp. 74–111), but until print is well established there are no dictionaries that undertake generalized comprehensive accounts of the words in use in any language. It is easy to understand why this is so if you think of what it would mean to make even a few dozen relatively accurate handwritten copies of *Webster's Third* or even of the much smaller *Webster's New Collegiate Dictionary*. Dictionaries such as these are light-years away from the world of oral cultures. Nothing illustrates more strikingly how it is that writing and print alter states of consciousness.

Where grapholects exist, 'correct' grammar and usage are popularly interpreted as the grammar and usage of the grapholect itself to the exclusion of the grammar and usage of other dialects. The sensory bases of the very concept of order are largely visual (Ong 1967b, pp. 108, 136–7), and the fact that the grapholect is written or, *a fortiori*, printed encourages attributing to it a special normative power for keeping language in order. But when other dialects of a given language besides the grapholect vary from the grammar of the grapholect, they are not ungrammatical: they are simply using a different grammar, for language is structure, and it is impossible to use language without a grammar. In the light of this fact, linguists today commonly make the point that all dialects are equal in the sense that none has a grammar intrinsically more 'correct' than that of others. But Hirsch (1977, pp. 43–50) makes the further point that in a profound sense no other dialect, for example, in English or German or Italian, has anything remotely like the resources of the grapholect. It is bad pedagogy to insist that because there is nothing 'wrong' with other dialects, it makes no difference whether or not speakers of another dialect learn the grapholect, which has resources of a totally different order of magnitude.

## INTERACTIONS: RHETORIC AND THE PLACES

Two special major developments in the West derive from and affect the interaction of writing and orality. These are academic rhetoric and Learned Latin.

In his Volume III of the *Oxford History of English Literature*, C. S. Lewis observed that 'rhetoric is the greatest barrier between us and our ancestors' (1954, p. 60). Lewis honors the magnitude of the subject by refusing to treat it, despite its overwhelming relevance for the culture of all ages at least up to the Age of Romanticism (Ong 1971, pp. 1–22, 255–83). The study of rhetoric dominant in all western cultures until that time had begun as the core of ancient Greek education and culture. In ancient Greece, the study of 'philosophy', represented by Socrates, Plato and Aristotle, for all its subsequent fecundity, was a relatively minor element in the total Greek culture, never competitive with rhetoric either in the number of its practitioners or in its immediate social effects (Marrou 1956, pp. 194–205), as Socrates' unhappy fate suggests.

Rhetoric was at root the art of public speaking, of oral address, for persuasion (forensic and deliberative rhetoric) or exposition (epideictic rhetoric). The Greek *rhetor* is from the same root as the Latin *orator* and means a public speaker. In the perspectives worked out by Havelock (1963) it would appear obvious that in a very deep sense the rhetorical tradition represented the old oral world and the philosophical tradition the new chirographic structures of thought. Like Plato, C. S. Lewis was in effect unwittingly turning his back on the old oral world. Over the centuries, until the Age of Romanticism (when the thrust of rhetoric was diverted, definitively if not totally, from oral performance to writing), explicit or even implicit commitment to the formal study and formal practice of rhetoric is an index of the amount of residual primary orality in a given culture (Ong 1971, pp. 23–103).

Homeric and the pre-Homeric Greeks, like oral peoples generally, practiced public speaking with great skill long before their skills were reduced to an 'art', that is, to a body of sequentially organized, scientific principles which explained and abetted what verbal persuasion consisted in. Such an 'art' is presented in Aristotle's Art of Rhetoric (technē rhētorikē). Oral cultures, as has been seen, can have no 'arts' of this scientifically organized sort. No one could or can simply recite extempore a treatise such as Aristotle's Art of Rhetoric, as someone in an oral culture would have to do if this sort of understanding were to be implemented. Lengthy oral productions follow more agglomerative, less analytic, patterns. The 'art' of rhetoric, though concerned with oral speech, was, like other 'arts', the product of writing.

Persons from a high-technology culture who become aware of the vast literature of the past dealing with rhetoric, from classical antiquity through the Middle Ages, the Renaissance, and on into the Age of the Enlightenment (e.g. Kennedy 1980; Murphy 1974; Howell 1956, 1971), of the universal and obsessive interest in the subject through the ages and the amount of time spent studying it, of its vast and intricate terminology for classifying hundreds of figures of speech in Greek and Latin – antinomasia or pronominatio, paradiastole or distinctio, anticategoria or accusatio concertativa, and so on and on and on – (Lanham 1968; Sonnino 1968) are likely to react with, 'What a waste of time!' But for its first discoverers or inventors, the Sophists of fifth-century Greece, rhetoric was a marvelous thing. It provided a rationale for what was dearest to their hearts, effective and often showy oral performance, something which had been a distinctively human part of human existence for ages but which, before writing, could never have been so reflectively prepared for or accounted for.

Rhetoric retained much of the old oral feeling for thought and expression as basically agonistic and formulaic. This shows clearly in rhetorical teaching about the 'places' (Ong 1967b, pp. 56–87; 1971, pp. 147–87; Howell 1956, Index). With its agonistic heritage, rhetorical teaching assumed that the aim of more or less all discourse was to prove or disprove a point, against some opposition. Developing a subject was thought of as a process of 'invention', that is, of finding in the store of arguments that others had always exploited those arguments which were applicable to your case. These arguments were considered to be lodged or 'seated' (Quintilian's term) in the 'places' (topoi in Greek, loci in Latin), and were often called the loci communes or commonplaces when they were thought of as providing arguments common to any and all subject matter.

From at least the time of Quintilian, loci communes was taken in two different senses. First, it referred to the 'seats' of arguments, considered as abstract 'headings' in today's parlance, such as definition, cause, effect, opposites, likenesses, and so on (the assortment varied in length from one author to another). Wanting to develop a 'proof' – we should say simply to develop a line of thought – on any subject, such as loyalty, evil, the guilt of an accused criminal, friendship, war, or whatever, one could always find something to say by defining, looking to causes, effects, opposites, and all the rest. These headings can be styled the 'analytic commonplaces'. Secondly, loci communes or commonplaces referred to collections of sayings (in effect, formulas) on various topics – such as loyalty, decadence, friendship, or whatever – that could be worked into one's own speech-making or writing. In this sense the loci communes can be styled 'cumulative commonplaces'. Both the analytic and the cumulative commonplaces, it is clear, kept alive the old oral feeling for thought and expression essentially made up of formulaic or otherwise fixed materials inherited from the past. To say this is not to explicate the whole of the complex doctrine, which itself was integral to the massive art of rhetoric.

Rhetoric of course is essentially antithetical (Durand 1960, pp. 451, 453–9), for the orator speaks in the face of at least implied adversaries. Oratory has deep agonistic roots (Ong 1967b, pp. 192–222; 1981, pp. 119–48). The development of the vast rhetorical tradition was distinctive of the West and was related, whether as cause or effect or both, to the tendency among the Greeks and their cultural epigoni to maximize oppositions, in the mental as in the extramental world: this by contrast with Indians and Chinese, who programmatically minimized them (Lloyd 1966; Oliver 1971).

From Greek antiquity on, the dominance of rhetoric in the academic background produced throughout the literate world an impression, real if often vague, that oratory was the paradigm of all verbal expression, and kept the agonistic pitch of discourse exceedingly high by present-day standards. Poetry itself was often assimilated to epideictic oratory, and was considered to be concerned basically with praise or blame (as much oral, and even written, poetry is even today).

Into the nineteenth century most literary style throughout the West was formed by academic rhetoric, in one way or another, with one notable exception: the literary style of female authors. Of the females who became published writers, as many did from the 1600s on, almost none had any such training. In medieval times and after, the education of girls was often intensive and produced effective managers of households, of sometimes fifty to eighty persons, which were often sizable businesses (Markham 1675, *The English House-Wife*), but this education was not acquired in academic institutions, which taught rhetoric and all other subjects in Latin. When they began to enter schools in some numbers during the seventeenth century, girls entered not the mainline Latin schools but the newer vernacular schools. These were practically oriented, for commerce and domestic affairs, whereas the older schools with Latin-based instruction were for those aspiring to be clergy, lawyers, physicians, diplomats, and other public servants. Women writers were no doubt influenced by works that they had read emanating from the Latin-based, academic, rhetorical tradition, but they themselves normally expressed themselves in a different, far less oratorical voice, which had a great deal to do with the rise of the novel.

## INTERACTIONS: LEARNED LANGUAGES

The second massive development in the West affecting the interaction of writing and orality was Learned Latin. Learned Latin was a direct result of writing. Between about AD 550 and 700 the Latin spoken as a vernacular in various parts of Europe had evolved into various early forms of Italian, Spanish, Catalan, French, and the other Romance languages. By AD 700, speakers of these offshoots of Latin could no longer understand the old written Latin, intelligible perhaps to some of their greatgrandparents. Their spoken language had moved too far away from its origins. But schooling, and with it most official discourse of Church or state, continued in Latin. There was really no alternative.

Europe was a morass of hundreds of languages and dialects, most of them never written to this day. Tribes speaking countless Germanic and Slavic dialects, and even more exotic, non-Indo-European languages such as Magyar and Finnish and Turkish, were moving into western Europe. There was no way to translate the works, literary, scientific, philosophical, medical or theological, taught in schools and universities, into the swarming, oral vernaculars which often had different, mutually unintelligible forms among populations perhaps only fifty miles apart. Until one or another dialect for economic or other reasons became dominant enough to gain adherents even from other dialectical regions (as the East Midland dialect did in England or Hochdeutsch in Germany), the only practical policy was to teach Latin to the limited numbers of boys going to school. Once a mother tongue, Latin thus became a school language only, spoken not only in the classroom but also, in principle if far from always in fact, everywhere else on the school premises. By prescription of school statutes Latin had become Learned Latin, a language completely controlled by writing, whereas the new Romance vernaculars had developed out of Latin as languages had always developed, orally. Latin had undergone a sound-sight split.

Because of its base in academia, which was totally male − with exceptions so utterly rare as to be quite negligible − Learned Latin had another feature in common with rhetoric besides its classical provenance. For well over a thousand years, it was sex-linked, a language written and spoken only by males, learned outside the home in a tribal setting which was in effect a male puberty rite setting, complete with physical punishment and other kinds of deliberately imposed hardships (Ong 1971, pp. 113–41; 1981, pp. 119–48). It had no direct connection with anyone's unconscious of the sort that mother tongues, learned in infancy, always have.

Learned Latin related to orality and literacy, however, in paradoxical ways. On the one hand, as just noted, it was a chirographically controlled language. Of the millions who spoke it for the next 1400 years, every one was able also to write it. There were no purely oral users. But chirographic control of Learned Latin did not preclude its alliance with orality. Paradoxically, the textuality that kept Latin rooted in classical antiquity thereby kept it rooted also in orality, for the classical ideal of education had been to produce not the effective writer but the *rhetor*, the *orator*, the public speaker. The grammar of Learned Latin came from this old oral world. So did its basic vocabulary, although, like all languages actually in use, it incorporated thousands of new words over the centuries.

Devoid of baby-talk, insulated from the earliest life of childhood where language has its deepest psychic roots, a first language to none of its users, pronounced across Europe in often mutually unintelligible ways but always written the same way, Learned Latin was a striking exemplification of the power of writing for isolating discourse and of the unparalleled productivity of such isolation. Writing, as has earlier been seen, serves to separate and distance the knower and the known and thus to establish objectivity. It has been suggested (Ong 1977, pp. 24–9) that Learned Latin effects even greater objectivity by establishing knowledge in a medium insulated from the emotion-charged depths of one's mother tongue, thus reducing interference from the human life-world and making possible the exquisitely abstract world of medieval scholasticism and of the new mathematical modern science which followed on the scholastic experience. Without Learned Latin, it appears that modern science would have got under way with greater difficulty, if it had got under way at all. Modern science grew in Latin soil, for philosophers and scientists through the time of Sir Isaac Newton commonly both wrote and did their abstract thinking in Latin.

Interaction between such a chirographically controlled language as Learned Latin and the various vernaculars (mother tongues) is still far from being completely understood. There is no way simply to 'translate' a language such as Learned Latin into languages like the vernaculars. Translation was transformation. Interaction produced all sorts of special results. Bäuml (1980, p. 264) has called attention, for example, to some of the effects when metaphors from a consciously metaphorical Latin were shifted into less metaphoricized mother tongues.

During this period, other chirographically controlled, sexlinked male languages developed in Europe and Asia where sizable literate populations wanted to share a common intellectual heritage. Pretty much coeval with Learned Latin were Rabbinic Hebrew, Classical Arabic, Sanskrit, and Classical Chinese, with Byzantine Greek a sixth, much less definitively learned language, for vernacular Greek kept close contact with it (Ong 1977, pp. 28–34). These languages were all no longer in use as mother tongues (that is, in the straightforward sense, not used by mothers in raising children). They were never first languages for any individual, were controlled exclusively by writing, were spoken by males only (with negligible exceptions, though perhaps with more exceptions for Classical Chinese than for the others), and were spoken only by those who could write them and who, indeed, had learned them initially by the use of writing. Such languages are no more, and it is difficult today to sense their earlier power. All languages used for learned discourse today are also mother tongues (or, in the case of Arabic, are more and more assimilating to themselves mother tongues). Nothing shows more convincingly than this disappearance of chirographically controlled language how writing is losing its earlier power monopoly (though not its importance) in today's world.

## TENACIOUSNESS OF ORALITY

As the paradoxical relationships of orality and literacy in rhetoric and Learned Latin suggest, the transition from orality to literacy was slow (Ong 1967b, pp. 53–87; 1971, pp. 23–48). The Middle Ages used texts far more than ancient Greece and Rome, teachers lectured on texts in the universities, and yet never tested knowledge or intellectual prowess by writing, but always by oral dispute – a practice continued in diminishing ways into the nineteenth century and today still surviving vestigially in the defense of the doctoral dissertation in the fewer and fewer places where this is practiced. Though Renaissance humanism invented modern textual scholarship and presided over the development of letterpress printing, it also harked back to antiquity and thereby gave new life to orality. English style in the Tudor period (Ong 1971, pp. 23–47) and even much later carried heavy oral residue in its use of epithets, balance, antithesis, formulary structures, and commonplace materials. And so with western European literary styles generally.

In western classical antiquity, it was taken for granted that a written text of any worth was meant to be and deserved to be read aloud, and the practice of reading texts aloud continued, quite commonly with many variations, through the nineteenth century (Balogh 1926). This practice strongly influenced literary style from antiquity until rather recent times (Balogh 1926; Crosby 1936; Nelson 1976–7; Ahern

1982). Still yearning for the old orality, the nineteenth century developed 'elocution' contests, which tried to repristinate printed texts, using careful artistry to memorize the texts verbatim and recite them so that they would sound like extempore oral productions (Howell 1971, pp. 144–256). Dickens read selections from his novels on the orator's platform. The famous *McGuffey's Readers*, published in the United States in some 120 million copies between 1836 and 1920, were designed as remedial readers to improve not the reading for comprehension which we idealize today, but oral, declamatory reading. The *McGuffey's* specialized in passages from 'sound-conscious' literature concerned with great heroes ('heavy' oral characters). They provided endless oral pronunciation and breathing drills (Lynn 1973, pp. 16, 20).

Rhetoric itself gradually but inevitably migrated from the oral to the chirographic world. From classical antiquity the verbal skills learned in rhetoric were put to use not only in oratory but also in writing. By the sixteenth century rhetoric textbooks were commonly omitting from the traditional five parts of rhetoric (invention, arrangement, style, memory and delivery) the fourth part, memory, which was not applicable to writing. They were also minimizing the last part, delivery (Howell 1956, pp. 146–72, 270, *et passim*). By and large, they made these changes with specious explanations or no explanation at all. Today, when curricula list rhetoric as a subject, it usually means simply the study of how to write effectively. But no one ever consciously launched a program to give this new direction to rhetoric: the 'art' simply followed the drift of consciousness away from an oral to a writing economy. The drift was completed before it was noticed that anything was happening. Once it was completed, rhetoric was no longer the all-pervasive subject it had once been: education could no longer be described as fundamentally rhetorical as it could be in past ages. The three Rs – reading, 'riting, and 'rithmetic – representing an essentially nonrhetorical, bookish, commercial and domestic education, gradually took over from the traditional orally grounded, heroic, agonistic education that had generally prepared young men in the past for teaching and professional, ecclesiastical, or political public service. In the process, as rhetoric and Latin went out, women entered more and more into academia, which also became more and more commercially oriented (Ong 1967b, pp. 241–55).

# 5

## PRINT, SPACE AND CLOSURE

### HEARING-DOMINANCE YIELDS TO SIGHT-DOMINANCE

Although this book attends chiefly to oral culture and to the changes in thought and expression introduced by writing, it must give some brief attention to print, for print both reinforces and transforms the effects of writing on thought and expression. Since the shift from oral to written speech is essentially a shift from sound to visual space, here the effects of print on the use of visual space can be the central, though not the only, focus of attention. This focus brings out not only the relationship between print and writing, but also the relationship of print to the orality still residual in writing and early print culture. Moreover, while all the effects of print do not reduce to its effects on the use of visual space, many of the other effects do relate to this use in various ways.

In a work of this scope there is no way even to enumerate all the effects of print. Even a cursory glance at Elizabeth Eisenstein's two volumes, *The Printing Press as an Agent of Change* (1979), makes abundantly evident how diversified and vast the particular effects of print have been. Eisenstein spells out in detail how print made the Italian Renaissance a permanent European Renaissance, how it implemented the Protestant Reformation and reoriented Catholic religious practice, how it affected the development of modern capitalism, implemented western European exploration of the globe, changed family life and politics, diffused knowledge as never before, made universal literacy a serious objective, made possible the rise of modern sciences, and otherwise altered social and intellectual life. In *The Gutenberg Galaxy* (1962) and *Understanding Media* (1964) Marshall McLuhan has called attention to many of the subtler ways print has affected consciousness, as George Steiner has also done in *Language and Silence* (1967) and as I have undertaken to do elsewhere (Ong 1958b; 1967b; 1971; 1977). These subtler effects of print on consciousness, rather than readily observable social effects, concern us particularly here.

For thousands of years human beings have been printing designs from variously carved surfaces, and since the seventh or eighth century Chinese, Koreans and Japanese have been printing verbal texts, at first from wood blocks engraved in relief (Carter 1955). But the crucial development in the global history of printing was the invention of alphabetic letterpress print in fifteenth-century Europe. Alphabetic writing had broken the word up into spatial equivalents of phonemic units (in principle, though the letters never quite worked out as totally phonemic indicators). But the letters used in writing do not exist before the text in which they occur. With alphabetic letterpress print it is otherwise. Words are made out of units (types) which pre-exist as units before the words which they will constitute. Print suggests that words are things far more than writing ever did.

Like the alphabet, alphabetic letterpress print was a nonce invention (Ong 1967b, and references there cited). The Chinese had had movable type, but no alphabet, only characters, basically pictographic. Before the mid-1400s the Koreans and Uigur Turks had both the alphabet and movable type, but the movable types bore not separate letters but whole words. Alphabet letterpress printing, in which each letter was cast on a separate piece of metal, or type, marked a psychological breakthrough of the first order. It embedded the word itself deeply in the manufacturing process and made it into a kind of commodity. The first assembly line, a technique of manufacture which in a series of set steps produces identical complex objects made up of replaceable parts, was not one which produced stoves or shoes or weaponry but one which produced the printed book. In the late 1700s, the industrial revolution applied to other manufacturing the replaceable-part techniques which printers had worked with for three hundred years. Despite the assumptions of many semiotic structuralists, it was print, not writing, that effectively reified the word, and, with it, noetic activity (Ong 1958b, pp. 306–18).

Hearing rather than sight had dominated the older noetic world in significant ways, even long after writing was deeply interiorized. Manuscript culture in the West remained always marginally oral. Ambrose of Milan caught the earlier mood in his *Commentary on Luke* (iv. 5): 'Sight is often deceived, hearing serves as guarantee.' In the West through the Renaissance, the oration was the most taught of all verbal productions and remained implicitly the basic paradigm for all discourse, written as well as oral. Written material was subsidiary to hearing in ways which strike us today as bizarre. Writing served largely to recycle knowledge back into the oral world, as in medieval university disputations, in the reading of literary and other texts to groups (Crosby 1936; Ahern 1981; Nelson 1976–7), and in reading aloud even when reading to oneself. At least as late as the twelfth century in England, checking even written financial accounts was still done aurally, by having them read aloud. Clanchy (1979, pp. 215, 183) describes the practice and draws attention to the fact that it still registers in our vocabulary: even today, we speak of 'auditing', that is, 'hearing' account books, though what an accountant actually does today is examine them by sight. Earlier, residually oral folk could understand even figures better by listening than by looking.

Manuscript cultures remained largely oral-aural even in retrieval of material preserved in texts. Manuscripts were not easy to read, by later typographic standards, and what readers found in manuscripts they tended to commit at least somewhat to memory. Relocating material in a manuscript was not always easy. Memorization was encouraged and facilitated also by the fact that in highly oral manuscript cultures, the verbalization one encountered even in written texts often continued the oral mnemonic patterning that made for ready recall. Moreover, readers commonly vocalized, read slowly aloud or *sotto voce*, even when reading alone, and this also helped fix matter in the memory.

Well after printing was developed, auditory processing continued for some time to dominate the visible, printed text, though it was eventually eroded away by print. Auditory dominance can be seen strikingly in such things as early printed title pages, which often seem to us crazily erratic in the their inattention to visual word units. Sixteenth-century title pages very commonly divide even major words, including the author's name, with hyphens, presenting the first part of a word in one line in large type and the latter part in smaller type, as in the edition of Sir Thomas Elyot's *The Boke Named the Gouernour* published in London by Thomas Berthelet in 1534 (Figure 1 here; see Steinberg 1974, p. 154). Inconsequential words may be set in huge type faces: on the title page shown here the initial 'THE' is by far the most prominent

Figure 1

word of all. The result is often aesthetically pleasing as a visual design, but it plays havoc with our present sense of textuality. Yet this practice, not our practice, is the original practice from which our present practice has deviated. Our attitudes are the ones that have changed, and thus that need to be explained. Why does the original, presumably more 'natural' procedure seem wrong to us? Because we feel the printed words before us as visual units (even though we sound them at least in the imagination when we read). Evidently, in processing text for meaning, the sixteenth century was concentrating less on the sight of the word and more on its sound than we do. All text involves sight and sound. But whereas we feel reading as a visual activity cueing in sounds for us, the early age of print still felt it as primarily a listening process, simply set in motion by sight. If you felt yourself as reader to be listening to words, what difference did it make if the visible text went its own visually aesthetic way? It will be recalled that pre-print manuscripts commonly ran words together or kept spaces between them minimal.

Eventually, however, print replaced the lingering hearing-dominance in the world of thought and expression with the sight-dominance which had its beginnings with writing but could not flourish with the support of writing alone. Print situates words in space more relentlessly than writing ever did. Writing moves words from the sound world to a world of visual space, but print locks words into position in this space. Control of position is everything in print. 'Composing' type by hand (the original form of typesetting) consists in positioning by hand preformed letter types, which, after use, are carefully repositioned, redistributed for future use into their proper compartments in the case (capitals or 'upper case' letters in the upper compartments, small or 'lower case' letters in the lower compartments). Composing on the linotype consists in using a machine to position the separate matrices for individual lines so that a line of type can be cast from the properly positioned matrices. Composing on a computer terminal or wordprocesser positions electronic patterns (letters) previously programmed into the computer. Printing from 'hot metal' type (that is, from cast type – the older process) calls for locking up the type in an absolutely rigid position in the chase, locking the chase firmly onto a press, affixing and clamping down the makeready, and squeezing the forme of type with great pressure onto the paper printing surface in contact with the platen.

Most readers are of course not consciously aware of all this locomotion that has produced the printed text confronting them. Nevertheless, from the appearance of the printed text they pick up a sense of the word-in-space quite different from that conveyed by writing. Printed texts look machine-made, as they are. Chirographic control of space tends to be ornamental, ornate, as in calligraphy. Typographic control typically impresses more by its tidiness and inevitability: the lines perfectly regular, all justified on the right side, everything coming out even visually, and without the aid of the guidelines or ruled borders that often occur in manuscripts. This is an insistent world of cold, non-human, facts. 'That's the way it is' – Walter Cronkite's television signature comes from the world of print that underlies the secondary orality of television (Ong 1971, pp. 284–303).

By and large, printed texts are far easier to read than manuscript texts. The effects of the greater legibility of print are massive. The greater legibility ultimately makes for rapid, silent reading. Such reading in turn makes for a different relationship between the reader and the authorial voice in the text and calls for different styles of writing. Print involves many persons besides the author in the production of a work – publishers, literary agents, publishers' readers, copy editors and others. Before as well as after scrutiny by such persons, writing for print often calls for painstaking revisions by the author of an order of magnitude virtually unknown in a manuscript culture. Few lengthy prose works from manuscript cultures could pass editorial scrutiny as original works today: they are not organized for rapid assimilation from a printed page. Manuscript culture is producer-oriented, since every individual copy of a work represents great expenditure of an individual copyist's time. Medieval manuscripts are turgid with abbreviations, which favor the copyist although they inconvenience the reader. Print is consumer-oriented, since the individual copies of a work represent a much smaller investment of time: a few hours spent in producing a more readable text will immediately improve thousands upon thousands of copies. The effects of print on thought and style have yet to be assessed fully. The journal *Visible Language* (formerly called the *Journal of Typographic Research*) published many articles contributory to such an assessment.

## SPACE AND MEANING

Writing had reconstituted the originally oral, spoken word in visual space. Print embedded the word in space more definitively. This can be seen in such developments as lists, especially alphabetic indexes, in the use of words (instead of iconographic signs) for labels, in the use of printed drawings of all sorts to convey information, and in the use of abstract typographic space to interact geometrically with printed words in a line of development that runs from Ramism to concrete poetry and to Derrida's logomachy with the (printed, typically, not simply written) text.

### (i) Indexes

Lists begin with writing. Goody has discussed (1977, pp. 741 1 1) the use of lists in the Ugaritic script of around 1300 BC and in other early scripts. He notes (1977, pp. 87–8) that the information in the lists is abstracted from the social situation in which it had been embedded ('fattened kids', 'pastured ewes', etc., with no further specifications) and also from linguistic context (normally in oral utterance nouns are not free-floating as in lists, but are embedded in sentences: rarely do we hear an oral recitation of simply a string of nouns – unless they are being read off a written or printed list). In this sense, lists as such have 'no oral equivalent' (1977, pp. 86–7) though of course the individual written words sound in the inner ear to yield their meanings. Goody also notes the initially awkward, *ad hoc* way in which space was utilized in making these lists, with word-dividers to separate items from numbers, ruled lines, wedged lines, and elongated lines. Besides administrative lists, he discusses also event lists, lexical lists (words are listed in various orders, often hierarchically by meaning – gods, then kin of the gods, next gods' servants), and Egyptian onomastica or name-lists, which were often memorized for oral recitation. Still highly oral manuscript culture felt that having written series of things readied for oral recall was of itself intellectually improving. (Educators in the West until recently had the same feeling, and across the world most educators probably still do.) Writing is here once more at the service of orality.

Goody's examples show the relatively sophisticated processing of verbalized material in chirographic cultures so as to make the material more immediately retrievable through its spatial organization. Lists range names of related items in the same physical, visual space. Print develops far more sophisticated use of space for visual organization and for effective retrieval.

Indexes are a prime development here. Alphabetic indexes show strikingly the disengagement of words from discourse and their embedding in typographic space. Manuscripts can be alphabetically indexed. They rarely are (Daly 1967, pp. 81–90; Clanchy 1979, pp. 28–9, 85). Since two manuscripts of a given work, even if copied from the same dictation, almost never correspond page for page, each manuscript of a given work would normally require a separate index. Indexing was not worth the effort. Auditory recall through memorization was more economical, though not thorough-going. For visual location of materials in a manuscript text, pictorial signs were often preferred to alphabetic indexes. A favorite sign was the 'paragraph', which originally meant this mark ¶, not a unit of discourse at all. When alphabetic indexes occurred, they were rare, often crude, and commonly not understood, even in thirteenth-century Europe, when sometimes an index made for one manuscript was appended without change of page numbers to another manuscript with a different pagination (Clanchy 1979, p. 144). Indexes seem to have been valued at times for their beauty and mystery rather than for their utility. In 1286, a Genoese compiler could marvel at the alphabetical catalogue he had devised as due not to his own prowess but 'the grace of God working in me' (Daly 1967, p. 73). Indexing was long by first letter only – or, rather, by first sound: for example, in a Latin work published as late as 1506 in Rome, since in Italian and Latin as spoken by Italian-speakers the letter h is not pronounced, 'Halyzones' is listed under a (discussed in Ong 1977, pp. 169–72). Here even visual retrieval functions aurally. Ioannes Ravisius Textor's Specimen epithetorum (Paris, 1518), alphabetizes 'Apollo' before all other entries under a, because Textor considers it fitting that in a work concerned with poetry, the god of poetry should get top billing.

Clearly, even in a printed alphabetic index, visual retrieval was given low priority. The personalized, oral world still could overrule processing words as things.

The alphabetic index is actually a crossroads between auditory and visualist cultures. 'Index' is a shortened form of the original *index locorum* or *index locorum communium*, 'index of places' or 'index of commonplaces'. Rhetoric had provided the various *loci* or 'places' — headings, we would style them — under which various 'arguments' could be found, headings such as cause, effect, related things, unlike things, and so on. Coming with this orally based, formulary equipment to the text, the indexer of 400 years ago simply noted on what pages in the text one or another *locus* was exploited, listing there the locus and the corresponding pages in the *index locorum*. The loci had originally been thought of as, vaguely, 'places' in the mind where ideas were stored. In the printed book, these vague psychic 'places' became quite physically and visibly localized. A new noetic world was shaping up, spatially organized.

In this new world, the book was less like an utterance, and more like a thing. Manuscript culture had preserved a feeling for a book as a kind of utterance, an occurrence in the course of conversation, rather than as an object. Lacking title pages and often titles, a book from pre-print, manuscript culture is normally catalogued by its 'incipit' (a Latin verb meaning 'it begins'), or the first words of its text (referring to the Lord's Prayer as the 'Our Father' is referring to it by its incipit and evinces a certain residual orality). With print, as has been seen, come title pages. Title pages are labels. They attest a feeling for the book as a kind of thing or object. Often in medieval western manuscripts, instead of a title page the text proper might be introduced by an observation to the reader, just as a conversation might start with a remark of one person to another: 'Hic habes, carissime lector, librum quem scripset quidam de. . . .' (Here you have, dear reader, a book which so-and-so wrote about. . . .) The oral heritage is at work here, for, although oral cultures of course have ways of referring to stories or other traditional recitations (the stories of the Wars of Troy, the Mwindo stories, and so on), label-like titles as such are not very operational in oral cultures: Homer would hardly have begun a recitation of episodes from the *Iliad* by announcing '*The Iliad*'.

## (ii) Books, contents and labels

Once print has been fairly well interiorized, a book was sensed as a kind of object which 'contained' information, scientific, fictional or other, rather than, as earlier, a recorded utterance (Ong 1958b, p. 313). Each individual book in a printed edition was physically the same as another, an identical object, as manuscript books were not, even when they presented the same text. Now, with print, two copies of a given work did not merely say the same thing, they were duplicates of one another as objects. The situation invited the use of labels, and the printed book, being a lettered object, naturally took a lettered label, the title page (new with print – Steinberg 1974, pp. 145–8). At the same time the iconographic drive was still strong, as is seen in the highly emblematic engraved title pages that persisted through the 1660s, filled with allegorical figures and other nonverbal designs.

## (iii) Meaningful surface

Ivins (1953, p. 31) has pointed out that, although the art of printing designs from various carved surfaces had been known for centuries, only after the development of movable letterpress type in the mid-1400s were prints used systematically to convey information. Hand-done technical drawings, as Ivins has shown (1953, pp. 14–16, 40–5) soon deteriorated in manuscripts because even skilled artists miss the point of an illustration they are copying unless they are supervised by an expert in the field the illustrations refer to. Otherwise, a sprig of white clover copied by a succession of artists unfamiliar with real white clover can end up looking like asparagus. Prints might have solved the problem in a manuscript culture, since print-making had been practiced for centuries for decorative purposes. Cutting an accurate printing block for white clover would have been quite feasible long before the invention of letterpress printing, and would have provided just what was needed, an 'exactly repeatable visual statement'. But manuscript production was not congenial to such manufacture. Manuscripts were produced by handwriting, not from pre-existing parts. Print was congenial. The verbal text was reproduced from pre-existing parts, and so could prints be. A press could print an 'exactly repeatable visual statement' as easily as a forme set up from type.

One consequence of the new exactly repeatable visual statement was modern science. Exact observation does not begin with modern science. For ages, it has always been essential for survival among, for example, hunters and craftsmen of many sorts. What is distinctive of modern science is the conjuncture of exact observation and exact verbalization: exactly worded descriptions of carefully observed complex objects and processes. The availability of carefully made, technical prints (first woodcuts, and later even more exactly detailed metal engravings) implemented such exactly worded descriptions. Technical prints and technical verbalization reinforced and improved each other. The resulting hypervisualized noetic world was brand new. Ancient and medieval writers are simply unable to produce exactly worded descriptions of complex objects at all approximating the descriptions that appear after print and, indeed, that mature chiefly with the Age of Romanticism, that is, the age of the Industrial Revolution. Oral and residually oral verbalization directs its attention to action, not to the visual appearance of objects or scenes or persons (Fritschi 1981, pp. 65–6; cf. Havelock 1963, pp. 61–96). Vitruvius' treatise on architecture is notoriously vague. The kinds of exactitude aimed at by the long-standing rhetorical tradition were not of a visual–vocal sort. Eisenstein (1979, p. 64) suggests how difficult it is today to imagine earlier cultures where relatively few persons had ever seen a physically accurate picture of anything.

The new noetic world opened by exactly repeatable visual statement and correspondingly exact verbal description of physical reality affected not just science but literature as well. No pre-Romantic prose provides the circumstantial description of landscape found in Gerard Manley Hopkins's notebooks (1937) and no pre-Romantic poetry proceeds with the close, meticulous, clinical attention to natural phenomena found, for example, in Hopkins's description of a plunging brook in *Inversnaid*. As much as Darwin's evolutionary biology or Michelson's physics this kind of poetry grows out of the world of print.

### (iv) Typographic space

Because visual surface had become charged with imposed meaning and because print controlled not only what words were put down to form a text but also the exact situation of the words on the page and their spatial relationship to one another, the space itself on a printed sheet – 'white space' as it is called – took on high significance that leads directly into the modern and post-modern world. Manuscript lists and charts, discussed by Goody (1977, pp. 74–111), can situate words in specific spatial relationships to one another, but if the spatial relationships are extremely complicated, the complications will not survive the vagaries of successive copiers. Print can reproduce with complete accuracy and in any quantity indefinitely complex lists and charts. Early in the age of print, extremely complex charts appear in the teaching of academic subjects (Ong 1958b, pp. 80, 81, 202, *et passim*).

Typographic space works not only on the scientific and philosophic imagination, but also on the literary imagination, which shows some of the complicated ways in which typographic space is present to the psyche. George Herbert exploits typographic space to provide meaning in his 'Easter Wings' and 'The Altar', where the lines, of varying lengths, give the poems a visualized shape suggesting wings and an altar respectively. In manuscripts, this kind of visual structure would be only marginally viable. In *Tristram Shandy* (1760–7), Laurence Sterne uses typographic space with calculated whimsy, including in his book blank pages, to indicate his unwillingness to treat a subject and to invite the reader to fill in. Space here is the equivalent of silence. Much later, and with greater sophistication, Stéphane Mallarmé designs his poem 'Un Coup de dés' to be set in varying fonts and sizes of type with the lines scattered calculatingly across the pages in a kind of typographical free-fall suggesting the chance that rules a throw of dice (the poem is reproduced and discussed in Bruns 1974, pp. 115–38). Mallarmé's declared objective is to 'avoid narrative' and 'space out' the reading of the poem so that the page, with its typographic spaces, not the line, is the unit of verse. E. E. Cummings's untitled Poem No. 276 (1968) about the grasshopper disintegrates the words of its text and scatters them unevenly about the page until at last letters come together in the final word 'grasshopper' – all this to suggest the erratic and optically dizzying flight of a grasshopper until he finally reassembles himself straightforwardly on the blade of grass before us. White space is so integral to Cummings's poem that it is utterly impossible to read the poem aloud. The sounds cued in by the letters have to be present in the imagination but their presence is not simply auditory: it interacts with the visually and kinesthetically perceived space around them.

Concrete poetry (Solt 1970) climaxes in a certain way the inter-action of sounded words and typographic space. It presents exquisitely complicated or exquisitely uncomplicated visual displays of letters and/or words some of which can be viewed but not read aloud at all, but none of which can be appropriated without some awareness of verbal sound. Even when concrete poetry cannot be read at all, it is still not merely a picture. Concrete poetry is a minor genre, often merely gimmicky – a fact which makes it all the more necessary to explain the drive to produce it.

Hartman (1981, p. 35) has suggested a connection between con-crete poetry and Jacques Derrida's on-going logomachy with the text. The connection is certainly real and deserves more attention. Concrete poetry plays with the dialectic of the word locked into space as opposed to the sounded, oral word which can never be locked into space (every text is pretext), that is, it plays with the absolute limita-tions of textuality which paradoxically reveal the built-in limitations of the spoken word, too. This is Derrida's terrain, though he moves over it at his own calculated gait. Concrete poetry is not the product of writing but of typography, as has been seen. Deconstruction is tied to typog-raphy rather than, as its advocates seem often to assume, merely to writing.

## MORE DIFFUSE EFFECTS

One can list without end additional effects, more or less direct, which print had on the noetic economy or the 'mentality' of the West. Print eventually removed the ancient art of (orally based) rhetoric from the center of academic education. It encouraged and made possible on a large scale the quantification of knowledge, both through the use of mathematical analysis and through the use of diagrams and charts. Print eventually reduced the appeal of iconography in the management

of knowledge, despite the fact that the early ages of print put iconographic illustrations into circulation as they had never been before.
Iconographic figures are akin to the 'heavy' or type characters of oral
discourse and they are associated with rhetoric and with the arts of
memory that oral management of knowledge needs (Yates 1966).

Print produced exhaustive dictionaries and fostered the desire to
legislate for 'correctness' in language. This desire in great part grew out
of a sense of language based on the study of Learned Latin. Learned
tongues textualize the idea of language, making it seem at root something written. Print reinforces the sense of language as essentially textual. The printed text, not the written text, is the text in its fullest,
paradigmatic form.

Print established the climate in which dictionaries grew. From their
origins in the eighteenth century until the past few decades, dictionaries of English have commonly taken as their norm for language only
the usage of writers producing text for print (and not quite all of
them). The usage of all others, if it deviates from this typographic
usage, has been regarded as 'corrupt'. *Webster's Third New International
Dictionary* (1961) was the first major lexicographical work to break
cleanly with this old typographical convention and to cite as sources
for usage persons not writing for print – and of course many persons,
formed in the old ideology, immediately wrote off this impressive
lexicographical achievement (Dykema 1963) as a betrayal of the 'true'
or 'pure' language.

Print was also a major factor in the development of the sense of
personal privacy that marks modern society. It produced books smaller
and more portable than those common in a manuscript culture,
setting the stage psychologically for solo reading in a quiet corner, and
eventually for completely silent reading. In manuscript culture and
hence in early print culture, reading had tended to be a social activity,
one person reading to others in a group. As Steiner (1967, p. 383) has
suggested, private reading demands a home spacious enough to provide for individual isolation and quiet. (Teachers of children from
poverty areas today are acutely aware that often the major reason for
poor performance is that there is nowhere in a crowded house where a
boy or girl can study effectively.)

Print created a new sense of the private ownership of words. Persons in a primary oral culture can entertain some sense of proprietary rights to a poem, but such a sense is rare and ordinarily enfeebled by the common share of lore, formulas, and themes on which everyone draws. With writing, resentment at plagiarism begins to develop. The ancient Latin poet Martial (i. 53.9) uses the word *plagiarius*, a torturer, plunderer, oppressor, for someone who appropriates another's writing. But there is no special Latin word with the exclusive meaning of plagiarist or plagiarism. The oral commonplace tradition was still strong. In the very early days of print, however, a royal decree or *privilegium* was often secured forbidding the reprinting of a printed book by others than the original publisher. Richard Pynson secured such a *privilegium* in 1518 from Henry VIII. In 1557 the Stationers' Company was incorporated in London to oversee authors' and printers' or printer-publishers' rights, and by the eighteenth century modern copyright laws were shaping up over western Europe. Typography had made the word into a commodity. The old communal oral world had split up into privately claimed freeholdings. The drift in human consciousness toward greater individualism had been served well by print. Of course, words were not quite private property. They were still shared property to a degree. Printed books did echo one another, willy-nilly. At the onset of the electronic age, Joyce faced up to the anxieties of influence squarely and in *Ulysses* and *Finnegans Wake* undertook to echo everybody on purpose.

By removing words from the world of sound where they had first had their origin in active human interchange and relegating them definitively to visual surface, and by otherwise exploiting visual space for the management of knowledge, print encouraged human beings to think of their own interior conscious and unconscious resources as more and more thing-like, impersonal and religiously neutral. Print encouraged the mind to sense that its possessions were held in some sort of inert mental space.

## PRINT AND CLOSURE: INTERTEXTUALITY

Print encourages a sense of closure, a sense that what is found in a text has been finalized, has reached a state of completion. This sense affects literary creations and it affects analytic philosophical or scientific work.

Before print, writing itself encouraged some sense of noetic closure.

By isolating thought on a written surface, detached from any interlocutor, making utterance in this sense autonomous and indifferent to attack, writing presents utterance and thought as uninvolved with all else, somehow self-contained, complete. Print in the same way situates utterance and thought on a surface disengaged from everything else, but it also goes farther in suggesting self-containment. Print encloses thought in thousands of copies of a work of exactly the same visual and physical consistency. Verbal correspondence of copies of the same printing can be checked with no resort to sound at all but simply by sight: a Hinman collator superimposed corresponding pages of two copies of a text and signal variations to the viewer with a blinking light.

The printed text is supposed to represent the words of an author in definitive or 'final' form. For print is comfortable only with finality. Once a letterpress forme is closed, locked up, or a photolithographic plate is made, and the sheet printed, the text does not accommodate changes (erasures, insertions) so readily as do written texts. By contrast, manuscripts, with their glosses or marginal comments (which often got worked into the text in subsequent copies) were in dialogue with the world outside their own borders. They remained closer to the give-and-take of oral expression. The readers of manuscripts are less closed off from the author, less absent, than are the readers of those writing for print. The sense of closure or completeness enforced by print is at times grossly physical. A newspaper's pages are normally all filled – certain kinds of printed material are called 'fillers' – just as its lines of type are normally all justified (i.e. all exactly the same width). Print is curiously intolerant of physical incompleteness. It can convey the impression, unintentionally and subtly, but very really, that the material the text deals with is similarly complete or self-consistent.

Print makes for more tightly closed verbal art forms, especially in narrative. Until print, the only linearly plotted lengthy story line was that of the drama, which from antiquity had been controlled by writing. Euripides' tragedies were texts composed in writing and then memorized verbatim to be presented orally. With print, tight plotting is extended to the lengthy narrative, in the novel from Jane Austen's time on, and reaches its peak in the detective story. These forms will be discussed in the next chapter.

In literary theory, print gives rise ultimately to Formalism and the

New Criticism, with their deep conviction that each work of verbal art is closed off in a world of its own, a 'verbal icon'. Significantly, an icon is something seen, not heard. Manuscript culture felt works of verbal art to be more in touch with the oral plenum, and never very effectively distinguished between poetry and rhetoric. More will be said of Formalism and the New Criticism also in the next chapter.

Print ultimately gives rise to the modern issue of intertextuality, which is so central a concern in phenomenological and critical circles today (Hawkes 1977, p. 144). Intertextuality refers to a literary and psychological commonplace: a text cannot be created simply out of lived experience. A novelist writes a novel because he or she is familiar with this kind of textual organization of experience.

Manuscript culture had taken intertextuality for granted. Still tied to the commonplace tradition of the old oral world, it deliberately created texts out of other texts, borrowing, adapting, sharing the common, originally oral, formulas and themes, even though it worked them up into fresh literary forms impossible without writing. Print culture of itself has a different mindset. It tends to feel a work as 'closed', set off from other works, a unit in itself. Print culture gave birth to the romantic notions of 'originality' and 'creativity', which set apart an individual work from other works even more, seeing its origins and meaning as independent of outside influence, at least ideally. When in the past few decades doctrines of intertextuality arose to counteract the isolationist aesthetics of a romantic print culture, they came as a kind of shock. They were all the more disquieting because modern writers, agonizingly aware of literary history and of the de facto intertextuality of their own works, are concerned that they may be producing nothing really new or fresh at all, that they maybe totally under the 'influence' of others' texts. Harold Bloom's work The Anxiety of Influence (1973) treats this modern writer's anguish. Manuscript cultures had few if any anxieties about influence to plague them, and oral cultures had virtually none.

Print creates a sense of closure not only in literary works but also in analytic philosophical and scientific works. With print came the catechism and the 'textbook', less discursive and less disputatious than most previous presentations of a given academic subject. Catechisms and textbooks presented 'facts' or their equivalents: memorizable, flat statements that told straightforwardly and inclusively how matters stood in a given field. By contrast, the memorable statements of oral cultures and of residually oral manuscript cultures tended to be of a proverbial sort, presenting not 'facts' but rather reflections, often of a gnomic kind, inviting further reflection by the paradoxes they involved.

Peter Ramus (1515–72) produced the paradigms of the textbook genre: textbooks for virtually all arts subjects (dialectic or logic, rhetoric, grammar, arithmetic, etc.) that proceeded by cold-blooded definitions and divisions leading to still further definitions and more divisions, until every last particle of the subject had been dissected and disposed of. A Ramist textbook on a given subject had no acknowledged interchange with anything outside itself. Not even any difficulties or 'adversaries' appeared. A curriculum subject or 'art', if presented properly according to Ramist method, involved no difficulties at all (so Ramists maintained): if you defined and divided in the proper way, everything in the art was completely self-evident and the art itself was complete and self-contained. Ramus relegated difficulties and refutations of adversaries to separate 'lectures' (*scholae*) on dialectic, rhetoric, grammar, arithmetic, and all the rest. These lectures lay outside the self-enclosed 'art'. Moreover, the material in each of the Ramist textbooks could be presented in printed dichotomized outlines or charts that showed exactly how the material was organized spatially in itself and in the mind. Every art was in itself completely separate from every other, as houses with intervening open spaces are separate from one another, though the arts were mingled in 'use' – that is to say, in working up a given passage of discourse, one used simultaneously logic, grammar, rhetoric, and possible other arts as well (Ong 1958b, pp. 30–1, 225–69, 280).

A correlative of the sense of closure fostered by print was the fixed point of view, which as Marshall McLuhan pointed out (1962, pp. 126–7, 135–6), came into being with print. With the fixed point of view, a fixed tone could now be preserved through the whole of a lengthy prose composition. The fixed point of view and fixed tone showed in one way a greater distance between writer and reader and in another way a greater tacit understanding. The writer could go his or her own way confidently (greater distance, lack of concern). There was no need to make everything a kind of Menippean satire, a mixture of various points of view and tone for various sensibilities. The writer could be confident that the reader would adjust (greater understanding). At this point, the 'reading public' came into existence – a sizable clientele of readers unknown personally to the author but able to deal with certain more or less established points of view.

## POST-TYPOGRAPHY: ELECTRONICS

The electronic transformation of verbal expression has both deepened the commitment of the word to space initiated by writing and intensified by print and has brought consciousness to a new age of secondary orality. Although the full relationship of the electronically processed word to the orality–literacy polarity with which this book concerns itself is too vast a subject to be considered in its totality here, some few points need to be made.

Despite what is sometimes said, electronic devices are not eliminating printed books but are actually producing more of them. Electronically taped interviews produce 'talked' books and articles by the thousands which would never have seen print before taping was possible. The new medium here reinforces the old, but of course transforms it because it fosters a new, self-consciously informal style, since typographic folk believe that oral exchange should normally be informal (oral folk believe it should normally be formal – Ong 1977, pp. 82–91). Moreover, as earlier noted, composition on computer terminals is replacing older forms of typographic composition, so that soon virtually all printing will be done in one way or another with the aid of electronic equipment. And of course information of all sorts electronically gathered and/or processed makes its way into print to swell the typographic output. Finally, the sequential processing and spatializing of the word, initiated by writing and raised to a new order of intensity by print, is further intensified by the computer, which maximizes commitment of the word to space and to (electronic) local motion and optimizes analytic sequentiality by making it virtually instantaneous.

At the same time, with telephone, radio, television and various kinds of sound tape, electronic technology has brought us into the age of 'secondary orality'. This new orality has striking resemblances to the old in its participatory mystique, its fostering of a communal sense, its concentration on the present moment, and even its use of formulas (Ong 1971, pp. 284–303; 1977, pp. 16–49, 305–41). But it is essentially a more deliberate and self-conscious orality, based permanently on the use of writing and print, which are essential for the manufacture and operation of the equipment and for its use as well.

Secondary orality is both remarkably like and remarkably unlike primary orality. Like primary orality, secondary orality has generated a strong group sense, for listening to spoken words forms hearers into a group, a true audience, just as reading written or printed texts turns individuals in on themselves. But secondary orality generates a sense for groups immeasurably larger than those of primary oral culture – McLuhan's 'global village'. Moreover, before writing, oral folk were group-minded because no feasible alternative had presented itself. In our age of secondary orality, we are groupminded self-consciously and programmatically. The individual feels that he or she, as an individual, must be socially sensitive. Unlike members of a primary oral culture, who are turned outward because they have had little occasion to turn inward, we are turned outward because we have turned inward. In a like vein, where primary orality promotes spontaneity because the analytic reflectiveness implemented by writing is unavailable, secondary orality promotes spontaneity because through analytic reflection we have decided that spontaneity is a good thing. We plan our happenings carefully to be sure that they are thoroughly spontaneous.

The contrast between oratory in the past and in today's world well highlights the contrast between primary and secondary orality. Radio and television have brought major political figures as public speakers to a larger public than was ever possible before modern electronic developments. Thus in a sense orality has come into its own more than ever before. But it is not the old orality. The old-style oratory coming from primary orality is gone forever. In the Lincoln-Douglas debates of 1858, the combatants – for that is what they clearly and truly were – faced one another often in the scorching Illinois summer sun outdoors, before wildly responsive audiences of as many as 12,000 or 15,000 persons (at Ottawa and Freeport, Illinois, respectively – Sparks 1908, pp. 137–8, 189–90), speaking for an hour and a half each. The first speaker had one hour, the second an hour and a half, and the first another half hour of rebuttal – all this with no amplifying equipment. Primary orality made itself felt in the additive, redundant, carefully balanced, highly agonistic style, and the intense interplay between speaker and audience. The debaters were hoarse and physically exhausted at the end of each bout. Presidential debates on television today are completely out of this older oral world. The audience is absent, invisible, inaudible. The candidates are ensconced in tight little booths, make short presentations, and engage in crisp little conversations with each other in which any agonistic edge is deliberately kept dull. Electronic media do not tolerate a show of open antagonism. Despite their cultivated air of spontaneity, these media are totally dominated by a sense of closure which is the heritage of print: a show of hostility might break open the closure, the tight control. Candidates accommodate themselves to the psychology of the media. Genteel, literate domesticity is rampant. Only quite elderly persons today can remember what oratory was like when it was still in living contact with its primary oral roots. Others perhaps hear more oratory, or at least more talk, from major public figures than people commonly heard a century ago. But what they hear will give them very little idea of the old oratory reaching back from pre-electronic times through two millennia and far beyond, or of the oral lifestyle and oral thought structures out of which such oratory grew.

# 6

---

# ORAL MEMORY, THE STORY LINE AND CHARACTERIZATION

## THE PRIMACY OF THE STORY LINE

The shift from orality to literacy registers in many genres of verbal art – lyric, narrative, descriptive discourse, oratory (purely oral through chirographically organized oratory to television-styled public address), drama, philosophical and scientific works, historiography, and biography, to mention only a few. Of these, the genre most studied in terms of the orality–literacy shift has been narrative. It will be of use here to consider some of the work done on narrative to suggest some newer insights offered by orality–literacy studies. To narrative we can for present purposes assimilate drama, which, while it presents action with no narrative voice, still has a story line, as narrative does.

Obviously, other developments in society besides the orality–literacy shift help determine the development of narrative over the ages – changing political organization, religious development, intercultural exchanges, and much else, including developments in the other verbal genres. This treatment of narrative is not intended to reduce all causality to the orality–literacy shift but only to show some of the effects which this shift produces.

Narrative is everywhere a major genre of verbal art, occurring all the way from primary oral cultures into high literacy and electronic information processing. In a sense narrative is paramount among all verbal art forms because of the way it underlies so many other art forms, often even the most abstract. Human knowledge comes out of time. Behind even the abstractions of science, there lies narrative of the observations on the basis of which the abstractions have been formulated. Students in a science laboratory have to 'write up' experiments, which is to say, they have to narrate what they did and what happened when they did it. From the narration, certain generalizations or abstract conclusions can be formulated. Behind proverbs and aphorisms and philosophical speculation and religious ritual lies the memory of human experience strung out in time and subject to narrative treatment. Lyric poetry implies a series of events in which the voice in the lyric is embedded or to which it is related. All of this is to say that knowledge and discourse come out of human experience and that the elemental way to process human experience verbally is to give an account of it more or less as it really comes into being and exists, embedded in the flow of time. Developing a story line is a way of dealing with this flow.

## NARRATIVE AND ORAL CULTURES

Although it is found in all cultures, narrative is in certain ways more widely functional in primary oral cultures than in others. First, in a primary oral culture, as Havelock pointed out (1978a; cf. 1963), knowledge cannot be managed in elaborate, more or less scientifically abstract categories. Oral cultures cannot generate such categories, and so they use stories of human action to store, organize, and communicate much of what they know. Most, if not all, oral cultures generate quite substantial narratives or series of narratives, such as the stories of the Trojan wars among the ancient Greeks, the coyote stories among various Native American populations, the Anansi (spider) stories in Belize and other Caribbean cultures with some African heritage, the Sunjata stories of old Mali, the Mwindo stories among the Nyanga, and so on. Because of their size and complexity of scenes and actions, narratives of this sort are often the roomiest repositories of an oral culture's lore.

Second, narrative is particularly important in primary oral cultures because it can bond a great deal of lore in relatively substantial, lengthy forms that are reasonably durable – which in an oral culture means forms subject to repetition. Maxims, riddles, proverbs, and the like are of course also durable, but they are usually brief. Ritual formulas, which may be lengthy, have most often specialized content. Genealogies, which can be relatively long, present only highly specialized information. Other lengthy verbal performance in a primary oral culture tends to be topical, a nonce occurrence. Thus an oration might be as substantial and lengthy as a major narrative, or a part of a narrative that would be delivered at one sitting, but an oration is not durable: it is not normally repeated. It addresses itself to a particular situation and, in the total absence of writing, disappears from the human scene for good with the situation itself. Lyric tends to be either brief or topical or both. And so with other forms.

In a writing or print culture, the text physically bonds whatever it contains and makes it possible to retrieve any kind of organization of thought as a whole. In primary oral cultures, where there is no text, the narrative serves to bond thought more massively and permanently than other genres.

## ORAL MEMORY AND THE STORY LINE

Narrative itself has a history. Scholes and Kellogg (1966) surveyed and schematized some of the ways in which narrative in the West has developed from some of its ancient oral origins into the present, with full attention to complex social, psychological, aesthetic, and other factors. Acknowledging the complexities of the full history of narrative, the present account will simply call attention to some salient differences that set off narrative in a totally oral cultural setting from literate narrative, with particular attention to the functioning of memory.

The retention and recall of knowledge in primary oral culture, described in Chapter 3, calls for noetic structures and procedures of a sort quite unfamiliar to us and often enough scorned by us. One of the places where oral mnemonic structures and procedures manifest themselves most spectacularly is in their effect on narrative plot, which in an oral culture is not quite what we take plot typically to be. Persons from

today's literate and typographic cultures are likely to think of consciously contrived narrative as typically designed in a climactic linear
plot often diagramed as the well-known 'Freytag's pyramid' (i.e. an
upward slope, followed by a downward slope): an ascending action
builds tension, rising to a climactic point, which consists often of a
recognition or other incident bringing about a *peripeteia* or reversal of
action, and which is followed by a dénouement or untying – for this
standard climactic linear plot has been likened to the tying and untying
of a knot. This is the kind of plot Aristotle finds in the drama (*Poetics*
1451b–1452b) – a significant locale for such plot, since Greek drama,
though orally performed, was composed as a written text and in the
West was the first verbal genre, and for centuries was the only verbal
genre, to be controlled completely by writing.

Ancient Greek oral narrative, the epic, was not plotted this way. In
his *Ars Poetica*, Horace writes that the epic poet 'hastens into the action
and precipitates the hearer into the middle of things' (lines 148–9).
Horace has chiefly in mind the epic poet's disregard for temporal
sequence. The poet will report a situation and only much later explain,
often in detail, how it came to be. He probably has also in mind
Homer's conciseness and vigor (Brink 1971, pp. 221–2): Homer
wants to get immediately to 'where the action is'. However this may be,
literate poets eventually interpreted Horace's *in medias res* as making
*hysteron proteron* obligatory in the epic. Thus John Milton explains in the
'Argument' to Book I of *Paradise Lost* that, after proposing 'in brief the
whole subject' of the poem and touching upon 'the prime cause' of
Adam's fall 'the Poem hasts into the midst of things.'

Milton's words here show that he had from the start a control of his
subject and of the causes powering its action that no oral poet could
command. Milton has in mind a highly organized plot, with a beginning, middle and end (Aristotle, *Poetics* 1450b) in a sequence corresponding temporally to that of the events he was reporting. This plot he
deliberately dismembered in order to reassemble its parts in a
consciously contrived anachronistic pattern.

Exegesis of oral epic by literates in the past has commonly seen oral
epic poets as doing this same thing, imputing to them conscious deviation from an organization which was in fact unavailable without writing. Such exegesis smacks of the same chirographic bias evident in the

term 'oral literature'. As oral performance is thought of as a variant of writing, so the oral epic plot is thought of as a variant of the plot worked out in writing for drama. Aristotle was already thinking this way in his *Poetics* (1447–1448a, 1451a, and elsewhere), which for obvious reasons shows a better understanding of the drama, written and acted in his own chirographic culture, than of the epic, the product of a primary oral culture long vanished.

In fact, an oral culture has no experience of a lengthy, epic-size or novel-size climactic linear plot. It cannot organize even shorter narrative in the studious, relentless climactic way that readers of literature for the past 200 years have learned more and more to expect – and, in recent decades, self-consciously to depreciate. It hardly does justice to oral composition to describe it as varying from an organization it does not know, and cannot conceive of. The 'things' that the action is supposed to start in the middle of have never, except for brief passages, been ranged in a chronological order to establish a 'plot'. Horace's *res* is a construct of literacy. You do not find climactic linear plots ready-formed in people's lives, although real lives may provide material out of which such a plot may be constructed by ruthless elimination of all but a few carefully highlighted incidents. The full story of all the events in Othello's whole life would be a complete bore.

Oral poets characteristically experience difficulty in getting a song under way: Hesiod's *Theogony*, on the borderline between oral performance and written composition, makes three tries at the same material to get going (Peabody 1975, pp. 432–3). Oral poets commonly plunged the reader in *medias res* not because of any grand design, but perforce. They had no choice, no alternative. Having heard perhaps scores of singers singing hundreds of songs of variable lengths about the Trojan War, Homer had a huge repertoire of episodes to string together but, without writing, absolutely no way to organize them in strict chronological order. There was no list of the episodes nor, in the absence of writing, was there any possibility even of conceiving of such a list. If he were to try to proceed in strict chronological order, the oral poet would on any given occasion be sure to leave out one or another episode at the point where it should fit chronologically and would have to put it in later on. If, on the next occasion, he remembered to put the episode in at the right chronological order, he would be sure to leave out other episodes or get them in the wrong chronological order.

Moreover, the material in an epic is not the sort of thing that would of itself readily yield a climactic linear plot. If the episodes in the *Iliad* or the *Odyssey* are rearranged in strict chronological order, the whole has a progression, but it does not have the tight climactic structure of the typical drama. Whitman's chart of the organization of the *Iliad* (1965) suggests boxes within boxes created by thematic recurrences, not Freytag's pyramid.

What made a good epic poet was not mastery of a climactic linear plot which he deconstructed by dint of a sophisticated trick called plunging his hearer *in medias res*. What made a good epic poet was, among other things of course, first, tacit acceptance of the fact that episodic structure was the only way and the totally natural way of imagining and handling lengthy narrative, and, second, possession of supreme skill in managing flashbacks and other episodic techniques. Starting in 'the middle of things' is not a consciously contrived ploy but the original, natural, inevitable way to proceed for an oral poet approaching a lengthy narrative (very short accounts are perhaps another thing). If we take the climactic linear plot as the paradigm of plot, the epic has no plot. Strict plot for lengthy narrative comes with writing.

Why is it that lengthy climactic plot comes into being only with writing, comes into being first in the drama, where there is no narrator, and does not make its way into lengthy narrative until more than 2000 years later with the novels of the age of Jane Austen? Earlier so-called 'novels' were all more or less episodic, although Mme de la Fayette's *La Princesse de Clèves* (1678) and a few others are less so than most. The climactic linear plot reaches a plenary form in the detective story – relentlessly rising tension, exquisitely tidy discovery and reversal, perfectly resolved dénouement. The detective story is generally considered to have begun in 1841 with Edgar Allan Poe's *The Murders in the Rue Morgue*. Why was all lengthy narrative before the early 1800s more or less episodic, so far as we know, all over the world (even Lady Murasaki Shikibu's otherwise precocious *The Tale of Genji*)? Why had no one written a tidy detective story before 1841? Some answers to these questions – though of course not all the answers – can be found in a deeper understanding of the dynamics of the orality–literacy shift.

Berkley Peabody opened new insights into the relationship of memory and plot in his lengthy work, *The Winged Word: A Study in the Technique of Ancient Greek Oral Composition as Seen Principally through Hesiod's Works and Days* (1975). Peabody builds not only on the work of Parry, Lord and Havelock, and related work, but also on work of earlier Europeans such as Antoine Meillet, Theodor Bergk, Hermann Usener, and Ulrich von Wilamowitz-Moellendorff, and upon some cybernetic and structuralist literature. He situates the psychodynamics of Greek epos in the Indo-European tradition, showing intimate connections between Greek metrics and Avestan and Indian Vedic and other Sanskrit metrics and the connections between the evolution of the hexameter line and noetic processes. This larger ambience in which Peabody situates his conclusions suggests still wider horizons beyond. Very likely, what he has to say about the place of plot and about related matters in ancient Greek narrative song will be found to apply in various ways to oral narrative in cultures around the entire world. And indeed, in his abundant notes, Peabody makes reference from time to time to Native American and other non-Indo-European traditions and practices.

In part explicitly and in part by implication, Peabody brings out a certain incompatibility between linear plot (Freytag's pyramid) and oral memory, as earlier works were unable to do. He makes it clear that the true 'thought' or content of ancient Greek oral epos dwells in the remembered traditional formulaic and stanzaic patterns rather than in the conscious intentions of the singer to organize or 'plot' narrative in a certain remembered way (1975, pp. 172–9). 'A singer effects, not a transfer of his own intentions, but a conventional realization of traditional thought for his listeners, including himself' (1975, p. 176). The singer is not conveying 'information' in our ordinary sense of 'a pipeline transfer' of data from singer to listener. Basically, the singer is remembering in a curiously public way – remembering not a memorized text, for there is no such thing, nor any verbatim succession of words, but the themes and formulas that he has heard other singers sing. He remembers these always differently, as rhapsodized or stitched together in his own way on this particular occasion for this particular audience. 'Song is the remembrance of songs sung' (1975, p. 216).

The oral epic (and by hypothetical extension other forms of narrative in oral cultures) has nothing to do with creative imagination in the modern sense of this term, as applied to written composition. 'Our own pleasure in deliberately forming new concepts, abstractions and patterns of fancy must not be attributed to the traditional singer' (1975, p. 216). When a bard adds new material, he processes it in the traditional way. The bard is always caught in a situation not entirely under his control: these people on this occasion want him to sing (1975, p.174). (We know from present-day experience how a performer, unexpectedly pressed by a group to perform, will normally at first demur, thereby provoking renewed invitations until finally he has established a workable relationship with his audience: 'All right. If you insist . . .'.) The oral song (or other narrative) is the result of interaction between the singer, the present audience, and the singer's memories of songs sung. In working with this interaction, the bard is original and creative on rather different grounds from those of the writer.

Since no one had ever sung the songs of the Trojan wars, for example, in full chronological sequence, no Homer could even think of singing them that way. Bardic objectives are not framed in terms of a tight over-all plot. In modern Zaïre (then the Democratic Republic of the Congo), Candi Rureke, when asked to narrate all the stories of the Nyanga hero Mwindo, was astonished (Biebuyck and Mateene 1971, p. 14): never, he protested, had anyone performed all the Mwindo episodes in sequence. We know how this performance was elicited from Rureke. As the result of previous negotiations with Biebuyck and Mateene, he narrated all the Mwindo stories, now in prose, now in verse, with occasional choral accompaniment, before a (somewhat fluid) audience, for twelve days, as three scribes, two Nyanga and one Belgian, took down his words. This is not much like writing a novel or a poem. Each day's performance tired Rureke both psychologically and physically, and after the twelve days he was totally exhausted.

Peabody's profound treatment of memory throws bright new light on many of the characteristics of orally based thought and expression earlier discussed here in Chapter 3, notably on its additive, aggregative character, its conservatism, its redundancy or copia, and its participatory economy.

Of course, narrative has to do with the temporal sequence of events, and thus in all narrative there is some kind of story line. As the result of a sequence of events, the situation at the end is subsequent to what it was at the beginning. Nevertheless, memory, as it guides the oral poet, often has little to do with strict linear presentation of events in temporal sequence. The poet will get caught up with the description of the hero's shield and completely lose the narrative track. In our typographic and electronic culture, we find ourselves today delighted by exact correspondence between the linear order of elements in discourse and the referential order, the chronological order in the world to which the discourse refers. We like sequence in verbal reports to parallel exactly what we experience or can arrange to experience. When today narrative abandons or distorts this parallelism, as in Robbe-Grillet's Marienbad or Julio Cortázar's Rayuela, the effect is clearly self-conscious: one is aware of the absence of the normally expected parallelism.

Oral narrative is not greatly concerned with exact sequential parallelism between the sequence in the narrative and the sequence in extra-narrative referents. Such a parallelism becomes a major objective only when the mind interiorizes literacy. It was precociously exploited, Peabody points out, by Sappho, and it gives her poems their curious modernity as reports on temporally lived personal experience (1975, p. 221). Of course by Sappho's time (fl. c. 600 BC) writing was already structuring the Greek psyche.

## CLOSURE OF PLOT: TRAVELOGUE TO DETECTIVE STORY

The effects of literacy and later of print on the plotting of narrative are too vast to treat here in full detail. But some of the more generic effects are illuminated by considering the transit to literacy from orality. As the experience of working with text as text matures, the maker of the text, now properly an 'author', acquires a feeling for expression and organization notably different from that of the oral performer before a live audience. The 'author' can read the stories of others in solitude, can work from notes, can even outline a story in advance of writing it. Though inspiration continues to derive from unconscious sources, the writer can subject the unconscious inspiration to far greater conscious control than the oral narrator. The writer finds his written words accessible for reconsideration, revision, and other manipulation until they are finally released to do their work. Under the author's eyes the text lays out the beginning, the middle and the end, so that the writer is encouraged to think of his work as a self-contained, discrete unit, defined by closure.

Because of increased conscious control, the story line develops tighter and tighter climactic structures in place of the old oral episodic plot. The ancient Greek drama, as has earlier been noted, was the first western verbal art form to be fully controlled by writing. It was the first – and for centuries the only – genre to have typically a tight, Freytag-pyramid structure. Paradoxically, although the drama was presented orally, it had been composed before presentation as a written text. It is significant that dramatic presentation lacks a narrative voice. The narrator has buried himself completely in the text, disappeared beneath the voices of his characters. A narrator in an oral culture, as has been seen, normally and naturally operated in episodic patterning, and the elimination of narrative voice appears to have been essential at first to rid the story line of such patterning. We must not forget that episodic structure was the natural way to talk out a lengthy story line if only because the experience of real life is more like a string of episodes than it is like a Freytag pyramid. Careful selectivity produces the tight pyramidal plot, and this selectivity is implemented as never before by the distance that writing establishes between expression and real life.

Outside drama, in narrative as such, the original voice of the oral narrator took on various new forms when it became the silent voice of the writer, as the distancing effected by writing invited various fictionalizations of the decontextualized reader and writer (Ong 1977, pp. 53–81). But, until print appeared and eventually had its fuller effects, the voice's allegiance to episode always remained firm.

Print, as has been seen, mechanically as well as psychologically locked words into space and thereby established a firmer sense of closure than writing could. The print world gave birth to the novel, which eventually made the definitive break with episodic structure, though the novel may not always have been so tightly organized in climactic form as many plays. The novelist was engaged more specifically with a text and less with auditors, imagined or real (for printed prose romances were often written to be read aloud). But his or her position was a bit unsettled still. The nineteenth-century novelist's recurrent 'dear reader' reveals the problem of adjustment: the author still tends to feel an audience, listeners, somewhere, and must frequently recall that the story is not for listeners but for readers, each one alone in his or her own world. The addiction of Dickens and other nineteenth-century novelists to declamatory reading of selections from their novels also reveals the lingering feeling for the old oral narrator's world. An especially persistent ghost from this world was the itinerant hero, whose travels served to string episodes together and who survived through medieval romances and even through Cervantes' otherwise unbelievably precocious *Don Quixote* into Defoe (Robinson Crusoe was a stranded itinerant) and into Fielding's *Tom Jones*, Smollett's episodic narratives, and even some of Dickens, such as *The Pickwick Papers*.

The pyramidally structured narrative, as has been seen, reaches its peak in the detective story, beginning with Poe's *The Murders in the Rue Morgue*, published in 1841. In the ideal detective story, ascending action builds relentlessly to all but unbearable tension, the climactic recognition and reversal releases the tension with explosive suddenness, and the dénouement disentangles everything totally − every single detail in the story turns out to have been crucial − and, until the climax and dénouement, effectively misleading. Chinese 'detective novels', which began in the seventeenth century and matured in the eighteenth and nineteenth, share narrative materials with Poe, but never achieved Poe's climactic concision, interlarding their texts with 'lengthy poems, philosophical digressions, and what not' (Gulik 1949, p. iii).

Detective-story plots are deeply interior in that a full closure is commonly achieved inside the mind of one of the characters first and then diffused to the reader and the other fictional characters. Sherlock Holmes had it all figured out in his head before anyone else did, including especially the reader. This is typical of the detective story as against the simple 'mystery' story, which does not have so tidy a closed organization. The 'inward turn of narrative', in Kahler's term (1973), is strikingly illustrated here by contrast with the old oral narrative. The oral narrator's protagonist, distinguished typically for his external exploits, has been replaced by the interior consciousness of the typographic protagonist.

Not infrequently the detective story shows some direct connection between plot and textuality. In *The Gold-Bug* (1843), Edgar Allan Poe not only places the key to the action inside Legrand's mind but also presents as its external equivalent a text, the written code that interprets the map locating the hidden treasure. The immediate problem that Legrand directly solves is not an existential problem (Where is the treasure?) but a textual one (How is this writing to be interpreted?). Once the textual problem is solved, everything else falls into place. And, as Thomas J. Farrell once pointed out to me, although the text is handwritten, the code in the text is largely typographic, made up not simply of letters of the alphabet but also of punctuation marks, which are minimal or nonexistent in manuscript but abundant in print. These marks are even farther from the oral world than letters of the alphabet are: though part of a text, they are unpronounceable, nonphonemic. The effect of print in maximizing the sense of isolation and closure is evident. What is inside the text and the mind is a complete unit, self-contained in its silent inner logic. Later, varying this same theme in a kind of quasi-detective story, Henry James creates in *The Aspern Papers* (1888) a mysterious central character whose entire identity is bound up in a cache of his unpublished letters, which at the end of the story are incinerated, unread by the man who had dedicated his life to pursuing them to discover what sort of person Jeffrey Aspern really was. With the papers, the mystery of Aspern's person in his pursuivant's mind goes up in smoke. Textuality is incarnated in this haunting story. 'The letter kills; the spirit gives life' (2 Corinthians 3:6).

The very reflectiveness of writing – enforced by the slowness of the writing process as compared to oral delivery as well as by the isolation of the writer as compared to the oral performer – encourages growth of consciousness out of the unconscious. A detective-story writer is exquisitely more reflectively conscious than one of Peabody's epic narrators, as Edgar Allan Poe's own theorizing makes evident.

Writing, as has been seen, is essentially a consciousness-raising activity. The tightly organized, classically plotted story both results from and encourages heightened consciousness, and this fact expresses itself symbolically when, with the arrival of the perfectly pyramidal plot in the detective story, the action is seen to be focused within the consciousness of the protagonist – the detective. In recent decades, as typographic culture has been transmuted into electronic culture, the tightly plotted story has fallen out of favor as too 'easy' (that is, too fully controlled by consciousness) for author and reader. Avantgarde literature is now obliged to deplot its narratives or to obscure their plots. But deplotted stories of the electronic age are not episodic narratives. They are impressionistic and imagistic variations on the plotted stories that preceded them. Narrative plot now permanently bears the mark of writing and typography. When it structures itself in memories and echoes, suggestive of early primary oral narrative with its heavy reliance on the unconscious (Peabody 1975), it does so inevitably in a self-conscious, characteristically literate way, as in Alain Robbe-Grillet's *La Jalousie* or James Joyce's *Ulysses*.

## THE 'ROUND' CHARACTER, WRITING AND PRINT

The modern reader has typically understood effective 'characterization' in narrative or drama as the production of the 'round' character, to use E. M. Forster's term (1974, pp. 46–54), the character that 'has the incalculability of life about it'. Opposed to the 'round' character is the 'flat' character, the type of character that never surprises the reader but, rather, delights by fulfilling expectations copiously. We know now that the type 'heavy' (or 'flat') character derives originally from primary oral narrative, which can provide characters of no other kind. The type character serves both to organize the story line itself and to manage the non-narrative elements that occur in narrative. Around Odysseus (or, in other cultures, Brer Rabbit or the spider Anansi) the lore concerning cleverness can be made use of, around Nestor the lore about wisdom, and so on.

As discourse moves from primary orality to greater and greater chirographic and typographic control, the flat, 'heavy' or type character yields to characters that grow more and more 'round', that is, that perform in ways at first blush unpredictable but ultimately consistent in terms of the complex character structure and complex motivation with which the round character is endowed. Complexity of motivation and internal psychological growth with the passage of time make the round character like a 'real person'. The round character that emerged out of the novel depended for its appearance upon a great many developments. Scholes and Kellogg (1966, pp. 165–77) suggest such influences as the interiorizing drive in the Old Testament and its intensification in Christianity, the Greek dramatic tradition, the Ovidian and Augustinian traditions of introspection, and the inwardness fostered by the medieval Celtic romances and the courtly-love tradition. But they also point out that the ramification of personal character traits was not perfected until the novel appeared with its sense of time not simply as a framework but as a constituent of human action.

All these developments are inconceivable in primary oral cultures and in fact emerge in a world dominated by writing with its drive toward carefully itemized introspection and elaborately worked out analyses of inner states of soul and of their inwardly structured sequential relationships. Fuller explanation of the emergence of the 'round' character must include an awareness of what writing, and later print, did to the old noetic economy. The first approximations we have of the round character are in the Greek tragedies, the first verbal genre controlled entirely by writing. These deal still with essentially public leaders rather than with the ordinary, domestic characters that can flourish in the novel, but Sophocles' Oedipus and, even more, Pentheus and Agave and Iphigenia and Orestes in Euripides' tragedies are incomparably more complex and interiorly anguished than any of Homer's characters. In orality-literacy perspectives, what we are dealing with here is the increasing interiorization of the world opened up by writing. Watt (1967, p. 75) calls attention to the 'internalization of conscience' and the introspective habits that produced the feeling for human character found already in Defoe, and traces this to Defoe's Calvinist Puritan background. There is something distinctively Calvinistic in the way Defoe's introspective characters relate to the secular world. But introspection and greater and greater internalization of conscience mark the entire history of Christian asceticism, where their intensification is clearly connected with writing, from St Augustine's *Confessions* to the *Autobiography* of St Thérèse of Lisieux (1873–97). Miller and Johnson (1938, p. 461), quoted by Watt, note that 'almost every literate Puritan kept some sort of journal'. The advent of print intensified the inwardness fostered by script. The age of print was immediately marked in Protestant circles by advocacy of private, individual interpretation of the Bible, and in Catholic circles was marked by the growth of frequent private confession of sins, and concomitantly a stress on the examination of conscience. The influence of writing and print on Christian asceticism cries for study.

Writing and reading, as has been seen, are solo activities (though reading at first was often enough done communally). They engage the psyche in strenuous, interiorized, individualized thought of a sort inaccessible to oral folk. In the private worlds that they generate, the feeling for the 'round' human character is born – deeply interiorized in motivation, powered mysteriously, but consistently, from within. First emerging in chirographically controlled ancient Greek drama, the 'round' character is further developed in Shakespeare's age after the coming of print, and comes to its peak with the novel, when, after the advent of the Age of Romanticism, print is more fully interiorized (Ong 1971).

Writing and print do not entirely do away with the flat character. In accordance with the principle that a new technology of the word reinforces the old while at the same time transforming it, writing cultures may in fact generate at certain points the epitome of type characters, that is, abstract characters. These occur in the morality plays of the late Middle Ages, which employ abstract virtues and vices as characters – type characters intensified as only writing can intensify them – and in the drama of the humors in the seventeenth century, which, as in Ben Jonson's *Every Man in His Humor* or *Volpone*, introduce slightly fleshed out virtues and vices as characters in more complex plots. Defoe, Richardson, Fielding, and other early novelists (Watt 1967, pp. 19–21), and even at times Jane Austen, give characters names that type them: Lovelace, Heart-free, Allworthy, or Square. Late high-technology, electronic cultures still produce type characters in regressive genres such as Westerns or in contexts of self-conscious humor (in the modern sense of this word). The Jolly Green Giant works well enough in advertising script because the anti-heroic epithet 'jolly' advertises to adults that they are not to take this latterday fertility god seriously. The story of type characters and the complex ways they relate written fiction to oral tradition has not yet been told.

Just as the deplotted story of the late-print or electronic age builds on classical plot and achieves its effect because of a sense that the plot is masked or missing, so in the same age the bizarrely hollowed characters that represent extreme states of consciousness, as in Kafka, Samuel Beckett or Thomas Pynchon, achieve their effects because of the contrast felt with their antecedents, the 'round' characters of the classical novel. Such electronic-age characters would be inconceivable had narrative not gone through a 'round' character stage.

The development of the round character registers changes in consciousness that range far beyond the world of literature. Since Freud, the psychological and especially the psychoanalytic understanding of all personality structure has taken as its model something like the 'round' character of fiction. Freud understands real human beings as psychologically structured like the dramatic character Oedipus, not like Achilles, and indeed like an Oedipus interpreted out of the world of nineteenth-century novels, more 'round' than anything in ancient Greek literature. It would appear that the development of modern depth psychology parallels the development of the character in drama and the novel, both depending on the inward turning of the psyche produced by writing and intensified by print. Indeed, just as depth psychology looks for some obscure but highly significant deeper meaning hidden beneath the surface of ordinary life, so novelists from Jane Austen to Thackeray and Flaubert invite the reader to sense some truer meaning beneath the flawed or fraudulent surface they portray. The insights of 'depth' psychology were impossible earlier for the same reasons that the fully 'round' character of the nineteenth-century novel was not possible before its time. In both cases, textual organization of consciousness was required, though of course other forces were also in play – the movement away from the holist therapy of the 'old' (pre-Pasteur) medicine and the need for a new holism, the democratization and privatization of culture (itself an effect of writing and, later, print), the rise of the so-called 'nuclear' family or 'family of affection' in place of the extended family organized to preserve the 'line' of descent, advanced technology relating larger groups of persons more intimately to one another, and so on.

But whatever these other forces behind the development of depth psychology, one major force was the new feeling for the human lifeworld and the human person occasioned by writing and print. Epithetically delineated characters do not yield well to psychoanalytic criticism, nor do characters delineated in a faculty psychology of competing 'virtues' and 'vices'. Insofar as modern psychology and the 'round' character of fiction represent to present-day consciousness what human existence is like, the feeling for human existence has been processed through writing and print. This is by no means to fault the present-day feeling for human existence. Quite the contrary. The present-day phenomenological sense of existence is richer in its conscious and articulate reflection than anything that preceded it. But it is salutary to recognize that this sense depends on the technologies of writing and print, deeply interiorized, made a part of our own psychic resources. The tremendous store of historical, psychological and other knowledge which can go into sophisticated narrative and characterization today could be accumulated only through the use of writing and print (and now electronics). But these technologies of the word do not merely store what we know. They style what we know in ways which made it quite inaccessible and indeed unthinkable in an oral culture.

# 7

## SOME THEOREMS

Study of the contrast between orality and literacy is largely unfinished business. What has recently been learned about this contrast continues to enlarge understanding not only of the oral past, but also of the present, liberating our text-bound minds and setting much of what has long been familiar in new perspectives. Here I shall suggest some of the seemingly more interesting new perspectives and insights, but only some, for it is impossible to be inclusive or complete. I shall present the matter here in the form of theorems; more or less hypothetical statements that connect in various ways with what has already been explained here about orality and the orality–literacy shift. If the foregoing chapters have been even moderately successful, the reader should be able to carry the theorems farther as well as to generate his or her own theorems and supplementary insights.

Some of these theorems will attend especially to the ways in which certain present-day schools of literary interpretation and/or philosophy relate to the orality–literacy shift. Most of these schools are treated in Hawkes (1977). For the reader's convenience, wherever possible, references will be given directly to Hawkes, in whom the various primary sources can be traced.

## LITERARY HISTORY

Literary history has begun to exploit the possibilities which orality–literacy studies open to it. Important studies have reported on a wide scatter of specific traditions treating either their primary oral performances or the oral elements in their literary texts. Foley (1980b) cites works on Sumerian myth, biblical Psalms, various West and Central African oral productions, medieval English, French and Germanic literature (see Curschmann 1967), the Russian *bylina*, and American folk preaching. Haymes's listings (1973) add studies on Ainu, Turkic, and still other traditions. But literary history on the whole still proceeds with little if any awareness of orality–literacy polarities, despite the importance of these polarities in the development of genres, plot, characterization, writer–reader relationships (see Iser 1978), and the relationship of literature to social, intellectual and psychic structures.

Texts can represent all sorts of different adjustments to orality–literacy polarities. Manuscript culture in the West was always marginally oral, and, even after print, textuality only gradually achieved the place it has today in cultures where most reading is silent. We have not yet come to full terms with the fact that from antiquity well through the eighteenth century many literary texts, even when composed in writing, were commonly for public recitation; originally by the author himself (Hadas 1954, p. 40; Nelson 1976–7, p. 77). Reading aloud to family and other small groups was still common in the early twentieth century until electronic culture mobilized such groups around radio and television sets rather than around a present group member.

Medieval literature is particularly intriguing in its relation to orality because of the greater pressures of literacy on the medieval psyche brought about not only by the centrality of the biblical text (the ancient Greeks and Romans had had no sacred texts, and their religions are virtually empty of formal theology) but also by the strange new mixture of orality (disputations) and textuality (commentaries on written works) in medieval academia (Hajnal 1954). Probably most medieval writers across Europe continued the classical practice of writing their literary works to be read aloud (Crosby 1936; Nelson 1976–7; Ahern

1981). This helped determine the always rhetorical style as well as the nature of plot and characterization.

The same practice persisted to a notable degree through the Renaissance. William Nelson (1976–7, pp. 119–20) calls attention to Alamanni's revision of his originally unsuccessful *Giron Cortese* to make it more episodic and thus better fitted for oral reading to groups, as Ariosto's successful *Orlando* had been. Nelson goes on to conjecture that the same motivation prompted Sir Philip Sidney's revision of the *Old Arcadia*, suitable for oral delivery. He points out also (1976–7, p. 117) that through the Renaissance the practice of oral reading brings authors to express themselves 'as though real people . . . were listening' to them – not the 'hypotheses' to whom present-day authors normally address themselves. Hence the style of Rabelais and Thomas Nashe. This study of Nelson's is one of the richest in pointing out orality–literacy dynamisms in English literature from the Middle Ages to the nineteenth century and in suggesting how much more there is to do in studying the orality–literacy polarities. Who has yet assessed Lyly's *Euphues* as a work to read aloud?

The Romantic Movement marks the beginning of the end of the old orality-grounded rhetoric (Ong 1971), yet orality echoes, sometimes hauntingly, sometimes awkwardly, in the style of early American writers such as Hawthorne (Bayer 1980), not to mention the Founding Fathers of the United States of America, and it echoes clearly through the historiography of Thomas Babington Macaulay into that of Winston Churchill. In these writers the stagey conceptualization and semi-oratorical style register the highly effective residual orality in British public schools. Literary history has still to examine what is involved here.

Over the centuries, the shift from orality through writing and print to electronic processing of the word has profoundly affected and, indeed, basically determined the evolution of verbal art genres, and of course simultaneously the successive modes of characterization and of plot. In the West, for example, the epic is basically and irremediably an oral art form. Written and printed epics, the so-called 'art' epics, are self-conscious, archaizing imitations of procedures demanded by the psychodynamics of oral storytelling – for example, plunging at the beginning *in medias res*, elaborate formulaic descriptions of armor and agonistic behavior, other formulary development of other oral themes. As orality diminishes with writing and print, the epic irresistibly changes shape despite the author's best intentions and efforts. The narrator of the *Iliad* and the *Odyssey* is lost in the oral communalities: he never appears as 'I'. The writer Virgil begins his *Aeneid* with 'Arma, virumque cano', 'I sing of arms and the man'. Spenser's letter to Sir Walter Raleigh introducing *The Faerie Queene* shows that Spenser actually thought he was composing a work like Homer's: but writing and print had determined that he could not. Eventually, the epic loses even imaginary credibility: its roots in the noetic economy of oral culture are dried up. The only way the eighteenth century can relate seriously to the epic is by making fun of it in mock-epics. These are produced by the hundreds. After that, the epic in effect is dead. Kazantzakis's continuation of the *Odyssey* is an alien literary form.

Romances are the product of chirographic culture, creations in a new written genre heavily reliant on oral modes of thought and expression, but not consciously imitating earlier oral forms as the 'art' epic did. Popular ballads, as the Border ballads in English and Scots, develop on the edge of orality. The novel is clearly a print genre, deeply interior, de-heroicized, and tending strongly to irony. Present-day de-plotted narrative forms are part of the electronic age, deviously structured in abstruse codes (like computers). And so on. These are some general overall patterns. What the detailed patterns have been, for the most part no one yet knows. But study and understanding of them will throw light not only on verbal art forms and thought forms of the past but also on those of the present and possibly even of the future.

A great gap in our understanding of the influence of women on literary genre and style could be bridged or closed through attention to the orality–literacy–print shift. An earlier chapter here noted that early women novelists and other women writers generally worked from outside the oral tradition because of the simple fact that girls were not commonly subjected to the orally based rhetorical training that boys got in school. The style of women writers was distinctively less formally oral than that of men, yet no major studies, so far as I know, have examined the consequences of this fact, which must certainly be massive. Certainly, non-rhetorical styles congenial to women writers helped make the novel what it is: more like a conversation than a platform performance. Steiner (1967, pp. 387–9) has called attention to the origins of the novel in mercantile life. This life was thoroughly literate, but its literacy was vernacular, not grounded in Latin rhetoric. The dissenters' schools, which trained for business life, were the first to admit girls to the classroom.

Various kinds of residual orality as well as the 'literate orality' of the secondary oral culture induced by radio and television await in-depth study (Ong 1971, pp. 284–303; 1977, pp. 53–81). Some of the most interesting work on orality–literacy contrasts today has been done in studies of modern anglophone West African literature (Fritschi 1981).

At a more practical level our deeper understanding of the psychodynamics of orality in relation to the psychodynamics of writing is improving the teaching of writing skills, particularly in cultures today moving rapidly from virtually total orality into literacy, as many African cultures are doing (Essien 1978), and in residually oral subcultures in dominantly high-literacy societies (Farrell 1978a; 1978b) such as urban black subcultures or Chicano subcultures in the United States.

## NEW CRITICISM AND FORMALISM

The orality-to-literacy shift throws clear light on the meaning of the New Criticism (Hawkes 1977, pp. 151–6) as a prime example of text-bound thinking. The New Criticism insisted on the autonomy of the individual work of textual art. Writing, it will be remembered, has been called 'autonomous discourse' by contrast with oral utterance, which is never autonomous but always embedded in non-verbal existence. The New Critics have assimilated the verbal art work to the visual object-world of texts rather than to the oral–aural event-world. They have insisted that the poem or other literary work be regarded as an object, a 'verbal icon'.

It is hard to see how this visualist-tactile model of a poem or other verbal creation could apply effectively to an oral performance, which presumably could be a true poem. Sound resists reduction to an 'object' or an 'icon' – it is an on-going event, as has been seen. Moreover, the divorce between poem and context would be difficult to imagine in an oral culture, where the originality of the poetic work consists in the way this singer or narrator relates to this audience at this time. Although it is of course in some way a special event, distinguishable from other kinds of event, in a special setting, its aim and/or result is seldom if ever simply aesthetic: performance of an oral epic, for example, can serve also simultaneously as an act of celebration, as *paideia* or education for youth, as a strengthener of group identity, as a way of keeping alive all sorts of lore – historical, biological, zoological, sociological, venatic, nautical, religious – and much else. Moreover, the narrator typically identifies with the characters he treats and interacts freely with his real audience, who by their responses in turn help determine what he says – the length and style of his narrative. In his performance of *The Mwindo Epic*, Candi Rureke not only himself addresses the audience but even has the hero, Mwindo, address the scribes who are recording Rureke's performance in writing, telling them to hurry on with their work (Biebuyck and Mateene 1971). Hardly an icon, this. At the end of the epic, Rureke summarizes the real-life messages that he feels the story conveys (1971, p. 44). The romantic quest for 'pure poetry', sealed off from real-life concerns, derives from the feel for autonomous utterance created by writing and, even more, the feel for closure created by print. Nothing shows more strikingly the close, mostly unconscious, alliance of the Romantic Movement with technology.

The slightly older Russian Formalism (Hawkes 1977, pp. 59–73) took much the same position as the New Criticism, although the two schools developed independently. Formalists have made much of poetry as 'foregrounded' language, language that calls attention to the words themselves in their relationship to one another within the closure that is the poem, which has its own autonomous, inner being. Formalists minimize or eliminate from criticism any concern with the poem's 'message', 'sources', 'history', or relationship to the biography of its author. They are obviously also text-bound, too, focused exclusively (and unreflectively for the most part) on poems composed in writing.

To say that the New Critics and Russian Formalists have been text-bound is not to downgrade them. For they were in fact dealing with poems that were textual creations. Moreover, given the preceding state of criticism, which had devoted itself in great part to the biography and psychology of the author, to the neglect of the text, they had warrant to stress the text. The preceding criticism had come out of a residually oral, rhetorical tradition, and was in fact unskilled in treating autonomous, properly textual, discourse. Seen in the perspectives suggested by orality–literacy contrasts, the shift from earlier criticism to Formalism and the New Criticism thus appears as a shift from a residually oral (rhetorical, contextual) mentality to a textual (non-contextual) mentality. But the textual mentality was relatively unreflective. For, although texts are autonomous by contrast with oral expression, ultimately no text can stand by itself independent of the extratextual world. Every text builds on pretext.

For all texts have extratextual supports. Roland Barthes (Hawkes 1977, pp. 154–5) has pointed out that any interpretation of a text has to move outside the text so as to refer to the reader: the text has no meaning until someone reads it, and to make sense it must be interpreted, which is to say related to the reader's world – which is not to say read whimsically or with no reference to the writer's world. One might describe the situation this way: since any given time is situated in the totality of all time, a text, deposited by its author in a given time, is *ipso facto* related to all times, having implications which can be unfolded only with the passage of time, inaccessible to the consciousness of the author or author's coevals, though not necessarily absent from their subconscious. Marxist criticism (from which Barthes in part derives – Hawkes 1977, pp. 267–71) maintains that the self-reference of the New Critics is class-determined and sycophantic: it identifies the 'objective' meaning of the text with something actually outside the text, namely the interpretations it imagines to be the ones supported by the sophistication, wit, sense of tradition and poise of what is essentially a decaying aristocracy (Hawkes 1977, p. 155). The New Criticism, in this view, proved most successful with the sycophantic middle classes who look up to this aristocratic milieu.

The New Criticism also grew out of another major realignment of oral–literate forces, that which took place as academia shifted from a chirographically controlled Learned Latin base to a more freely oral vernacular base. Although there had been a few scattered courses in English literature in American colleges and universities by around 1850, the subject became a sizable academic subject only in the early twentieth century and at the graduate level only after World War I (Parker 1967). At Oxford and Cambridge Universities undergraduate study of English began timidly only in the late nineteenth century and became a self-sufficient subject also only after World War I (Potter 1937; Tillyard 1958). By the 1930s the New Criticism was under way, a spin-off from the new academic study of English, the first major vernacular criticism of English-language literature to develop in an academic environment (Ong 1962, pp. 177–205). Academia had known no 'old criticism' of English. Earlier criticism of vernacular works, however astute, was extra-academic, occasional and often amateur, for earlier academic, professional study of literature had been restricted to Latin, with some Greek, and had been grounded in the study of rhetoric.

Latin, as has been seen, had for well over a thousand years been a chirographically controlled language, no longer a mother tongue. Although it was tied in to a residually oral mentality, it provided no direct access to the unconscious of the sort that a mother tongue provides. Under these conditions, a literary text in Latin, however complex, and however learnedly understood, was bound to be opaque by comparison with a text in one's own mother's tongue, written out of a richer mix of unconscious and conscious elements. Given the relative intrinsic opacity of Latin texts, it was not surprising that comment on the text should be deflected somewhat from the text itself to the author, his psychology, the historical background, and all the externals that so annoyed advocates of the New Criticism.

The New Criticism itself zeroed in from the first on English-language texts and did so mostly in an academic setting where discussions could develop on a scale larger, more continuous, and more organized than that of earlier occasional criticism of vernacular works. Never before had texts been attended to in this exhaustive way, partly because by the 1930s and 1940s the recesses beneath consciousness had been opened by depth psychology and the psyche turned reflectively in on itself as never before, but also because a text in the vernacular had a different relationship to the early oral world of childhood than did a text in a language which for well over a millennium had been spoken by no one who did not know also how to write it. Textual studies, so far as I know, have never exploited the implications here

(Ong 1977, pp. 22–34). The implications are massive. Semiotic structuralism and deconstructionism generally take no cognizance at all of
the various ways that texts can relate to their oral substratum. They
specialize in texts marked by the late typographic point of view
developed in the Age of Romanticism, on the verge of the electronic
age (1844 marked Morse's successful demonstration of the telegraph).

## STRUCTURALISM

Structuralist analysis as developed by Claude Lévi-Strauss (1970;
Hawkes 1977, pp. 32–58) has focused largely on oral narrative and has
achieved a certain freedom from chirographic and typographic bias by
breaking down oral narrative in abstract binary terms rather than in
terms of the sort of plot developed in written narrative. Lévi-Strauss's
fundamental analogue for narrative is language itself with its system of
contrastive elements: phoneme, morpheme, etc. He and his many
followers generally have paid little if any attention to the specific
psychodynamics of oral expression as worked out by Parry, Lord, and
particularly Havelock and Peabody. Attention to such work would add
another dimension to Structuralist analysis, which is often accused of
being overly abstract and tendentious – all structures discerned turn
out to be binary (we live in the age of the computer), and binarism is
achieved by passing over elements, often crucial elements, that do
not fit binary patterning. Moreover, the binary structures, however
interesting the abstract patterns they form, seem not to explain the
psychological urgency of a narrative and thus they fail to account for
why the story is a story.

Studies of orality as such have brought out that oral narrative is not
always put together in terms which admit of ready Structuralist binary
analysis, or even of the rigid thematic analysis which Propp (1968)
applies to the folktale. The structure of oral narrative collapses at times,
though this fact does not hamper a good narrator skilled in digression
and flashback techniques. The straightforward narrative 'line', as Peabody has made clear (1975, pp. 179, 235 and *passim*), is much less
operative in primary oral performance than in written composition (or
in oral performance by persons influenced by written composition).
Oral composition works with 'informational cores' in which the

formulas do 'not show the degree of organization that we commonly associate with thought', although the themes do so more or less (Peabody 1975, p. 179).

Oral performers, especially but not exclusively performers in verse, are beset with distractions. A word may set off a chain of associations which the performer follows into a *cul de sac* from which only the skilled narrator can extricate himself. Homer gets himself into such predicaments not infrequently – 'Homer nods'. The ability to correct mistakes gracefully and make them appear as not mistakes at all is one of the things that separates the expert singers from the bunglers (Peabody 1975, pp. 235, 457–64; Lord 1960, p. 109). The modes of organization and disorganization here seem not to be a matter of mere *bricolage* (handiman's work, *ad hoc* improvization), a favorite term in structuralist semiotics, coming from Levi-Strauss's *Totemism* (1963) and *The Savage Mind* (1966). *Bricolage* is the literate's term for what he himself would be guilty of if he produced an oral-styled poem. But oral organization is not literate organization put together in makeshift fashion. Subtle connections can exist, for example, in ancient Greek narrative of oral provenance, between the structure of the hexameter line and thought forms themselves.

## TEXTUALISTS AND DECONSTRUCTIONISTS

The growing knowledge of the psychodynamics of orality and literacy also cuts across the work of the group we may here call textualists, notably A. J. Greimas, Tzvetan Todorov, the late Roland Barthes, Philippe Sollers and Jacques Derrida, as well as Michel Foucault and Jacques Lacan (Hawkes 1977). These critic-philosophers, who derive largely from a Husserlian tradition, specialize in texts, and in fact in printed texts, and mostly in latter-day printed texts from the Age of Romanticism – a significant specialization when this age is recognized as marking a new state of consciousness associated with the definite interiorization of print and the atrophy of the ancient rhetorical tradition (Ong 1971 and 1977). Most textualists show little concern with historical continuities (which are also psychological continuities). Cohen (1977, p. xxii) has noted how Foucault's 'archaeology' is concerned chiefly with correcting modern views rather than with explaining the past on its own terms. Similarly, the Marxist semiotics and literary theory related to structuralism and textualism, as represented, for example, in Pierre Macherey (1978), rests on detailed examples all drawn from the nineteenth-century novel, as Macherey's translator notes (1978, p. lx).

A favorite point of departure for textualists has been Jean-Jacques Rousseau. Jacques Derrida (1976, pp. 164–268 and *passim*) has carried on a lengthy dialogue with Rousseau. Derrida insists that writing is 'not a supplement to the spoken word' but a quite different performance. By this insistence, he and others have rendered a great service in undercutting the chirographic and typographic bias that has also been the concern of this book. At its worst, as textualists see it, this bias can take this form: one assumes that there simply is a one-to-one correspondence between items in an extramental world and spoken words, and a similar one-to-one correspondence between spoken words and written words (which seem to be taken to include print; the textualists generally assimilate writing and print to each other and seldom if ever venture even to glance at electronic communication). On this assumption of one-to-one correspondence, the naive reader presumes the prior presence of an extramental referent which the word presumably captures and passes on through a kind of pipeline to the psyche.

In a variation on Kant's noumenon-phenomenon theme (itself related to the sight-dominance brought on by writing and confirmed by print – Ong 1967b, p. 74), Derrida excoriates this metaphysics of presence. He styles the pipeline model 'logocentrism' and diagnoses it as deriving from 'phonocentrism', that is, from taking the logos or sounded word as primary, and thereby debasing writing by comparison with oral speech. Writing breaks the pipeline model because it can be shown that writing has an economy of its own so that it cannot simply transmit unchanged what it receives from speech. Moreover, looking back from the break made by writing, one can see that the pipeline is broken even earlier by spoken words, which do not themselves transmit an extramental world of presence as through transparent glass. Language is structure, and its structure is not that of the extramental world. The end result for Derrida is that literature – and indeed language itself – is not at all 'representational' or 'expressive' of something outside itself. Since it does not refer to anything in the manner of a pipeline, it refers to, or means, nothing.

Yet it hardly follows that because A is not B, it is nothing. Culler (1975, pp. 241–54) discusses the work of many of the textualists, as I have styled them here, or structuralists, as he styles them, and shows that, despite their denial that literature is representational or referential, the structuralists (or textualists) who have made up the *Tel Quel* group in Paris (Barthes, Todorov, Sollers, Julia Kristeva, and others) actually – and unavoidably – use language representationally, for they 'would not want to claim that their analyses are no better than any other' (1975, p. 252).

There is little doubt, on the other hand, that today many persons do rely on a logocentric model in thinking about noetic and communication processes. In breaking up what he calls phonocentrism and logocentrism, Derrida is performing a welcome service, in the same territory that Marshall McLuhan swept through with his famous dictum, 'The medium is the message'.

However, recent work on the orality–literacy contrasts treated in the present book complicates the roots of phonocentrism and of logocentrism beyond the textualists' account, especially in the case of Plato. Plato's relationship to orality was thoroughly ambiguous. On the one hand, in the *Phaedrus* and the *Seventh Letter* he downgraded writing in favor of oral speech, and thus is phonocentric. On the other hand, when, in his *Republic*, he proscribed poets, he did so, as Havelock shows, because they stood for the old oral, mnemonic world of imitation, aggregative, redundant, copious, traditionalist, warmly human, participatory – a world antipathetic to the analytic, sparse, exact, abstract, visualist, immobile world of the 'ideas' which Plato was touting. Plato did not consciously think of his antipathy to poets as an antipathy to the old oral noetic economy, but that is what it was, as we can now discern. Plato felt this antipathy because he lived at the time when the alphabet had first become sufficiently interiorized to affect Greek thought, including his own, the time when patiently analytic, lengthily sequential thought processes were first coming into existence because of the ways in which literacy enabled the mind to process data.

Paradoxically, Plato could formulate his phonocentrism, his preference for orality over writing, clearly and effectively only because he could write. Plato's phonocentrism is textually contrived and textually defended. Whether this phonocentrism translates into logocentrism and a metaphysic of 'presence' is at least disputable. The Platonic doctrine of 'ideas' suggests that it does not, since in this doctrine the psyche deals only with shadows or shadows of shadows, not with the presences of true 'ideas'. Perhaps Plato's 'ideas' were the first 'grammatology'.

The implication of connecting logocentrism to phonocentrism is that logocentrism, a kind of gross realism, is fostered chiefly by attention to the primacy of sound. But logocentrism is encouraged by textuality and becomes more marked shortly after chirographic textuality is reinforced by print, reaching its peak in the noetics of the sixteenth-century French philosopher and educational reformer Peter Ramus (Ong 1958b). In his dialectic or logic Ramus provided a virtually unsurpassable example of logocentrism. In *Ramus, Method, and the Decay of Dialogue* (1958b, pp. 203–4), I called it not logocentrism but 'corpuscular epistemology', a one-to-one gross correspondence between concept, word and referent which never really got to the spoken word at all but took the printed text, not oral utterance, as the point of departure and the model for thought.

The textualists, so far as I know, have not provided any description of the detailed historical origins of what they style logocentrism. In his *Saving the Text: Literature/Derrida/Philosophy* (1981, p. 35) Geoffrey H. Hartman has called attention to the absence of any account in Derrida of the passage from the (orally grounded) world of 'imitation' to the later (print grounded) world of 'dissemination'. In the absence of such an account, it would appear that the textualist critique of textuality, brilliant and to a degree serviceable as it is, is still itself curiously text-bound. In fact, it is the most text-bound of all ideologies, because it plays with the paradoxes of textuality alone and in historical isolation, as though the text were a closed system. The only way out of the bind would be through a historical understanding of what primary orality was, for primary orality is the only verbal source out of which textuality could initially grow. As Hartman suggests (1981, p. 66), 'If thinking is for us, today, textual, then we should understand the grounding. . . . Texts are false bottom.' Or, I would say (write), text is fundamentally pretext – though this does not mean that text can be reduced to orality.

'Deconstruction' of literary texts has grown out of the work of textualists such as those mentioned here. Deconstructionists like to point out that 'languages, our western languages at least, both affirm logic and at the same time turn it on edge' (Miller 1979, p. 32). This point is made by showing that if all the implications in a poem are examined, it will be seen that the poem is not completely consistent with itself.

But why should all the implications suggested by language be consistent? What leads one to believe that language can be so structured as to be perfectly consistent with itself, so as to be a closed system? There are no closed systems and never have been. The illusion that logic is a closed system has been encouraged by writing and even more by print. Oral cultures hardly had this kind of illusion, though they had others. They had no sense of language as 'structure'. They did not conceive of language by analogy with a building or other object in space. Language and thought for the ancient Greeks grew out of memory. Mnemosyne, not Hephaestus, is the mother of the Muses. Architecture had nothing to do with language and thought. For 'structuralism' it does, by ineluctable implication.

The work of the deconstructionists and other textualists mentioned above derives its appeal in part from historically unreflective, uncritical literacy. What is true in this work can often be represented more readily and forcefully by a more fully knowledgeable textualism – we cannot do away with texts, which shape our thought processes, but we can understand their weaknesses. L'écriture and orality are both 'privileged', each in its own distinctive way. Without textualism, orality cannot even be identified; without orality, textualism is rather opaque and playing with it can be a form of occultism, elaborate obfuscation – which can be endlessly titillating, even at those times when it is not especially informative.

## SPEECH-ACT AND READER-RESPONSE THEORY

Two other specialized approaches to literature invite rethinking in terms of orality–literacy contrasts. One of these grows out of the speech-act theory elaborated by J. L. Austin, John R. Searle and H. P. Grice, which Mary Louise Pratt (1977) has used to construct tentatively a definition of literary discourse as such. Speech-act theory distinguishes the 'locutionary' act (the act of producing an utterance, of producing a structure of words), the 'illocutionary' act (expressing an interactive setting between utterer and recipient – e.g. promising, greeting, asserting, boasting, and so on), and the 'perlocutionary' act (one producing intended effects in the hearer such as fright, conviction or courage). The theory involves Grice's 'cooperative principle', which implicitly governs discourse by prescribing that one's contribution to a conversation should follow the accepted direction of the exchange of speech one is engaged in, and it involves his concept of 'implicature', which refers to various kinds of calculation that we use in order to make sense of what we hear. It is apparent that the co-operative principle and implicature will have quite different bearings in oral communication from those they have in written. So far as I know, these different bearings have never been spelt out. If they were, they might well show that promising, responding, greeting, asserting, threatening, commanding, protesting and other illocutionary acts do not mean quite the same thing in an oral culture that they mean in a literate culture. Many literate persons with experience of highly oral cultures feel that they do not: they regard oral peoples, for example, as dishonest in fulfillment of promises or in responses to queries.

This is only one indication of the light that orality–literacy contrasts might throw on the fields which speech-act theories study. Speech-act theory could be developed not only to attend more to oral communication but also to attend more reflectively to textual communication precisely as textual. Winifred B. Horner (1979) begun development along these lines by suggesting that writing a 'composition' as an academic exercise is a special kind of act which she calls a text-act.

Another approach to literature especially inviting to orality–literacy contrasts is the reader-response criticism of Wolfgang Iser, Norman Holland, Stanley Fish, David Bleich, Michael Riffaterre and others, including Jacques Derrida and Paul Ricoeur. Reader-response criticism is intimately aware that writing and reading differ from oral communication, and in terms of absence: the reader is normally absent when the writer writes and the writer is normally absent when the reader reads, whereas in oral communication speaker and hearer are present to one another. They also react vigorously against the New Criticism's apotheosis of the physical text. 'The objectivity of the text is an illusion' (Fish

1972, p. 400). Little has thus far been done, however, to understand reader response in terms of what is now known of the evolution of noetic processes from primary orality through residual orality to high literacy. Readers whose norms and expectancies for formal discourse are governed by a residually oral mindset relate to a text quite differently from readers whose sense of style is radically textual. The nineteenth-century novelists' nervous apostrophes to the 'dear reader', as has already been noted, suggest that the typical reader was felt by the writer to be closer to the old-style listener than most readers commonly are felt to be today. Even today, however, in the United States (and doubtless in other highliteracy societies across the globe) readers in certain subcultures are still operating in a basically oral framework, performance-oriented rather than information-oriented (Ong 1978). Opportunities for further work here are open and inviting, and they have practical implications for the teaching of both reading skills and writing skills, as well as implications for heady theorizing.

It appears obvious that speech-act theory and reader-response theory could be extended and adapted to throw light on the use of radio and television (and the telephone as well). These technologies belong to the age of secondary orality (an orality not antecedent to writing and print, as primary orality is, but consequent upon and dependent upon writing and print). To be adapted to them, speech-act and reader-response theory need to be related first to primary orality.

## SOCIAL SCIENCES, PHILOSOPHY, BIBLICAL STUDIES

Other fields open to orality-literacy studies can only be mentioned here. Anthropology and linguistics, as has been seen, have already felt the effects and contributed greatly to our knowledge of orality in its contrasts with literacy. Sociology has thus far felt the effects less strongly. Historiography has yet to feel the effects: How interpret ancient historians, such as Livy, who wrote to be read aloud? What is the relation of Renaissance historiography and the orality embalmed in rhetoric? Writing created history. What did print do to what writing created? The fuller answer cannot be simply quantitative, in terms of increased 'facts'. What does the feeling for closure fostered by print have to do with the plotting of historical writing, the selection of the kinds of theme that historians use to break into the seamless web of events around them so that a story can be told? In keeping with the agonistic structures of old oral cultures, early history, though written, was largely the story of wars and political confrontation. Today we have moved to the history of consciousness. This shift in focus here obviously relates to the interiorizing drift in the chirographic mentality. In what ways?

So far as I know, philosophy, and, with it, intellectual history, has done little with orality studies. Philosophy and all the sciences and 'arts' (analytic studies of procedures, such as Aristotle's *Art of Rhetoric*) depend for their existence on writing, which is to say they are produced not by the unaided human mind but by the mind making use of a technology that has been deeply interiorized, incorporated into mental processes themselves. The mind interacts with the material world around it more profoundly and creatively than has hitherto been thought. Philosophy, it seems, should be reflectively aware of itself as a technological product – which is to say a special kind of very human product. Logic itself emerges from the technology of writing.

Analytic explicatory thought has grown out of oral wisdom only gradually, and perhaps is still divesting itself of oral residue as we accommodate our conceptualizations to the computer age. Havelock (1978a) has shown how a concept such as Platonic justice develops under the influence of writing out of archaic evaluative accounts of human operations (oral 'situational thinking') innocent of the concept of 'justice' as such. Further comparative orality–literacy studies would be illuminating in philosophy.

It is likely enough that an orality–literacy study of the conceptual apparatus of medieval philosophy would find it less orally grounded than ancient Greek philosophy and far more orally grounded than Hegelian or later phenomenological thought. But in what way are the virtues and vices that intrigue ancient and medieval thinkers akin to 'heavy' type-characters in oral narrative as compared to more complexly nuanced abstract psychologizing in Hegelian or later phenomenological thought? These kinds of question can be answered only by detailed comparative studies, which would certainly throw light on the nature of philosophical problems in various ages.

In sum, if philosophy is reflective about its own nature, what is it to make of the fact that philosophical thinking cannot be carried on by the unaided human mind but only by the human mind that has familiarized itself with and deeply interiorized the technology of writing? What does this precisely intellectual need for technology have to say about the relationship of consciousness to the external universe? And what does it have to say about Marxist theories concentrating on technologies as means of production and alienation? Hegelian philosophy and its sequels are packed with orality–literacy problems. The fuller reflective discovery of the self on which so much of Hegel's and other phenomenology depends is the result not only of writing but also of print: without these technologies the modern privatization of the self and the modern acute, doubly reflexive self-awareness are impossible.

Orality-literacy theorems challenge biblical study perhaps more than any other field of learning, for, over the centuries, biblical study has generated what is doubtlessly the most massive body of textual commentary in the world. Since the form criticism of Hermann Gunkel (1862–1932), biblical scholarship has become increasingly aware of such specifics as oral-formulaic elements in the text (Culley 1967). But as Werner Kelber noted (1980, 1983), biblical studies, like other textual studies, are inclined unwittingly to model the noetic and verbal economy of oral cultures on literacy, projecting oral memory as a variant of verbatim literate memory and thinking of what is preserved in oral tradition as a kind of text that is only waiting to be set down in writing. Kelber's major work, *The Oral and the Written Gospel*, addresses for the first time, head-on, in the full light of then recent orality–literacy studies, the question of what oral tradition truly was before the Synoptic written texts came into being. One can be aware that texts have oral backgrounds without being entirely aware of what orality really is. O'Connor (1980) has broken with the dominant trend here in his reassessment of Hebrew verse structure in terms of truly oral psychodynamics. It does appear that an in-depth appreciation of the noetic and communication processes of primary orality could open to biblical studies new depths of textual and doctrinal understanding.

## ORALITY, WRITING AND BEING HUMAN

'Civilized' peoples have long contrasted themselves with 'primitive' or 'savage' peoples, not only in drawing-room conversation or at cocktail parties but also in sophisticated historical works and anthropological studies. One of the pivotal anthropological works of recent decades, a work cited often in these pages, is Claude Lévi-Strauss's *The Savage Mind* (1966 – first French edition, *La Pensée sauvage*, 1962). One thinks also of the earlier works of Lucien Lévy-Bruhl, *Les Fonctions mentales dans les sociétés inférieures* (1910) and *La Mentalité primitive* (1923), and of Franz Boas's Lowell Lectures, *The Mind of Primitive Man* (1922). The terms 'primitive' and 'savage', not to mention 'inferior', are weighted terms. No one wants to be called primitive or savage, and it is comforting to apply these terms contrastively to other people to show what we are not. The terms are somewhat like the term 'illiterate': they identify an earlier state of affairs negatively, by noting a lack or deficiency.

In the current attention to orality and oral–literacy contrasts, a more positive understanding of earlier states of consciousness has replaced, or is replacing, these well-meant, but essentially limiting approaches. In a published series of radio lectures, Lévi-Strauss himself defended the 'people we call, usually and wrongly, "primitive"' against the common charge that their minds are of 'coarser quality' or 'fundamentally different' (1979, pp. 15–16). He suggests that the term 'primitive' should be replaced by 'without writing'. 'Without writing', however, is still a negative assessment, suggesting a chirographic bias. The present treatment would suggest using the less invidious and more positive term 'oral'. Lévi-Strauss's much quoted statement (1966, p. 245) that 'the savage mind totalizes' would be rendered 'the oral mind totalizes'.

Orality is not an ideal, and never was. To approach it positively is not to advocate it as a permanent state for any culture. Literacy opens possibilities to the word and to human existence unimaginable without writing. Oral cultures today value their oral traditions and agonize over the loss of these traditions, but I have never encountered or heard of an oral culture that does not want to achieve literacy as soon as possible. (Some individuals of course do resist literacy, but they are mostly soon lost sight of.) Yet orality is not despicable. It can produce creations beyond the reach of literates, for example, the *Odyssey*. Nor is orality ever completely eradicable: reading a text oralizes it. Both orality and the growth of literacy out of orality are necessary for the evolution of consciousness.

To say that a great many changes in the psyche and in culture connect with the passage from orality to writing is not to make writing (and/or its sequel, print) the sole cause of all the changes. The connection is not a matter of reductionism but of relationism. The shift from orality to writing intimately interrelates with more psychic and social developments than we have yet noted. Developments in food production, in trade, in political organization, in religious institutions, in technological skills, in educational practices, in means of transportation, in family organization, and in other areas of human life all play their own distinctive roles. But most of these developments, and indeed very likely every one of them, have themselves been affected, often at great depth, by the shift from orality to literacy and beyond, as many of them have in turn affected this shift.

## 'MEDIA' VERSUS HUMAN COMMUNICATION

In treating the technologizing of the word, for the most part this book has avoided the term media (with its now more and more fugitive singular, medium). The reason is that the term can give a false impression of the nature of verbal communication, and of other human communication as well. Thinking of a 'medium' of communication or of 'media' of communication suggests that communication is a pipeline transfer of units of material called 'information' from one place to another. My mind is a box. I take a unit of 'information' out of it, encode the unit (that is, fit it to the size and shape of the pipe it will go through), and put it into one end of the pipe (the medium, something in the middle between two other things). From the one end of the pipe the 'information' proceeds to the other end, where someone decodes it (restores its proper size and shape) and puts it in his or her own box-like container called a mind. This model obviously has something to do with human communication, but, on close inspection, very little, and it distorts the act of communication beyond recognition. Hence McLuhan's wry book title: *The Medium is the Massage* (not quite the 'message').

Human communication, verbal and other, differs from the 'medium' model most basically in that it demands anticipated feedback in order to take place at all. In the medium model, the message is moved from sender-position to receiver-position. In real human communication, the sender has to be not only in the sender position but also in the receiver position before he or she can send anything.

To speak, you have to address another or others. People in their right minds do not stray through the woods just talking at random to nobody. Even to talk to yourself you have to pretend that you are two people. The reason is that what I say depends on what reality or fancy I feel I am talking into, that is, on what possible responses I might anticipate. Hence I avoid sending quite the same message to an adult and to a small child. To speak, I have to be somehow already in communication with the mind I am to address before I start speaking. I can be in touch perhaps through past relationships, by an exchange of glances, by an understanding with a third person who has brought me and my interlocutor together, or in any of countless other ways. (Words are modifications of a more-than-verbal situation.) I have to sense something in the other's mind to which my own utterance can relate. Human communication is never one-way. Always, it not only calls for response but is shaped in its very form and content by anticipated response.

This is not to say that I am sure how the other will respond to what I say. But I have to be able to conjecture a possible range of responses at least in some vague way. I have to be somehow inside the mind of the other in advance in order to enter with my message, and he or she must be inside my mind. To formulate anything I must have another person or other persons already 'in mind'. This is the paradox of human communication. Communication is intersubjective. The media model is not. There is no adequate model in the physical universe for this operation of consciousness, which is distinctively human and which signals the capacity of human beings to form true communities wherein person shares with person interiorly, inter-subjectively.

Willingness to live with the 'media' model of communication shows chirographic conditioning. First, chirographic cultures regard speech as more specifically informational than do oral cultures, where speech is more performance-oriented, more a way of doing something to someone. Second, the written text appears *prima facie* to be a one-way informational street, for no real recipient (reader, hearer) is present when the texts come into being. But in speaking as in writing, some recipient must be present, or there can be no text produced: so, isolated from real persons, the writer conjures up a fictional person or persons. 'The writer's audience is always a fiction' (Ong 1977, pp. 54–81). For a writer any real recipient is normally absent (if a recipient is accidentally present, the inscribing of the message itself proceeds as though the person were somehow absent – otherwise, why write?). The fictionalizing of readers is what makes writing so difficult. The process is complex and fraught with uncertainties. I have to know the tradition – the intertextuality, if you wish – in which I am working so that I can create for real readers fictional roles that they are able and willing to play. It is not easy to get inside the minds of absent persons most of whom you will never know. But it is not impossible if you and they are familiar with the literary tradition they work in. I hope that I have somewhat succeeded in laying hold on tradition sufficiently to get inside the minds of readers of this present book.

## THE INWARD TURN: CONSCIOUSNESS AND THE TEXT

Since at least the time of Hegel, awareness has been growing that human consciousness evolves. Although being human means being a person and thus being unique and induplicable, growth in historical knowledge has made it apparent that the way in which a person feels himself or herself in the cosmos has evolved in a patterned fashion over the ages. Modern studies in the shift from orality to literacy and the sequels of literacy, print and the electronic processing of verbalization, make more and more apparent some of the ways in which this evolution has depended on writing.

The evolution of consciousness through human history is marked by growth in articulate attention to the interior of the individual person as distanced – though not necessarily separated – from the communal structures in which each person is necessarily enveloped. Self-consciousness is coextensive with humanity: everyone who can say 'I' has an acute sense of self. But reflectiveness and articulateness about the self take time to grow. Short-term developments show its growth: the crises in Euripides' plays are less crises of social expectations and more crises of interior conscience than are the crises in the plays of the earlier tragedian Aeschylus. Longer-term developments show a similar growth in explicit philosophical concern with the self, which becomes noticeable in Kant, central in Fichte, obtrusive in Kierkegaard, and pervasive in twentieth-century existentialists and personalists. In *The Inward Turn of Narrative* (1973) Erich Kahler reported in detail the way in which narrative in the West becomes more and more preoccupied with and articulate about inner, personal crises. The stages of consciousness described in a Jungian framework by Erich Neumann in *The Origins and History of Consciousness* (1954) move toward a selfconscious, articulate, highly personal, interiority.

The highly interiorized stages of consciousness in which the individual is not so immersed unconsciously in communal structures are stages which, it appears, consciousness would never reach without writing. The interaction between the orality that all human beings are born into and the technology of writing, which no one is born into, touches the depths of the psyche. Ontogenetically and phylogenetically, it is the oral word that first illuminates consciousness with articulate language, that first divides subject and predicate and then relates them to one another, and that ties human beings to one another in society. Writing introduces division and alienation, but a higher unity as well. It intensifies the sense of self and fosters more conscious interaction between persons. Writing is consciousness-raising.

The orality–literacy interaction enters into ultimate human concerns and aspirations. All the religious traditions of mankind have their remote origins in the oral past and it appears that they all make a great deal of the spoken word. Yet the major world religions have also been interiorized by the development of sacred texts: the Vedas, the Bible, the Koran. In Christian teaching orality–literacy polarities are particularly acute, probably more acute than in any other religious tradition, even the Hebrew. For in Christian teaching the Second Person of the One Godhead, who redeemed mankind from sin, is known not only as the Son but also as the Word of God. In this teaching, God the Father utters or speaks His Word, his Son. He does not inscribe him. The very Person of the Son is constituted as the Word of the Father. Yet Christian teaching also presents at its core the written word of God, the Bible, which, back of its human authors, has God as author as no other writing does. In what way are the two senses of God's 'word' related to one another and to human beings in history? The question is more focused today than ever before.

So are countless other questions involved in what we now know about orality and literacy. Orality–literacy dynamics enter integrally into the modern evolution of consciousness toward both greater interiorization and greater openness.

# BIBLIOGRAPHY

Besides works cited in the text, this bibliography lists also a few other works the reader may find particularly helpful.

The bibliography does not undertake to give complete coverage of the massive literature in all fields where orality and literacy are matters of concern (for example, African cultures), but only to list some significant works which can serve as entries into major fields. Many works listed here contain bibliographies that lead further into the various issues.

Most of the major work on orality–literacy contrasts has been done in English, much of the pioneering work by scholars in the United States and Canada. This bibliography concentrates on English-language works, but includes some few in other languages.

To avoid clutter, material in this book readily verifiable from ordinary reference sources, such as encyclopedias, is not provided with references in the text here.

Entries are annotated where some special reason appears to call for annotation.

Abrahams, Roger D. (1968) 'Introductory remarks to a rhetorical theory of folklore', *Journal of American Folklore*, 81, 143–58.
—— (1972) 'The training of the man of words in talking sweet', *Language in Society*, 1, 15–29.
Achebe, Chinua (1961) No *Longer at Ease* (New York: Ivan Obolensky).

Ahern, John (1982) 'Singing the book: orality in the reception of Dante's *Comedy'*, *Annals of Scholarship* (in press).

Antinucci, Francesco (1979) 'Notes on the linguistic structure of Somali poetry' in Hussein M. Adam (ed.), *Somalia and the World: Proceedings of the International Symposium … Oct. 15–21, 1979*, vol. I (Mogadishu: Halgan), 141–53.

Aristotle (1961) *Aristotle's Poetics*, trans. and analysis by Kenneth A. Telford (Chicago: Henry Regnery).

Balogh, Josef (1926) ' "Voces Paginarum": Beiträge zur Geschichte des lauten Lesens und Schreibens', *Philologus*, 82, 84–109, 202–40. Very early but still highly informative.

Basham, A. L. (1963) *The Wonder That Was India: A Study of the History and Culture of the Indian Sub-Continent before the coming of the Muslims*, new and rev. edn (New York: Hawthorn Books). 1st edn 1954.

Bäuml, Franz H. (1980). 'Varieties and consequences of medieval literacy and illiteracy', *Speculum*, 55, 237–65. Highly informed and informative. Medieval culture was basically literate in its leaders, but the access of many to the written text was not necessarily direct: many knew the text only because they had someone who knew how to read it to them. Medieval literacy and illiteracy were more 'determinants of different types of communication' than simply 'personal attributes' of individuals.

Bayer, John G. (1980) 'Narrative techniques and oral tradition in *The Scarlet Letter*', *American Literature*, 52, 250–63.

Berger, Brigitte (1978) 'A new interpretation of the IQ controversy', *The Public Interest*, 50 (Winter 1978), 29–44.

Bernstein, Basil (1974) *Class, Codes, and Control. Theoretical Studies towards a Sociology of Language*, vol. I, 2nd rev. edn (London: Routledge & Kegan Paul). 1st edn 1971.

Biebuyck, Daniel and Mateene, Kahombo C. (eds and trans.) (1971) *The Mwindo Epic from the Banyanga*, as narrated by Candi Rureke, English trans. with text of Nyanga original (Berkeley and Los Angeles: University of California Press).

Bloom, Harold (1973) *The Anxiety of Influence* (New York: Oxford University Press).

Boas, Franz (1922) *The Mind of Primitive Man*, A course of lectures delivered before the Lowell Institute, Boston, Mass., and the National University of Mexico, 1910–1911 (New York: Macmillan).

Boerner, Peter (1969) *Tagebuch* (Stuttgart: J. B. Metzler).

Bright, William (1981) 'Literature: written and oral' in Deborah Tannen (ed.), *Georgetown University Round Table on Languages and Linguistics 1981* (Washington, DC: Georgetown University Press), 270–83.

Brink, C[harles] O[scar] (1971) *Horace on Poetry: The 'Ars Poetica'* (Cambridge, England: Cambridge University Press).

Bruns, Gerald L. (1974) *Modern Poetry and the Idea of Language: A Critical and Historical Study* (New Haven and London: Yale University Press).

Bynum, David E. (1967) 'The generic nature of oral epic poetry', *Genre*, 2 (3) (September 1967), 236–58. Reprinted in Dan Ben-Amos (ed.), *Folklore Genres* (Austin and London: University of Texas Press, 1976), 35–58.

—— (1974) *Child's Legacy Enlarged: Oral Literary Studies at Harvard since 1856*, Publications of the Milman Parry Collection (Cambridge, Mass.: Center for the Study of Oral Literature). Reprinted from the types of *Harvard Library Bulletin*, xxii (3) (July 1974).

—— (1978) *The Daemon in the Wood: A Study of Oral Narrative Patterns* (Cambridge, Mass.: Center for the Study of Oral Literature). Distributed by Harvard University Press.

Carothers, J. C. (1959) 'Culture, psychiatry, and the written word', *Psychiatry*, 22, 307–20.

Carrington, John F. (1974) *La Voix des tambours: comment comprendre le langage tambouriné d'Afrique* (Kinshasa: Centre Protestant d'Editions et de Diffusion).

Carter, Thomas Francis (1955) *The Invention of Printing in China and Its Spread Westward*, rev. by L. Carrington Goodrich, 2nd edn (New York: Ronald Press).

Chadwick, H[ector] Munro and Chadwick, N[ora] Kershaw (1932–40) *The Growth of Literature*, 3 vols (Cambridge, England: Cambridge University Press).

Chafe, Wallace L. (1982) 'Integration and involvement in speaking, writing, and oral literature', in Deborah Tannen (ed.), *Spoken and Written Language: Exploring Orality and Literacy* (Norwood, NJ: Ablex).

Champagne, Roland A. (1977–8) 'A grammar of the languages of culture: literary theory and Yury M. Lotman's semiotics', *New Literary History*, ix, 205–10.

Chaytor, H[enry] J[ohn] (1945) *From Script to Print: An Introduction to Medieval Literature* (Cambridge, England: Cambridge University Press).

Clanchy, M. T. (1979) *From Memory to Written Record: England, 1066–1307* (Cambridge, Mass.: Harvard University Press).

Cohen, Murray (1977) *Sensible Words: Linguistic Practice in England 1640–1785* (Baltimore and London: Johns Hopkins University Press).

Cole, Michael and Scribner, Sylvia (1973) *Culture and Thought* (New York: John Wiley).

Cook-Gumperz, Jenny and Gumperz, John (1978) 'From oral to written culture: the transition to literacy', in Marcia Farr Whitehead (ed.), *Variation in Writing* (Hillsdale, NJ: Lawrence Erlbaum Associates).

Cormier, Raymond J. (1974) 'The problem of anachronism: recent scholarship on the French medieval romances of antiquity', *Philological Quarterly*, LIII, (2) (Spring 1974), 145–57. 'Only in part do the widely accepted features of preliterate society fit the new, precocious, emerging audience of romance. It would be most tempting to posit illiteracy as a cause for the anachronisms in the romances of antiquity and elsewhere. Only *in part*, I would submit, do the widely recognized features of non-literate society, orality, dynamism, polemicism, and externalized schizoid behavior, characterize that of the mid-twelfth century.'

Crosby, Ruth (1936) 'Oral delivery in the Middle Ages', *Speculum*, 11, 88–110.

Culler, Jonathan (1975) *Structuralist Poetics: Structuralism, Linguistics, and the Study of Literature* (Ithaca, NY: Cornell University Press).

Culley, Robert C. (1967) *Oral-Formulaic Language in the Biblical Psalms* (Toronto: University of Toronto Press).

Cummings, E. E. (Edward Estlin) (1968) *Complete Poems*, 2 vols (London: MacGibbon & Kee).

Curschmann, Michael (1967) 'Oral poetry in medieval English, French, and German literature: some notes on recent research', *Speculum*, 42, 36–53.

Daly, Lloyd S. (1967) *Contributions to a History of Alphabetization in Antiquity and the Middle Ages*, Collection Latomus, vol. XC (Brussels: Latomus, Revue d'études latines).

Derrida, Jacques (1976) *Of Grammatology*, trans. by Gayatri Chakravorty Spivak (Baltimore and London: Johns Hopkins University Press).

—— (1978) *Writing and Difference*, trans., with an introduction and additional notes, by Alan Bass (Chicago: University of Chicago Press).

Diringer, David (1953) *The Alphabet: A Key to the History of Mankind*, 2nd edn, rev. (New York: Philosophical Library).

—— (1960) *The Story of Aleph Beth* (New York and London: Yoseloff).

—— (1962) *Writing*, Ancient Peoples and Places, 25 (London: Thames & Hudson).

Durand, Gilbert (1960) *Les Structures anthropologiques de l'imaginaire* (Paris: Presses Universitaires de France).

Dykema, Karl (1963) 'Cultural lag and reviewers of *Webster III*', *AAUP Bulletin* 49, 364–69.

Edmonson, Munro E. (1971) *Lore: An Introduction to the Science of Folklore and Literature* (New York: Holt, Rinehart & Winston).

Eisenstein, Elizabeth (1979) *The Printing Press as an Agent of Change: Communications and Cultural Transformations in Early-Modern Europe*, 2 vols (New York: Cambridge University Press).

Eliade, Mircea (1958) *Patterns in Comparative Religion*, trans. by Willard R. Trask (New York: Sheed & Ward).

Elyot, Sir Thomas (1534) *The Boke Named the Gouernour* (London: Thomas Berthelet).

Eoyang, Eugene (1977). 'A taste for apricots: approaches to Chinese fiction', in Andrew H. Plaks (ed.), *Chinese Narrative: Critical and Theoretical Essays*, with a foreword by Cyril Birch (Princeton, NJ: Princeton University Press), 53–69.

Essien, Patrick (1978) 'The use of Annang proverbs as tools of education in Nigeria', dissertation, St Louis University.

Faik-Nzuji, Clémentine (1970) *Enigmes Lubas-Nshinga: Étude structurale* (Kinshasa: Editions de l'Université Lovanium).

Farrell, Thomas J. (1978a) 'Developing literacy: Walter J. Ong, and basic writing', *Journal of Basic Writing*, 2(1) (Fall/Winter 1978), 30–51.

—— (1978b) 'Differentiating writing from talking', *College Composition and Communication*, 29, 346–50.

Febvre, Lucien and Martin, Henri-Jean (1958) *L'Apparition du livre* (Paris: Editions Albin-Michel).

Fernandez, James (1980) in Ivan Karp and Charles S. Bird (eds), *Explorations in African Systems of Thought* (Bloomington, Ind.: Indiana University Press), 44–59.

Finnegan, Ruth (1970) *Oral Literature in Africa* (Oxford: Clarendon Press).

—— (1977) *Oral Poetry: Its Nature, Significance, and Social Context* (Cambridge, England: Cambridge University Press).

—— (1978) *A World Treasury of Oral Poetry*, ed. with an introduction by Ruth Finnegan (Bloomington and London: Indiana University Press).

Fish, Stanley (1972) *Self-Consuming Artifacts: The Experience of Seventeenth-Century Poetry* (Berkeley, Calif. and London: University of California Press).

Foley, John Miles (1977) 'The traditional oral audience', *Balkan Studies*, 18,

145–53. Describes the social, ritual, kinship and other structures in oral performance at a Serbian festival in 1973.

—— (1979) Review of *Oral Poetry: Its Nature, Significance, and Social Context* (1977) by Ruth Finnegan, *Balkan Studies*, 20, 470–5.

—— (1980a) '*Beowulf* and traditional narrative song: the potential and limits of comparison', in John D. Niles (ed.), *Old English Literature in Context: Ten Essays* (London, England, and Totowa, NJ: Boydell, Rowman & Littlefield), 117–36, 173–8. Suggests that exactly what an oral formula is and how it works depends on the tradition in which it is used. There are, however, ample resemblances to warrant the continued use of the term oral formula.

—— (1980b) 'Oral literature: premises and problems', *Choice*, 18, 487–96 Expertly focused article, with invaluable bibliography, including a list of sound recordings.

—— (ed.) (1981) *Oral Traditional Literature: A Festschrift for Albert Bates Lord* (Columbus, Ohio: Slavica Press).

Forster, E[dward] M[organ] (1974) *Aspects of the Novel and Related Writings* (London: Edward Arnold).

Fritschi, Gerhard (1981) 'Oral experience in some modern African novels', typescript, 282 pp. received from the author.

Frye, Northrop (1957) *Anatomy of Criticism* (Princeton, NJ: Princeton University Press).

Gelb, I[gnace] J. (1963). *A Study of Writing*, rev. edn (Chicago: University of Chicago Press). Originally published as *A Study of Writing: The Foundations of Grammatology* (1952).

Givón, Talmy (1979) 'From discourse to syntax: grammar as a processing strategy', *Syntax and Semantics*, 12, 81–112.

Gladwin, Thomas (1970) *East Is a Big Bird: Navigation and Logic on Puluwat Atoll* (Cambridge, Mass.: Harvard University Press).

Goldin, Frederick (ed.) (1973) *Lyrics of the Troubadours and Trouvères: An Anthology and a History*, trans and introduction by Frederick Goldin (Garden City, NY: Anchor Books).

Goody, Jack [John Rankin] (ed.) (1968a) *Literacy in Traditional Societies*, introduction by Jack Goody (Cambridge, England: Cambridge University Press).

—— (1968b) 'Restricted Literacy in Northern Ghana', in Jack Goody (ed.), *Literacy in Traditional Societies* (Cambridge, England: Cambridge University Press), 198–264.

—— (1977) *The Domestication of the Savage Mind* (Cambridge, England: Cambridge University Press).

Goody, Jack [John Rankine] and Watt, Ian (1968) 'The consequences of literacy,' in Jack Goody (ed.), *Literacy in Traditional Societies* (Cambridge, England: Cambridge University Press), 27–84.

Grimble, A. F. (1957) *Return to the Islands* (London: Murray).

Gulik, Robert Hans van (trans. and ed.) (1949) *Three Murder Cases Solved by Judge Dee: An Old Chinese Detective Novel* (Tokyo: Toppan Printing Co.). The original is an anonymous eighteenth-century Chinese work. The historical Dee Goong An, or 'Judge Dee' (AD 630–700), figures in earlier Chinese stories.

Gumperz, John J., Kaltmann, Hannah and O'Connor, Catherine (1982 or 1983) 'The transition to literacy' in Deborah Tannen (ed.), *Coherence in Spoken and Written Discourse* (Norwood, NJ: Ablex). This paper was presented at a pre-conference session of the thirty-second annual Georgetown University Round Table on Languages and Linguistics, March 19–21, 1981. Manuscript received from authors.

Guxman, M. M. (1970) 'Some general regularities in the formation and development of national languages', in Joshua A. Fishman (ed.), *Readings in the Sociology of Language* (The Hague: Mouton), 773–6.

Hadas, Moses (1954) *Ancilla to Classical Reading* (New York: Columbia University Press).

Hajnal, István (1954) *L'Enseignement de l'écriture aux universités médiévales* (Budapest: Academia Scientiarum Hungarica Budapestini).

Harms, Robert W. (1980) 'Bobangi oral traditions: indicators of changing perceptions', in Joseph C. Miller (ed.), *The African Past Speaks* (London: Dawson; Hamden, Conn.: Archon), 178–200. These approaches are predicated on the assumption that oral traditions are retained and passed down, not out of an idle curiosity about the past, but because they make significant statements about the present.

Hartman, Geoffrey (1981) *Saving the Text: Literature/Derrida/Philosophy* (Baltimore, Md: Johns Hopkins University Press).

Haugen, Einar (1966) 'Linguistics and language planning', in William Bright (ed.), *Sociolinguistics: Proceedings of the UCLA Sociolinguistics Conference 1964* (The Hague: Mouton), 50–71.

Havelock, Eric A. (1963) *Preface to Plato* (Cambridge, Mass.: Belknap Press of Harvard University Press).

—— (1973) 'Prologue to Greek literacy', in *Lectures in Memory of Louise Taft Sample*, University of Cincinnati Classical Studies, vol. 2 (Norman, Okla.: University of Oklahoma Press), 229–91.

—— (1976) *Origins of Western Literacy* (Toronto: Ontario Institute for Studies in Education).

—— (1978a) *The Greek Concept of Justice: From Its Shadow in Homer to Its Substance in Plato* (Cambridge, Mass., and London, England: Harvard University Press).

—— (1978b) 'The alphabetization of Homer', in Eric A. Havelock and Jackson F. Herschell (eds), *Communication Arts in the Ancient World* (New York: Hastings House), 3–21.

—— (1979) 'The ancient art of oral poetry', *Philosophy and Rhetoric*, 19, 187–202.

Havelock, Eric A. and Herschell, Jackson P. (eds) (1978) *Communication Arts in the Ancient World*, Humanistic Studies in the Communication Arts (New York: Hastings House).

Hawkes, Terence (1977) *Structuralism and Semiotics* (Berkeley and Los Angeles: University of California Press; London: Methuen).

Haymes, Edward R. (1973) *A Bibliography of Studies Relating to Parry's and Lord's Oral Theory*, Publications of the Milman Parry Collection: Documentation and Planning Series, 1 (Cambridge, Mass.: Harvard University Press). Invaluable. Over 500 items. See also Holoka 1973.

Henige, David (1980) ' "The disease of writing": Ganda and Nyoro kinglists in a newly literate world', in Joseph C. Miller (ed.), *The African Past Speaks* (London: Dawson; Hamden, Conn.: Archon), 240–61.

Hirsch, E. D., Jr (1977) *The Philosophy of Composition* (Chicago and London: University of Chicago Press).

Holoka, James P. (1973) 'Homeric originality: a survey', *Classical World*, 66, 257–93. Invaluable bibliography, annotated; 214 entries. See also Haymes 1973.

Hopkins, Gerard Manley (1937) *Note-Books and Papers of Gerard Manley Hopkins*, ed. Humphrey House (London: Oxford University Press).

Horner, Winifred Bryan (1979) 'Speech-act and text-act theory: "theme-ing" in freshman composition', *College Composition and Communication*, 30, 166–9.

—— (1980) *Historical Rhetoric: An Annotated Bibliography of Selected Sources in English* (Boston, Mass.: G. K. Hall).

Howell, Wilbur Samuel (1956) *Logic and Rhetoric in England, 1500–1700* (Princeton, NJ: Princeton University Press).

—— (1971) *Eighteenth-Century British Logic and Rhetoric* (Princeton, NJ: Princeton University Press).

Iser, Wolfgang (1978) *The Act of Reading: A Theory of Aesthetic Response* (Baltimore and London: Johns Hopkins University Press). Originally published as *Der Akt des Lesens: Theorie ästhetischer Wirkung* (Munich: Wilhelm Fink, 1976).

Ivins, William M., Jr (1953) *Prints and Visual Communication* (Cambridge, Mass.: Harvard University Press).

Jaynes, Julian (1977) *The Origins of Consciousness in the Breakdown of the Bicameral Mind* (Boston: Houghton Mifflin).

Johnson, John William (1979a) 'Somali prosodic systems', *Horn of Africa*, 2 (3) (July-September), 46–54.

—— (1979b) 'Recent contributions by Somalis and Somalists to the study of oral literature', in Hussein M. Adam (ed.), *Somalia and the World: Proceedings of the International Symposium . . . Oct. 15–21, 1979*, vol. 1 (Mogadishu: Halgan), 117–31.

Jousse, Marcel (1925) *Le Style oral rhythmique et mnémotechnique chez les Verbo-moteurs* (Paris: G. Beauchesne).

—— (1978) *Le Parlant, la parole, et le souffle*, préface by Maurice Houis, Ecole Pratique des Hautes Etudes, *L'Anthropologie du geste* (Paris: Gallimard).

Kahler, Erich (1973) *The Inward Turn of Narrative*, trans. by Richard and Clara Winston (Princeton, NJ: Princeton University Press).

Kelber, Werner (1980) 'Mark and oral tradition', *Semeia*, 16, 7–55.

—— (1983) *The Oral and the Written Gospel: The Hermeneutics of Speaking and Writing in the Synoptic Tradition, Mark, Paul and Q.* (Philadelphia: Fortress Press).

Kennedy, George A. (1980) *Classical Rhetoric and Its Christian and Secular Tradition from Ancient to Modern Times* (Chapel Hill, NC: University of North Carolina Press).

Kerckhove, Derrick de (1981) 'A theory of Greek tragedy', *Sub-Stance*, pub. by Sub-Stance, Inc., University of Wisconsin, Madison (Summer 1981).

Kiparsky, Paul (1976) 'Oral poetry: some linguistic and typological considerations', in Benjamin A. Stolz and Richard S. Shannon (eds), *Oral Literature and the Formula* (Ann Arbor, Mich.: Center for the Coordination of Ancient and Modern Studies), 73–106.

Kroeber, A. L. (1972) 'Sign language inquiry', in Garrick Mallery (ed.), *Sign Language among North American Indians* (The Hague: Mouton). Reprinted Washington, DC, 1981.

Lanham, Richard A. (1968) *A Handlist of Rhetorical Terms* (Berkeley: University of California Press).

Leakey, Richard E. and Lewin, Roger (1979) *People of the Lake: Mankind and Its Beginnings* (Garden City, NY: Anchor Press/Doubleday).

Lévi-Strauss, Claude (1963) *Totemism*, trans. by Rodney Needham (Boston: Beacon Press).

—— (1966) *The Savage Mind* (Chicago: University of Chicago Press). Originally published as *La Pensée sauvage* (1962).

—— (1970) *The Raw and the Cooked*, trans. by John and Doreen Weightman (New York: Harper & Row). Originally published as *Le Cru et le cuit* (1964),

—— (1979) *Myth and Meaning*, the 1977 Massey Lectures, CBS Radio series, 'Ideas' (New York: Schocken Books).

Lévy-Bruhl, Lucien (1910) *Les Fonctions mentales dans les sociétés inférieures* (Paris: F. Alcan).

—— (1923) *Primitive Mentality*, authorized trans. by Lilian A. Clare (New York: Macmillan). French original, *La Mentalité primitive*.

Lewis, C[live] S[taples] (1954) *English Literature in the Sixteenth Century (excluding Drama)*, vol. 3 of *Oxford History of English Literature* (Oxford: Clarendon Press).

Lloyd, G[eoffrey] E[dward] R[ichard] (1966) *Polarity and Analogy: Two Types of Argumentation in Early Greek Thought* (Cambridge, England: Cambridge University Press).

Lord, Albert B. (1960) *The Singer of Tales*, Harvard Studies in Comparative Literature, 24 (Cambridge, Mass.: Harvard University Press).

—— (1975) 'Perspectives on recent work in oral literature', in Joseph J. Duggan (ed.), *Oral Literature* (New York: Barnes & Noble), 1–24.

Lotman, Jurij (1977) *The Structure of the Artistic Text*, trans. by Ronald Vroon, Michigan Slavic Contributions, 7 (Ann Arbor, Mich.: University of Michigan Press).

Lowry, Martin (1979) *The World of Aldus Manutius: Business and Scholarship in Renaissance Venice* (Ithaca, NY: Cornell University Press).

Luria [also Lurriia], Aleksandr Romanovich (1976) *Cognitive Development: Its Cultural and Social Foundations*, ed. Michael Cole, trans. by Martin Lopez-Morillas and Lynn Solotaroff (Cambridge, Mass., and London: Harvard University Press).

Lynn, Robert Wood (1973) 'Civil catechetics in mid-Victorian America: some notes about American civil religion, past and present', *Religious Education*, 68, 5–27.

Macherey, Pierre (1978) *A Theory of Literary Production*, trans. by Geoffrey Wall (London and Boston: Routledge & Kegan Paul). Originally published as *Pour une Théorie de la production littéraire* (1966).

Mackay, Ian (1978) *Introducing Practical Phonetics* (Boston: Little, Brown).

McLuhan, Marshall (1962) *The Gutenberg Galaxy: The Making of Typographic Man* (Toronto: University of Toronto Press).
—— (1964) *Understanding Media: The Extensions of Man* (New York: McGraw-Hill).
McLuhan, Marshall and Fiore, Quentin (1967) *The Medium Is the Massage* (New York: Bantam Books).
Malinowski, Bronislaw (1923) 'The problem of meaning in primitive languages', in C. K. Ogden, and I. A. Richards (eds), *The Meaning of Meaning: A Study of the Influence of Language upon Thought and of the Science of Symbolism*, introduction by J. P. Postgate and supplementary essays by B. Malinowski and F. G. Crookshank (New York: Harcourt, Brace; London: Kegan Paul, Trench, Trubner), 451–10.
Mallery, Garrick (1972) *Sign Language among North American Indians compared with That among Other Peoples and Deaf-Mutes*, with articles by A. L. Kroeber and C. F. Voegelin, Approaches to Semiotics, 14 (The Hague: Mouton). Reprint of a monograph published in 1881 in the first Report of the Bureau of Ethnology.
Maranda, Pierre, and Maranda, Elli Köngäs (eds) (1971) *Structural Analysis of Oral Tradition* (Philadelphia: University of Pennsylvania Press). Studies by Claude Lévi-Strauss, Edmund R. Leach, Dell Hymes, A. Julien Greimas, Victor Turner, James L. Peacock, Alan Dundes, Elli Köngäs Maranda, Alan Lomax and Joan Halifax, Roberto de Matta, and David Maybury-Lewis.
Markham, Gervase (1675) *The English House-Wife, containing the inward and outward Vertues which ought to be in a Compleat Woman: As her Skill in Physick, Chirurgery, Cookery, Extraction of Oyls, Banquetting stuff, Ordering of great Feasts, Preserving all sorts of Wines, conceited Secrets, Distillations, Perfumes, Ordering of Wool, Hemp, Flax; Making Cloth and Dying; the knowledge of Dayries; Office of Malting; of Oats, their excellent uses in Families; of Brewing, Baking and all other things belonging to the Household. A Work generally approved, and now the Eighth Time much Augmented, Purged, and made the most profitable and necessary for all men, and the general good of this Nation* (London: George Sawbridge).
Marrou, Henri-Irénée (1956) *A History of Education in Antiquity*, trans. by George Lamb (New York: Sheed & Ward).
Meggitt, Mervyn (1968) 'Uses of literacy in New Guinea and Melanesia', in Jack Goody (ed.), *Literacy in Traditional Societies* (Cambridge, England: Cambridge University Press), 300–9.

Merleau-Ponty, Maurice (1961) 'L'Oeil et l'esprit', *Les Temps modernes*, 18, 184–5. Numéro spécial: 'Maurice Merleau-Ponty', 193–227.

Miller, Joseph C. (1980) *The African Past Speaks: Essays on Oral Tradition and History* (London: Dawson; Hamden, Conn.: Archon).

Miller, J[oseph] Hillis (1979) 'On edge: the crossways of contemporary criticism', *Bulletin of the American Academy of Arts and Sciences*, 32(2) (January), 13–32.

Miller, Perry and Johnson, Thomas H. (1938) *The Puritans* (New York: American Book Co.).

Murphy, James J. (1974) *Rhetoric in the Middle Ages: A History of Rhetorical Theory from St Augustine to the Renaissance* (Berkeley, Los Angeles, and London: University of California Press).

Nänny, Max (1973) *Ezra Pound: Poetics for an Electric Age* (Bern: A. Francke Verlag).

Nelson, William (1976–7) 'From "Listen, Lordings" to "Dear Reader"', *University of Toronto Quarterly*, 46, 111–24.

Neumann, Erich (1954) *The Origins and History of Consciousness*, foreword by C. G. Jung, trans. by R. F. C. Hull, Bollingen Series, XLII (New York: Pantheon Books). Originally published as *Ursprungsgeschichte des Bewusstseins* (1949).

Obiechina, Emmanuel (1975) *Culture, Tradition, and Society in the West African Novel* (Cambridge, England: Cambridge University Press). 'The blending of impulses from the oral and the literary traditions gives the West African novel its distinctive local color' (p. 34).

O'Connor, M[ichael Patrick] (1980) *Hebrew Verse Structure* (Winona Lake, Ind.: Eisenbrauns). With skill and remarkable verve, avails himself of the work of Parry, Lord, and Ong to reassess Hebrew verse in line with new discoveries about oral cultures and their psychodynamics.

Okpewho, Isidore (1979) *The Epic in Africa: Toward a Poetics of the Oral Performance* (New York: Columbia University Press).

Oliver, Robert T. (1971) *Communication and Culture in Ancient India and China* (Syracuse, NY: Syracuse University Press).

Olson, David R. (1977) 'From utterance to text: the bias of language in speech and writing', *Harvard Educational Review*, 47, 257–81.

—— (1980a) 'On the language and authority of textbooks', *Journal of Communication*, 30(4) (Winter), 186–96.

—— (ed.) (1980b) *Social Foundations of Language and Thought* (New York: Norton).

Ong, Walter J. (1958a) *Ramus and Talon Inventory* (Cambridge, Mass.: Harvard University Press).

—— (1958b) *Ramus, Method, and the Decay of Dialogue* (Cambridge, Mass.: Harvard University Press).

—— (1962) *The Barbarian Within* (New York: Macmillan).

—— (1967a) *In the Human Grain* (New York: Macmillan; London: Collier-Macmillan).

—— (1967b) *The Presence of the Word* (New Haven and London: Yale University Press).

—— (1971) *Rhetoric, Romance, and Technology* (Ithaca and London: Cornell University Press).

—— (1977) *Interfaces of the Word* (Ithaca and London: Cornell University Press).

—— (1978) 'Literacy and orality in our times', *ADE Bulletin*, 58 (September), 1–7.

—— (1981) *Fighting for Life: Contest, Sexuality, and Consciousness* (Ithaca and London: Cornell University Press).

Opie, Iona Archibald and Opie, Peter (1952) *The Oxford Dictionary of Nursery Rhymes* (Oxford: Clarendon Press).

Opland, Jeff[rey] (1975) '*Imbongi Nezibongo*: the Xhosa tribal poet and the contemporary poetic tradition', *PMLA*, 90, 185–208.

—— (1976) Discussion following the paper 'Oral Poetry: some linguistic and typological considerations', by Paul Kiparsky, in Benjamin A. Stoltz and Richard S. Shannon (eds), *Oral Literature and the Formula* (Ann Arbor, Mich.: Center for the Coordination of Ancient and Modern Studies), 107–25.

Oppenheim, A. Leo (1964) *Ancient Mesopotamia* (Chicago: University of Chicago Press).

Packard, Randall M. (1980) 'The study of historical process in African traditions of genesis: the Bashu myth of Muhiyi', in Joseph C. Miller (ed.), *The African Past Speaks* (London: Dawson; Hamden, Conn.: Archon), 157–77.

Parker, William Riley (1967) 'Where do English departments come from?', *College English*, 28, 339–51.

Parry, Adam (1971) Introduction, pp. ix–xlii, and footnotes, *passim*, in Milman Parry, *The Making of Homeric Verse: The Collected Papers of Milman Parry*, ed. Adam Parry (Oxford: Clarendon Press).

Parry, Anne Amory (1973) *Blameless Aegisthus: A Study of ἀμύμων and Other Homeric Epithets*, Mnemosyne: Bibliotheca Classica Batava, Supp. 26 (Leyden: E. J. Brill).

Parry, Milman (1928) *L'Epithète traditionelle dans Homère* (Paris: Société Éditrice Les Belles Lettres). In English translation, pp. 1–190 in

Milman Parry, *The Making of Homeric Verse*, ed. Adam Parry (Oxford: Clarendon Press, 1971).

—— (1971) *The Making of Homeric Verse: The Collected Papers of Milman Parry*, ed. [his son] Adam Parry (Oxford: Clarendon Press).

Peabody, Berkley (1975) *The Winged Word: A Study in the Technique of Ancient Greek Oral Composition as Seen Principally through Hesiod's Works and Days* (Albany, NY: State University of New York Press).

Plaks, Andrew H. (ed.) (1977) *Chinese Narrative: Critical and Theoretical Essays*, foreword by Cyril Birch (Princeton, NJ: Princeton University Press).

Plato. References to Plato are given by citing the usual Stephanus numbers, by which the references can be traced in any scholarly edition and in most popular editions.

Plato (1973) *Phaedrus and Letters VII and VIII*, trans. with introductions by Walter Hamilton (Harmondsworth, England: Penguin Books).

Potter, Stephen (1937) *The Muse in Chains: A Study in Education* (London: Jonathan Cape).

Pratt, Mary Louise (1977) *Toward a Speech Act Theory of Literary Discourse* (Bloomington and London: Indiana University Press).

Propp, V[ladimir Iakovlevich] (1968) *Morphology of the Folktale*, 2nd edn rev. (Austin and London: University of Texas Press, for the American Folklore Society and the Indiana University Research Center for the Language Sciences).

Reichert, John (1978) 'More than kin and less than kind: limits of genre theory', in Joseph P. Strelka (ed.), *Theories of Literary Genre. Yearbook of Comparative Criticism*, vol. VIII (University Park and London: Pennsylvania State University Press), 57–79.

Renou, Louis (1965) *The Destiny of the Veda in India*, ed. Dev Raj Chanana (Delhi, Patna, Varanasi: Motilal Banarsidass).

Richardson, Malcolm (1980) 'Henry V, the English chancery, and chancery English', *Speculum*, 55(4) (October), 726–50.

Rosenberg, Bruce A. (1970) *The Art of the American Folk Preacher* (New York: Oxford University Press).

—— (1978) 'The genres of oral narrative', in Joseph P. Strelka (ed.), *Theories of Literary Genre. Yearbook of Comparative Criticism*, vol. VIII (University Park and London: Pennsylvania State University Press), 150–65.

Rousseau, Jean Jacques (1821) 'Essai sur l'origine des langues: où il est parlé de la mélodie et de l'imitation musicale', in *Oeuvres de J. J.*

*Rousseau* (21 vols, 1820–3) vol. 13, *Écrits sur la musique* (Paris: E. A. Lequien), 143–221.

Rutledge, Eric (1981) 'The lessons of apprenticeship: music and textual variation in Japanese epic tradition', paper read at the ninety-sixth annual convention of the Modern Languages Association of America, New York, NY, 27–30 December, 1981, program item 487, 'Anthropological approaches to literature', 29 December. Manuscript from the author.

Sampson, Geoffrey (1980) *Schools of Linguistics* (Stanford, Calif.: Stanford University Press).

Saussure, Ferdinand de (1959) *Course in General Linguistics*, trans. by Wade Baskin, ed. by Charles Bally and Albert Sechehaye, in collaboration with Albert Reidlinger (New York: Philosophical Library). Originally published in French (1916). This, the most important of Saussure's works, was compiled and edited from students' notes from his course in general linguistics given at Geneva in 1906–7, 1908–9 and 1901–11. Saussure left no text of his lectures.

Scheub, Harold (1977) 'Body and image in oral narrative performance', *New Literary History*, 8, 345–67. Includes photographs of gesticulation with hands and other parts of the body by women narrative performers among the Xhosa.

Schmandt-Besserat, Denise (1978) 'The earliest precursor of writing', *Scientific American*, 238, (6) (June), 50–9. Treats the hollow clay bullae and enclosed clay tokens from the Neolithic period in Western Asia in and around 9000 BC and used for several thousands of years, it seems, largely to record holdings or shipments of cattle, grain, other commodities. Very likely a precursor of writing that perhaps led into real writing.

Scholes, Robert and Kellogg, Robert (1966) *The Nature of Narrative* (New York: Oxford University Press).

Scribner, Sylvia and Cole, Michael (1978) 'Literacy without schooling: testing for intellectual effects', *Harvard Educational Review*, 48, 448–61.

Sherzer, Joel (1974) '*Namakke, Sunmakke, Kormakke*: three types of Cuna speech event', in Richard Bauman and Joel Sherzer (eds), *Explorations in the Ethnography of Speaking* (Cambridge, England, and New York: Cambridge University Press), 263–82, 462–4, 489. Reprint with same pagination: Institute of Latin American Studies, University of Texas at Austin, Offprint Series, 174 (n.d.).

—— (1981) 'The interplay of structure and function in Kuna narrative, or, how to grab a snake in the Darien', in Deborah Tannen (ed.),

*Georgetown University Round Table on Languages and Linguistics 1981* (Washington, DC: Georgetown University Press), 306–22.

Siertsema, B. (1955) *A Study of Glossematics: Critical Survey of its Fundamental Concepts* (The Hague: Martinus Nijhoff).

Solt, Mary Ellen (ed.) (1970) *Concrete Poetry: A World View* (Bloomington: Indiana University Press).

Sonnino, Lee Ann (1968) A *Handbook for Sixteenth-Century Rhetoric* (London: Routledge & Kegan Paul).

Sparks, Edwin Erie (ed.) (1908) *The Lincoln-Douglas Debates of 1858*, Collections of the Illinois State Historical Library, vol. III, Lincoln Series, vol. 1 (Springfield, Ill.: Illinois State Historical Library).

Steinberg, S. H. (1974) *Five Hundred Years of Printing*, 3rd edn rev. by James Moran (Harmondsworth, England: Penguin Books).

Steiner, George (1967) *Language and Silence: Essays on Language, Literature, and the Inhuman* (New York: Athenaeum).

Stokoe, William, C., Jr (1972) *Semiotics and Human Sign Language* (The Hague and Paris: Mouton).

Stolz, Benjamin A. and Shannon, Richard S. (eds) (1976) *Oral Literature and the Formula* (Ann Arbor, Mich.: Center for the Coordination of Ancient and Modern Studies).

Tambiah, S. J. (1968) 'Literacy in a Buddhist village in north-east Thailand', in Jack Goody (ed.), *Literacy in Traditional Societies* (Cambridge, England: Cambridge University Press), 85–131.

Tannen, Deborah (1980a) 'A comparative analysis of oral narrative strategies: Athenian Greek and American English', in Wallace L. Chafe (ed.), *The Pear Stories: Cultural, Cognitive, and Linguistic Aspects of Narrative Production* (Norwood, NJ: Ablex), 51–87.

—— (1980b) 'Implications of the oral/literate continuum for crosscultural communication', in James E. Alatis (ed.), *Georgetown University Round Table on Languages and Linguistics 1980: Current Issues in Bilingual Education* (Washington, DC: Georgetown University Press), 326–47.

Tillyard, E. M. W. (1958) *The Muse Unchained: An Intimate Account of the Revolution in English Studies at Cambridge* (London: Bowes & Bowes).

Toelken, Barre (1976) 'The "Pretty Languages" of Yellowman: Genre, Mode, and Texture in Navaho Coyote Narratives', in Dan Ben-Amos (ed.), *Folklore Genres* (Austin, Texas, and London: University of Texas Press), 145–70.

*Visible Language* (formerly *Journal of Typographic Research*). Publishes many valuable articles about typography, its constitution and development, its psychological and cultural effects, etc.

Watt, Ian (1867) *The Rise of the Novel: Studies in Defoe, Richardson, and Fielding* (Berkeley: University of California Press). Rpt. 1957.

Whitman, Cedric M. (1958) *Homer and the Homeric Tradition* (Cambridge, Mass.: Harvard University Press). Reprinted New York: Norton, 1965. Discusses the 'geometric structure of the *Iliad*', 249–84 (and diagram in four-page appendix after p. 366). Through ring composition (concluding a passage with the formula that began it), Homer (unconsciously?) organizes the *Iliad* in a geometric pattern like boxes within boxes. The *Iliad* is spun out from slight episode, the *Odyssey* is more complex (pp. 306 ff.).

Wilks, Ivor (1968) 'The transmission of Islamic learning in the western Sudan', in Jack Goody (ed.), *Literacy in Traditional Societies* (Cambridge, England: Cambridge University Press), 162–97.

Wilson, Edward O. (1975) *Sociobiology: The New Synthesis* (Cambridge, Mass.: Belknap Press of Harvard University Press).

Wolfram, Walt (1972) 'Sociolinguistic premises and the nature of nonstandard dialects', in Arthur L. Smith (ed.), *Language, Communication, and Rhetoric in Black America* (New York: Harper & Row), 28–40.

Yates, Frances A. (1966) *The Art of Memory* (Chicago: University of Chicago Press).

Zwettler, Michael J. (1977) *The Oral Tradition of Classical Arabic Poetry* (Columbus, Ohio: Ohio State University Press).

# INDEX

# After Ongism

## The evolution of networked intelligence

## John Hartley

You only have to consult Google Scholar to see the continuing importance and impact of Walter J. Ong's *Orality and Literacy*, originally published in 1982. Last time I looked, it showed over 7600 citations, more
than any other New Accents book with which I am familiar, including
Dick Hebdige's (1979) *Subculture* at around 5000, Terence Hawkes'
(1977) *Structuralism and Semiotics* at over 1300, and John Fiske's and my
(1978) *Reading Television* at around 1100.[1] Small wonder that a reissue is
called for. But the case for its revival goes beyond potential sales. It
is justified by the continuing importance of the topic, which has if
anything increased since the book was first published in the 1980s,
during the era of audio-visual and electronic media like film, radio and
TV.

The convergence of media, telecommunications and computer
technologies has precipitated a further transformation in modes of
communication through participatory platforms, including social network media, mobile applications, and consumer co-created content.
Now, media audiences are also users, and every user is a potential
producer, publisher, journalist, performer or critic. Much of this user-
created micro-productivity is a fascinating mix of orality and literacy. It
can be claimed with equal persuasion that we are in the midst of what

Ong called a "secondary orality" based on electronic media, and simultaneously that:

> Reading, which was in decline due to the growth of television, tripled from 1980 to 2008, because it is the overwhelmingly preferred way to receive words on the Internet.
>
> (Bohn and Short 2010: 7)

Ong's work focuses our attention not only on "orality" and "literacy" as such, which is important enough as a field of scholarship, but also on the *relations* between them, and on their *dynamics of change* or evolution over the short and long term: Ong is a theorist of media change. Naturally, a book that has been in print for thirty years is liable to attract criticism as well as praise. Some have concluded that his work, and that of Marshall McLuhan, is "technically outdated" (Pettitt 2012), because both of these writers flourished in the analogue era, prior to the social uptake of digital media and the internet. Does that mean that his ideas are no longer relevant; that "Ongism" should be consigned to history? Or would it be wise to take the longer view? Ong himself favours the *longue durée*. He thinks in units of 5000 years, naming alphabetic writing, invented by the Sumerians around 3500 BCE, as "the technology which has shaped and powered the intellectual activity of *modern man*" (*Orality and Literacy*: 82). He asserted the importance of *writing*, which he thought "was and is the most momentous of all human technological inventions" (*Orality and Literacy*: 84).

To what extent was he right? Does the importance of each communicative technology decline with the invention and uptake of its successor? Marshall McLuhan may have thought so – in the *Gutenberg Galaxy* (1962) he grants precedence to the invention of printing. Some people now are inclined to nominate the internet, or what John Brockman, self-confessed McLuhanite and founder of *The Edge*, "the world's smartest website,"[2] calls "Distributed Networked Intelligence (DNI)." That is, not the internet itself, but what the internet enables (i.e. human thought in externalised form): the "collective externalized mind, the mind we all share, the infinite oscillation of our collective consciousness interacting with itself, adding a fuller, richer dimension to what it means to be human" (The Edge 1999; see also Brockman

2012). The significance of this choice is that Brockman makes it as the "last word" of a conversation in which he had asked over a hundred prominent thinkers to name "the most important invention of the past two thousand years," on the eve of the millennium itself.[3]

In short, the smart money is on long-haul thinking; and Walter Ong was good at that. Thus, given that his work does continue to resonate for contemporary scholarship and debate, we should locate it in a field of criticism. Once again, this is not the place to make an overall assessment of Ong's life and works. Excellent appraisals have already been performed by others, notably the Jesuit communication scholar Paul Soukup (2007); the cultural historian Tom Pettitt (2012); and by Thomas Farrell, whose extensive writings on Ong must inform any subsequent endeavour (see especially Farrell 2000; and Farrell's Introduction to Ong 2002: 1–68). Here, in the restricted context of *Orality and Literacy*, I will discuss some of the issues that arise "after Ongism," and some of the issues over which he has been taken to task.

## Gutenberg parenthesis

Some contemporary commentators such as Tom Pettitt have reinvigorated the Ong line of thought by arguing that the print era constitutes not so much an example of linear progress or "consciousness-raising" (*Orality and Literacy*: 175), but rather a kind of historical deviation. Pettitt (2007; 2012) calls attention to the "Gutenberg parenthesis" – a 500-year period (better known as modernity) between what may prove to be longer stretches of oral and chirographic culture, corresponding to what Ong called "primary orality" (pre-Gutenberg – or strictly speaking pre-writing) and "secondary orality" (post-Gutenberg media and digital literacies). This approach allows the topic of orality and literacy to be pursued in the era of the internet, digital media, mobile devices and social networks without reducing it to an argument about "primitivism versus civilisation" (see below). The "Gutenberg parenthesis" idea suggests that despite its dominance, prestige and ubiquity, print-literacy is an exception in a much longer trajectory of human thought, which may be in the process of restoring earlier modes of communication based on speech and instantaneity rather than space and time-delay.

One of the oddest things about printing was that it delivered monopoly control over the *expression of the truth* to those who controlled *publication* (see Eisenstein 2011).[4] It seemed to liberate thought for all, and was so hailed by many over centuries, but this was a *read-only* freedom. In fact, the institutional forms taken by printing, which include the publishing and marketing industries, scientific and other associations, government agencies, and of course "the press," concentrated the "power of speech" into fewer and fewer hands, even as it extended ideas to whole populations.

The era of publishing as a general alternative to speech was relatively short — stretching from the sixteenth century to the beginning of the twenty-first century at most. It was always in conflict with other modes of communication, especially in the oral expression of family relations, fictional imagination, social values, corporeal pleasures such as art, drama and music, and semiotic systems based on apparel, food, and sexual signalling. But with the Enlightenment and the modernising revolutions that accompanied democratisation, industrialisation and consumerism, print became the undisputed conveyor of both *truth* (religious, scientific, professional, journalistic) and *control* (regulation, censorship, and the extreme asymmetry between writers and readers). We may link a Foucauldian approach to the administration of everyday life via institutions of knowledge (such as medicine) with an Ongian approach to the ordering of knowledge via print (for instance, see Chartier 1994; and see Cavallo and Chartier 1999). In both cases, it is not so much the intrinsic or psychological "effect" of print that's at stake, but the institutional authority of what Ong himself (1958) called "the pedagogical juggernaut" and its control over the production, form and dissemination of knowledge.

It is only with the growth of the digital interactive media that this "parenthesis" can be seen as a discrete period in history, rather than an inevitable evolutionary step. In the era of the internet, vastly more people than before can make use of literacy, including print-literacy, by publishing it for themselves. So we are in a time of unprecedented *convergence* among oral, written and print-literate modes, where oral forms like phatic communication are migrating to the web, the turn-taking modes of speech are augmented by links, photos, and file-sharing, private conversations are also global publications, text is literally hyper-inflated, and these multi-modal uses of multimedia literacy extend across much wider sections of the population than heretofore (see Baron 2009; Rettberg 2008; Papacharissi 2011). It is clearly important to rethink the relations between orality and literacy – both written and print – for the new media age.

## Progressivist ethnocentrism

Given the history of Americanism outlined in the Chapter "Before Ongism," it has been seen by some as necessary to disturb or disrupt the historical narrative that leaves a whiff of Western progressivism in Ong's account of the transition from oral to literate cultures. Certainly some commentators have been tempted to accuse him of preferring literate modes of thought as more advanced or civilised, compared with oral ones (Svehla 2006: 106–8; Moje and Luke 2009). However, despite his generally relaxed habit of equating Western thought with the human mind, Ong's attachment to European historical traditions cannot be seen as a simple universalisation of "New England" Puritanism for contemporary science, commerce and media. For a start, like his mentor McLuhan, Ong was a Catholic; indeed, like that other radical thought-provocateur of the day, Ivan Illich, he was a Jesuit priest. He taught at the Jesuit St Louis University, and was at ease in the Latin tongue, unlike most contemporary Protestants. Therefore, he cannot be thought of as a simple apologist for the Reformation or "plain style," even though his magnum opus was devoted to the work of Peter Ramus, Protestant pedagogue and founder of modern method, who was himself murdered by Catholic terrorists in the St Bartholomew's Day Massacre of 1572 (Ong 1958: 29).

Ong may have had reason to see the Protestant Reformation as an unfortunate interruption to an admired system – a "parenthesis" – rather than an inevitable advance in rational knowledge. He sees an "antipathy" between the "old oral, mnemonic world of imitation, aggregative, redundant, copious, traditionalist, warmly human, participatory," and the "analytic, sparse, exact, abstract, visualist, immobile world of [platonic] 'ideas'" (*Orality and Literacy*: 164) that were, he argued, a consequence of alphabetic literacy (scaled up many-fold by print-literacy). This account does not imply a progressive

(Whiggish) narrative of technological and cognitive "advance." There is ample evidence of Ong's attachment to oral modes; in his hands one might even call them prelapsarian, and speculate that writing, together with its hyperactive progeny, printing, was seen by Ong as another Fall, consequent upon human over-consumption of the tree of knowledge. Ong characterised Ramism as "the final shower of sparks released by an old oral-aural world as it was plunging from the epic firmament into the sea of a typographical civilization" (Ong 2002: 303). This Fall is not that of Judeo-Christian Adam, perhaps, but of Classical Icarus, in a Promethean shower of sparks. Either way, it results from knowledge overreaching itself.

There is no need to conclude, therefore, as Lance Svehla does, that Ong's account of the difference between oral and written worlds amounts to a "modernist epistemology," from which educators in particular would be obliged to conclude that contemporary students, especially those in inner cities and poor neighbourhoods with low exposure to books, who are "saturated by multiple media modes" and "grounded as they are in the icon," are therefore "culturally deficient and cognitively impaired" (Svehla 2006: 108–9). Ong's work can equally be read as a *preference* for rhetorical (Catholic) Medievalism over the spatial abstractions of (Protestant) modernity; and thence, with McLuhan, as *welcoming* the re-Medievalisation of the contemporary world through the electronic media, which he named as "secondary orality."[5] Here, "secondary" does not imply inferiority; only sequence.

Of course, a charge of *ethnocentrism* may still be in order, because by his own admission Ong concentrates on the Classical invention of alphabetic writing and its uptake in Europe and Western cultures, rather than comparing this with very different traditions from Mesopotamia, East Asia, Meso-America "and so on" (*Orality and Literacy*: 3). In short, Ong universalises as human what may arguably be observed only in recent Western traditions; and not in all of their citizens.

Contemporary sensibilities are more "catholic" in their willingness to admit the role of the traditions Ong skates over; and the difficult work of seeking to tell an integrated story of human civilisation as a whole has begun to be attempted. A widely praised example is *A History of the World in 100 Objects* (MacGregor 2010). This project began life orally, as a spoken radio series, and it continues digitally, as a well-used website.[6] Neil MacGregor, director of the British Museum, narrates world history from all inhabited continents and many civilisations. He does this entirely through objects, from the Olduvai stone chopping tools of early hominins, made nearly two million years ago, to a recently made-in-China solar-powered lamp kit.

Not only does such an approach show how ethnocentrism might be superseded, it also shows the limits of a logocentric approach to knowledge. It cautions us against the assumption that knowledge is carried by words alone, whether written or not, and thus that changes in communication technologies by themselves can change human consciousness. Neil MacGregor (2010: 658) concludes that "objects force us to the humble recognition that since our ancestors left East Africa to populate the world we have changed very little." The question of how much the human mind has changed remains open. But over that span of time there's no denying that knowledge has grown exponentially, much of it encoded in things, relationships, institutions and practices, as well as words. Ong's work is at its most valuable as part of the history of knowledge, not consciousness.

## Binarism

When Ong proposes the oral world as "antipathetic" to literacy (*Orality and Literacy*: 164), it matters less whether his own predilections, religiously-inspired or not, swing one way or the other; whether he prefers one or the other. A deeper problem lies in the assumption that these categories are binarily opposed (which is what "antipathy" requires), and that the adoption of alphabetic writing systems, and then of printing with moveable type, causes changes in the way humans know. Despite the fact that he criticised binary thinking among the structuralists (*Orality and Literacy*: 161), this tendency does structure Ong's approach in *Orality and Literacy*. As an aspect of his thought it was shared with an influential group of writers whose work became prominent in the mid-1960s. These included the anthropologist Sir Jack Goody (e.g. 1977), whose views were influential in literary, cultural and media studies through a much-anthologised article that he co-authored with Ian Watt, the theorist of the novel, called "The Consequences of Literacy" (Goody and Watt 1963).[7]

Naturally binarism dovetailed with Continental structuralist anthropology, especially that of Claude Lévi-Strauss, for instance in his distinction between "bricolage" (oral) and "engineering" (literate) modes of thought in *La Pensée Sauvage* (1962). Binarism crossed into the Anglosphere with structural anthropology, via interpreters such as Sir Edmund Leach (1976). It underpinned McLuhan's work, especially *The Gutenberg Galaxy* (1962) and that of his mentor, Harold Innis (1950; 1951). It was strongly endorsed by Innis's contemporary in Canada, Eric Havelock (a major influence on Ong: see *Orality and Literacy*: 27–8), whose *Preface to Plato* (1963) was published after a stint at Harvard. Havelock held – increasingly rigidly – that the invention of the Greek alphabet changed everything:

> The invention of the Greek alphabet, as opposed to all previous systems, including the Phoenician, constituted an event in the history of human culture, the importance of which has not as yet been fully grasped. Its appearance divides all pre-Greek civilizations from those that are post-Greek.
>
> (1977: 369)

Analysis of binary oppositions became influential in media and cultural studies, not least through my own co-authored book in the New Accents series, *Reading Television* (Fiske and Hartley 1978). We posited a series of differences between oral and literate modes of thought. Our purpose was not to keep them opposed, but rather the reverse: we wanted to counter what we saw as the print-literate prejudices of scholars and professional elites against popular television, by demonstrating its oral or "bardic" logic. We wanted to reinstate "oral modes" as a legitimate object of study; i.e. not to create but to rebalance the "great divide" between the two. Nonetheless, the use of binarism, even for analytical purposes, has the effect of legitimating the idea that orality and literacy are somehow "antipathetic" – an untested assumption that Ong's book, published four years after ours in the same New Accents series, did nothing to dispel.

## Pedagogic primitivism

David Olson and Nancy Torrance (1991: 7) call this binary approach
the "great-divide" theory. The problems with "great-divide" theory –
beyond the challenge of testing it empirically – are most acute when it
is *applied*, specifically in the classroom. Among literacy professionals it
became known as "Great Leap" theory, following a remark of David
Olson (2003), who *needed* a "great divide" in order to argue for the
reform of schooling:

> What is required, then, is an advance in our understanding of schools
> as bureaucratic institutions that corresponds to the advances in our
> understanding of the development of the mind ... a better under-
> standing of the relation between psychological theory and educational
> reform.

> (2003: xi)

The "Great Leap" Theory of Literacy follows from this: "I had assumed
that if only we knew more about ... how people learn, educational
practice would take a great leap forward." (Olson 2003: ix). The perceived *gap* between schooling and learning, where the former fails to
entail the latter, is projected onto a perceived difference – based on
social class – between print literacy and oral modes of thought. At the
very least, it was thought, reformists needed *not* to wage class struggle
*against* the have-nots by universalising the values of the literate elite.
Instead, the agenda was to reform pedagogies in institutional settings
with oral modes of learning in mind (effectively the opposite of the
Ramist project of the sixteenth century, designed to undo its
pedagogical-institutional legacy), with a view to promoting the intellectual emancipation of the population as a whole (see Kintgen et al
1988 for these and opposing perspectives).

The culture of literate credentialism – of certificating individuals
through written examination – is if anything more dominant now than
it was when Ong wrote *Orality and Literacy*. The "pedagogical juggernaut" is now a global competitive market in educational certification.
Print literacy is the medium of science, research, teaching, and social
institutions accessible chiefly by certification and examination, i.e.

government, administration, commerce and business, intellectual life and the professions. This contrasts with what Ong calls "secondary orality," i.e. electronically mediated oral modes of expression and communication, the favoured mode of informal communication and learning among those students, including many from challenging environments, whose senses are nurtured in popular culture and media, fashion and consumption, social networks online and in the street. This attempt to theorise modes of communication in terms of class distinction is then applied through educational programs designed to upend the established hierarchies of knowledge within the very institutions that serve to reproduce them. This kind of educational emancipationism channels the radical pedagogies of Catholic savants like Paulo Freire (1970) and Ivan Illich (1971) as well as Walter Ong. It was motivated by a desire to value "oral" modes of thought equally with or even above "literate" ones; to draw a closing bracket around the Ramist parenthesis in pedagogy.

Some detect traces of tribalism in this endeavour, a kind of "noble savage" Romanticism to which the 1960s generation seemed peculiarly prey – à la Robert Pirsig and Carlos Casteneda.[8] Walter Ong was not exempt from it, even as he sought to value the ceremonial life of what he called "peoples of simpler culture" and "more primitive peoples" (Ong 1971: 115). Thus, he compares Latin language learning in the Renaissance to the puberty rite, which he sees as "essentially didactic":

> Among the Bechuans, the boys in a state of nudity engage in a dance during which the men of the village pummel them with long, whip-like rods while asking such questions as, "Will you guard the chief well?" or "Will you herd the cattle well."
>
> (Ong 1971: 117)

In the Renaissance, it was Latin, rather than literacy as such, that separated the men from the boys – and from women, domestic life, and vernacular literacy too. This meant that "learning" (i.e. knowledge in Latin) was an almost exclusively male accomplishment; and that schools and universities were "strongly reminiscent of male club-houses in primitive societies" (120). Thus, even while showing that the oral culture of pre-modern tribal societies continued into the literate era, Ong persisted with a model of "primitive" (presumably as opposed to "advanced") societies, and sometimes also with a model of oral accomplishments that confined them to the unlearned, vernacular world of women, hearth and home.

Nevertheless, Ong's purpose in this study was not to argue for progressive advance from primitive to American culture, but to demonstrate how much formal schooling in Latin *resembled* traditional puberty ceremonials. It's a fascinating insight, with resonance beyond the Renaissance.[9] Not only were the foundations of modern science laid by Renaissance thinkers who mastered (and administered) this kind of schooling, but the "puberty rite" aspect lingers on. Ong argues that the learning of Latin – a dead language not shared by family members (especially women) or used in the everyday life of society – added an extra dimension to the sense of exclusiveness, access to arcane knowledge and in-group identity-formation among those with Latin rather than merely vernacular learning. For Ong, the "social implications were large":

> For when Latin passed out of vernacular usage, a sharp distinction was set up in society between those who knew it and those who did not. The conditions for a "marginal environment" were present ... between the family (which as such used a language other than Latin) and an extrafamilial world of learning (which used Latin). The fact that the marginal environment was primarily a linguistic one only heightened the initiatory aspects of the situation, for the learning of secret meanings and means of communication is a common feature of initiatory rites. It is through ability to communicate that man achieves a sense of belonging.
>
> (119)

In what McLuhan dubbed the Global Village, perhaps we haven't "progressed" as far beyond tribal culture – never mind the Renaissance – as we might like to think. As they read Ong's description of how "a boy's education was basically a puberty rite, a process preparing him for adult life by communicating to him the heritage of a past in a setting which toughened him and thus guaranteed his guarding the heritage for the future" (1971: 140), contemporary scholars might like to think about how well such an analysis describes the experience of *graduate education*, at least in big American universities.

## Transforming consciousness? Not so fast...

Despite its well-meaning purpose, the idea that education can take a "great leap forward" by bridging the "great divide" between orality and literacy remains controversial, because scholars of both literacy history (Graff 1981) and human psychology (Scribner and Cole 1981) have expressed strong scepticism about whether literacy, either alphabetic or print, does in fact transform or "restructure" human consciousness as Ong so confidently asserts (*Orality and Literacy*: chapter 4).

One problem with that idea is that writing does not supplant orality; print does not supplant writing. Typically, new media technologies supplement those already in use. Thus, the historian of literacy Harvey Graff has pointed out that education itself "long remained an oral activity" (1991: 5), in an interactive process where oral and literate modes coexist. Graff has sought to de-couple the study of literacy from the idea of progressive change by emphasising *continuities* in the history of literacy (1991: 8; see also Graff 1987; Finnegan 1988: 139; 175).

In effect, recent educational approaches to literacy have tended to shy away from "great leap" theory (Street 1984; Daniell 1986). Educational activists in favour of the classroom use of non-print media, however, have often retained some version or vestige of it in order to press the case for updating pedagogies (and technologies) for the era of broadcast and digital media (Kellner 2002). But by the turn of the twenty-first century, Ong's influence on the teaching of "media literacy" had waned to the point where neither his name nor McLuhan's is mentioned, on either side of the Atlantic, in the most influential studies (e.g. Jenkins et al, n.d.; Buckingham 2003).

This turn away from Ong is regrettable, because it throws the baby out with the bathwater. As usual, academic criticism routinely looks for opponents' worst faults (while wishing to be judged on its own best features). Rejection of Ong's more exorbitant claims seems to have led to the neglect of his best work too. He had no evidential warrant to step from what he knew about, i.e. the history of rhetorical, technological and "noetic" distinctions between orality, writing (chirographic literacy) and print-literacy, to what he didn't know about: the mind. His claim, that the historical shift from one technology of knowledge (speech) to another (writing) "restructures" human consciousness, is a simple over-generalisation. It can't do this, unless the claim is made that even the consciousness of those who can't or don't read (much less write), and those from other cultures, is transformed by rhetorical traditions and media technologies they don't use. No matter how pervasive they may be, technologies like writing, print, broadcasting, electronic communication and digital media are all social institutions (culture) rather than human attributes (nature). Ong's talk about "human consciousness" was essentially a red herring, because what he contributed to scholarship was something substantial and fascinating in its own terms – the history of learning systems. He did not need to extrapolate from social learning to human consciousness.

Several times, even as he is trying to address gender issues, Ong seems to suggest that consciousness is in fact divided along gender lines (e.g. 1971: 119–20; Orality and Literacy: 111–12, 156–7; 2002: 483–4). But, just as he was no neuroscientist, so he didn't know much about girls: "We are concerned with the boys alone here, for, generally speaking, it is boys alone who are taught in Renaissance schools, or who are given a systematic formal education" (1971: 117). Here is technological determinism at its least thoughtful; seeming to suggest that because something was transformed (communications technologies), then everything was (human consciousness), even when it wasn't (women's consciousness). Ong was interested in the role of "ceremonial combat" in both education and masculinity. But the subtitle of his book-length treatment of this topic, Fighting For Life: Contest, Sexuality, and Consciousness (1981), shows how his reach exceeded his grasp: "contest" and "sexuality" may be linked in educational institutions, but that does not entail a transformation of human "consciousness" – here was knowledge overreaching itself.

But the opposite fault also needs to be avoided. Just because Ong's most extreme assumptions, which are caused by his habit of generalising or universalising from his topic to "mankind," are wrongheaded, it does not follow that everything else is wrong too. Silly statements are made, as they are by us all. But that should not blind us to what Ong did know about, which was the history of technologies of knowledge, whether hardware such as writing and the press, or software like rhetoric or spatialised method. Here he was definitely on to something, and that something was *cultural evolution*.

## The evolution of Ongism

Ong flirted with evolutionary theory. In fact he gave it the last word in *Orality and Literacy*:

> Since at least the time of Hegel, awareness has been growing that human consciousness evolves ... Orality-literacy dynamics enter integrally into the modern evolution of consciousness.
>
> *(Orality and Literacy*: 174–6)

At a time when merely to utter that word in a Humanities common-room could cause consternation (on the grounds that evolution = social Darwinism = Nazism), mention of evolution may be seen as a bold move. Nevertheless, strangely to our post-Dawkins ear, the passage it introduces heads off to religious interiority, not to Darwin. It is possible that Ong didn't mean Darwinian evolution at all: he writes of "the modern evolution of consciousness" rather than "the evolution of modern consciousness." Here, word order may make quite a difference, since "modern evolution of" may just mean "historic change" (5000 years max), where "evolution of modern" is a Darwinian question (50,000 years minimum). No matter; the media scholarship of the day, influenced by Marxist political economy, was more interested in changes wrought by industrialisation and class struggle. Here, changes in consciousness were certainly countenanced, but were explained as the outcome of economic and institutional processes not evolutionary ones: the object of study wasn't the "evolution of consciousness" but "the consciousness industry" (Enzensberger 1970; 1974).

But the cat was out of the bag: Ong had invoked evolution, "onto-genetically and phylogenetically" (*Orality and Literacy*: 175: and see Gould 1977), as the *causal mechanism* behind the changes he associated with oral, then literate and print-based consciousness. At the time, this was little more than a hunch. Ong was part of a phase in the history of ideas when some causal connection between media technologies, cognition, and cultural change was suspected but hard to prove given the then state of bioscience, cognitive psychology, and literary history. The thought-experiments of his generation, conducted by the likes of McLuhan, Goody and Watt, Havelock etc., were bold and influential but impossible to verify or even to triangulate with other sciences. The "evolution of consciousness" remained a provocative metaphor rather than a field of substantive inquiry. Biological science (genetics), psychology (the brain), and textual scholarship (complex-networked meaning systems) were not sufficiently developed, internally or in relation to each other, to attempt to isolate evolutionary causal mechanisms in the study of technologies of consciousness, whether internal like speech or external like writing (but see Lotman 2009).

Times have changed since 1982. Among the changes is an accelerating "consilience" (Wilson 1998) between sciences and humanities, including various attempts to study literary and cultural topics using approaches derived from evolutionary or neo-Darwinian theory, complexity or network theory, and genetic biosciences including neuroscience and evolutionary psychology. Ong's interest in evolution has been taken up in ways he could not have foreseen, in current work in the evolutionary sciences (Mesoudi 2011); work that suggests we may indeed be able to understand culture and consciousness through evolutionary theory, not simply as a loose metaphor for change, but as part of the neo-Darwinian turn in the social and cultural as well as the biological sciences (Boyd and Richerson 1985). Following rapid development of evolutionary and complex-systems approaches in the biosciences, neurosciences, evolutionary and complexity theory (e.g. Kauffman 1995) and eventually even in the humanities, it is timely to reopen the question of the "evolution of consciousness" in relation to changes in the technologies and media of communication. Guides to this work include Brian Arthur (2009), whose own compelling theorising about technological evolution cries out to be applied to technologies of communication; and Brian Boyd (2009), whose work on Homer and the evolution of stories, and on evolutionary approaches to literature, has set a standard that augurs well for the future of this nascent field. Many others are now contributing to an emergent colloquy on evolution and the arts, for instance Austin (2010); Boyd et al (2010); Carroll (2011); Dissanayake (2000) and Dutton (2009). For a critique of some of this work, see Kramnick (2011).[10]

Setting Ong's work in this wider, interdisciplinary context links his "noetic" history-of-ideas approach not only with evolutionary and systems thinking but also with the contemporary field of the "science of science."[11] Media technologies can be studied as part of the "evolutionary turn" affecting many fields, bringing together insights from biosciences, textual studies, and network or complexity theory to understand the extent to which our species is adapting to evolutionary changes in the technologies and growth of knowledge. When you read Ong's book now, you're thinking about what John Brockman (The Edge 1999) called "Distributed Networked Intelligence." You're not only thinking about it; you're participating in it too.

As you do, consider the words of the anonymous "First Citizen" listening to Mark Antony's famous "lend me your ears" speech in Shakespeare's Julius Caesar, who remarks: "Methinks there is much reason in his sayings."[12] The same might be said of Walter J. Ong.

## Notes

1   Google Scholar accessed June 2012.
2   John Naughton, in the Observer (8 January 2012): www. guardian .co.uk/technology/2012/jan/08/john-brockman-edge-interview-john-naughton?newsfeed=true. McLuhan's influence on Brockman is discussed in this interview.
3   See all 114 contributions at The Edge (1999).
4   Those who controlled publishing controlled "public thought," in Clay Shirky's excellent phrase: "The beneficiaries of the system where making things public was a privileged activity, whether academics or politicians, reporters or doctors, will complain about the way the new abundance of public thought upends the old order, but those complaints are like keening at a wake; the change they fear is already in the past. The real action is elsewhere." www.edge.org/q2010/q10_1.html#shirky (and see Brockman 2012).
5   Ong and McLuhan wouldn't be the only medievalists to cast a "catholic" eye over "protestant" America – Umberto Eco did it later, with his Travels in Hyperreality (1987), although Eco had left

the Catholic Church during his doctorate studies (on aesthetics in Thomas Aquinas). See: www.themodernword.com/eco/eco_biography.html.

6    See: www.bbc.co.uk/ahistoryoftheworld.

7    Even the historians began to think in paired oppositions: Peter Laslett's influential book *The World We Have Lost* (2004; first published 1965) touches on some of these issues in trying to describe a society where reading and writing were rare accomplishments, a difference from contemporary society that emphasises – and separates the "we" of his title from – what he called "the pastness of the past."

8    Robert Pirsig's *Zen and the Art of Motorcycle Maintenance* (1974) and Carlos Castaneda's *The Teachings of Don Juan* (1968), both sought to derive wisdom from non-Western or tribal models; interestingly, both started life as academic dissertations (see: davidlavery.net/Collected_Works/Essays/Dissertations_as_Fictions.pdf, p. 3).

9    I discuss such resonances further in Hartley (2012).

10    The Wikipedia entry on "Darwinian literary studies" (accessed January 2012) is good.

11    See for instance *The Economist* (2011).

12    William Shakespeare (1599) *Julius Caesar*, III.ii.108: shakespeare.mit.edu/julius_caesar/julius_caesar.3.2.html; and see note 2, p. xxiv, above.

# References for Hartley Chapters

Altegoer, D. (2000) *Reckoning Words: Baconian Science and the Construction of Truth in English Renaissance Culture.* Cranbury NJ: Associated University Presses.

Altick, R. (1957) *The English Common Reader: A Social History of the Mass Reading Public, 1800–1900.* Chicago: Chicago University Press.

Arthur, B. (2009) *The Nature of Technology: What It Is and How It Evolves.* New York: Free Press.

Atiyah, Sir M. (2006) 'Benjamin Franklin and the Edinburgh Enlightenment.' *Proceedings of the American Philosophical Society,* 150:4, 591–606.

Austin, M. (2010) *Useful Fictions: Evolution, Anxiety, and the Origins of Literature.* USA: University of Nebraska Press.

Bacon, Sir F. (1605) *The Advancement of Learning.* Accessible at: http://ebooks.adelaide.edu.au/b/bacon/francis/b12a/complete.html.

Baron, D. (2009) *A Better Pencil: Readers, Writers, and the Digital Revolution.* Oxford: Oxford University Press.

Bedford (1984) 'A Brief History of Rhetoric and Composition.' *The Bedford Bibliography for Teachers of Writing.* Online: www.bedfordstmartins.com/bb/history.html.

Berry, C. (1997) *Social Theory of the Scottish Enlightenment.* Edinburgh: Edinburgh University Press.

Bohn, R. and J. Short (2010) *How Much Information? 2009 Report on*

*American Consumers.* UC San Diego: Global Information Industry Center: hmi.ucsd.edu/pdf/HMI_2009_ConsumerReport_Dec9_2009.pdf.

Boyd, B. (2009) *On the Origin of Stories: Evolution, Cognition and Fiction.* Cambridge, MA: Harvard University Press.

Boyd, B., J. Carroll and J. Gottschall, eds. (2010) *Evolution, Literature, and Film: A Reader.* New York: Columbia University Press.

Boyd, R. and P. Richerson (1985) *Culture and the Evolutionary Process.* Chicago: University of Chicago Press.

Brockman, J., ed. (2012) *How is the Internet Changing the Way You Think?* London: Atlantic Books.

Buckingham, D. (2003) *Media Education: Literacy, Learning and Contemporary Culture.* Cambridge: Polity.

Carroll, J. (2011) *Reading Human Nature: Literary Darwinism in Theory and Practice.* Albany, NY: SUNY Press.

Castaneda, C. (1968) *The Teachings of Don Juan: A Yaqui Way of Knowledge.* Berkeley: University of California Press.

Cavallo, G. and R. Chartier, eds. (1999) *A History of Reading in the West.* Amherst, MA: University of Massachusetts Press.

Chartier, R. (1994) *The Order of Books: Readers, Authors, and Libraries in Europe Between the Fourteenth and Eighteenth Centuries.* London: Polity Press.

Cousins, J., ed. (1910) *A Short Biographical Dictionary of English Literature.* London: J.M. Dent and Co.

Daniell, B. (1986) 'Against the Great Leap Theory of Literacy.' *PRE/TEXT*, 7, 181–93.

Dissanayake, E. (2000) *Art and Intimacy: How the Arts Began.* Seattle: University of Washington Press.

Dutton, D. (2009) *The Art Instinct: Beauty, Pleasure, and Human Evolution.* Oxford: Oxford University Press.

Eco, U. (1987) *Travels in Hyperreality.* London: Picador.

*Economist, The* (2011, April 28) 'The science of science: How to use the web to understand the way ideas evolve.' Online: www.economist.com/node/18618025.

Edge, The (1999) 'What Is The Most Important Invention In The Past Two Thousand Years?' *The Edge.* Online: edge.org/documents/Invention.html.

Eisenstein, E. (2011) *Divine Art, Infernal Machine: The Reception of Printing in the West from First Impressions to the Sense of an Ending.* Philadelphia: University of Pennsylvania Press.

Empson, Sir W. (1930) *Seven Types of Ambiguity*. London: Chatto & Windus.

Enzensberger, H. M. (1970) 'Constituents of a Theory of the Media.' *New Left Review*, 64, 13–36.

Enzensberger, H. M. (1974). *The Consciousness Industry: On Literature, Politics and the Media*. New York: Continuum Books/Seabury Press.

Farrell, T. (2000) *Walter Ong's Contributions to Cultural Studies: The Phenomenology of the Word and I-Thou Communication*. Cresskill, NJ: Hampton Press.

Finnegan, R. (1988) *Literacy and Orality: Studies in the Technology of Communication*. Oxford: Blackwell.

Fiske, J. and J. Hartley (1978) *Reading Television*. London: Methuen.

Freire, P. (1970) *Pedagogy of the Oppressed*. New York: Continuum.

Gibbon, E. (1910, first published 1776–88) *The Decline and Fall of the Roman Empire*. London: Everyman's Library.

Gitlin, T. (1987) *The Sixties: Years of Hope, Days of Rage*. NY: Bantam Books.

Goody, Sir J. (1977) *The Domestication of the Savage Mind*. Cambridge: Cambridge University Press.

Goody, Sir J. and I. Watt (1963) 'The Consequences of Literacy.' *Comparative Studies in Society and History*, 5:3, 304–45.

Gould, S. J. (1977) *Ontogeny and Phylogeny*. Cambridge, MA: Harvard University Press.

Graff, H. (1981) *Literacy and Social Development in the West*. Cambridge: Cambridge University Press.

Graff, H. (1987) *The Labyrinths of Literacy*. London: Falmer.

Graff, H. (1991) *The Legacies of Literacy: Continuities and Contradictions in Western Culture and Society*. Bloomington: Indiana University Press.

Gurr, A. (2004) *Playgoing in Shakespeare's London*. 3rd revised edn. Cambridge: Cambridge University Press.

Harbage, A. (1941) *Shakespeare's Audience*. NY: Columbia University Press.

Harbage, A. (1947/1961) *As They Liked It*. New York: Harper Torchbooks edn. Accessible at: www.archive.org/stream/astheylikeditasto17764 mbp/astheylikeditasto17764mbp_djvu.txt.

Hartley, J. (2012) 'Remembering Expertise: From Puberty Rite to Irenic Media Studies.' In K. Darian-Smith and S. Turnbull, eds. *Remembering Television: History, Memory and Technologies*. Cambridge: Cambridge Scholars Press.

Havelock, E. (1963) *Preface to Plato*. Cambridge, MA: Harvard University Press.

Havelock, E. (1977) 'The Preliteracy of the Greeks.' *New Literary History*, 8:3, 369–91.

Havelock, E. (1986) *The Muse Learns to Write: Reflections on Orality and Literacy from Antiquity to the Present*. New Haven, CT: Yale University Press.

Hawkes, T. (1977) *Structuralism and Semiotics*. London: Methuen.

Hawkes, T. (2009) 'William Empson's influence on the CIA.' *Times Literary Supplement*, June 10. Accessible at: http://philosophysother.blog spot.com/2009/08/hawkes-terence-william-empsons.html.

Hebdige, D. (1979) *Subculture: The Meaning of Style*. London: Methuen.

Holzman, M. (1999) 'The Ideological Origins of American Studies at Yale.' *American Studies*, 40:2, 71–99, accessible at: https://journals. ku.edu/index.php/amerstud/article/viewFile/2679/2638.

Holzman, M. (2008) *James Jesus Angleton, the CIA and the Craft of Counterintelligence*. Amherst: University of Massachusetts Press.

Hymes, D. (1996) *Ethnography, Linguistics, Narrative Inequality: Toward an Understanding of Voice*. London: Taylor & Francis.

Illich, I. (1971) *Deschooling Society*. London: Calder & Boyars. Accessible at: ournature.org/~novembre/illich/1970_deschooling.html.

Innis, H. (1950) *Empire and Communications*. Oxford: Clarendon Press.

Innis, H. (1951) *The Bias of Communication*. Toronto: University of Toronto Press.

Jenkins, H., K. Clinton, R. Purushotma, A. J. Robison and M. Weigel (n.d.) *Confronting the Challenges of Participatory Culture: Media Education for the 21st Century*. Chicago: MacArthur Foundation. Accessible at: http://digitallearning.macfound.org/atf/cf/%7B7E45C7E0-A3E0– 4B89-AC9C-E807E1B0AE4E%7D/JENKINS_WHITE_PAPER.PDF.

Jones, R. F. (1953) *The Triumph of the English Language*. Palo Alto, CA: Stanford University Press.

Kauffman, S. (1995) *At Home in the Universe: The Search for the Laws of Self-Organization and Complexity*. Oxford: Oxford University Press.

Kellner, D. (2002) 'New Media and New Literacies: Reconstructing Education for the New Millennium.' In L. Lievrouw and S. Livingstone (eds) *The Handbook of New Media*. London: Sage.

Kintgen, E., B. Kroll and M. Rose (eds) (1988) *Perspectives on Literacy*. Carbondale: Southern Illinois University Press.

Kramnick, J. (2011) 'Against Literary Darwinism.' *Critical Inquiry* 37, 315–47. Accessible at: criticalinquiry.uchicago.edu/uploads/pdf/Kramnick,_ Against_Literary_Darwinism.pdf.

Krippner, S. (1970) 'The Effects of Psychedelic Experience on Language Functioning.' In B. Aaronson and H. Osmond, eds, *PSYCHE-DELICS, The Uses and Implications of Hallucinogenic Drugs*. NY:

Doubleday & Company. Accessible at: www.psychedelic-library.org/krippner.htm.

Laslett, P. (2004; first published 1965) *The World We Have Lost*. London: Routledge.

Leach, Sir E. (1976) *Culture and Communication*. Cambridge: Cambridge University Press.

Lévi-Strauss, C. (1962) *La Pensée Sauvage*. Paris: Plon. Accessible at: http://archive.org/details/lapenseesauvageoolevi.

Lotman, Y. (2009) *Culture and Explosion*. Berlin: Mouton de Gruyter.

MacGregor, N. (2010) *A History of the World in 100 Objects*. London: Penguin.

McLean, I. (2011) 'Scottish Enlightenment Influence on Thomas Jefferson's Book-Buying: Introducing Jefferson's Libraries.' Oxford University: Nuffield's Working Papers Series in Politics. Accessible at: www.nuff.ox.ac.uk/politics/papers/2011/Iain%20McLean_working%20paper%202011_01.pdf.

McLuhan, M. (1962) *The Gutenberg Galaxy: The Making of Typographic Man*. Toronto: University of Toronto Press.

McLuhan, M., Q. Fiore and J. Agel (1967) *The Medium is the Massage: An Inventory of Effects*. New York: Gingko Press.

Mesoudi, A. (2011) *Cultural Evolution: How Darwinian Theory Can Explain Human Culture and Synthesize the Social Sciences*. Chicago: Chicago University Press.

Miller, P. (1939) *The New England Mind: The Seventeenth Century*. Cambridge, MA: Harvard University Press.

Miller, P. (1953) *The New England Mind: From Colony to Province*. Cambridge, MA: Harvard University Press.

Moje, E. B. and A. Luke (2009) 'Literacy and Identity: Examining the metaphors in history and contemporary research.' *Reading Research Quarterly*, 44:4, 415–37.

Olson, D. (1993) *Psychological Theory and Educational Reform: How School Remakes Mind and Society*. Cambridge: Cambridge University Press.

Olson, D. and N. Torrance, eds. (1991) *Literacy and Orality*. Cambridge: Cambridge University Press.

Ong, W. J. (1953) 'Peter Ramus and the Naming of Methodism: Medieval Science Through Ramist Homiletic.' *Journal of the History of Ideas*, 14:2, 235–48.

Ong, W. J. (1958/2004) *Ramus, Method, and the Decay of Dialogue: From the Art of Discourse to the Art of Reason*. Chicago: Chicago University Press.

Ong, W. J. (1971) *Rhetoric, Romance, and Technology: Studies in the Interaction of Expression and Culture*. Ithaca, NY and London: Cornell University Press.

Ong, W. J. (1981) *Fighting For Life: Contest, Sexuality, and Consciousness*. Ithaca, NY: Cornell University Press.

Ong, W. J. (2002) *An Ong Reader: Challenges for Further Inquiry*. Ed. T. Farrell and P. Soukup. Cresskill, NJ: Hampton Press.

Papacharissi, Z., ed. (2011) *A Networked Self: Identity, Community, and Culture on Social Network Sites*. New York: Routledge.

Pettitt, T. (2007) 'Before the Gutenberg Parenthesis.' Plenary paper to *Media in Transition 5: Creativity, Ownership and Collaboration in the Digital Age*. MIT: web.mit.edu/comm-forum/mit5/papers/pettitt_plenary_gutenberg.pdf.

Pettitt, T. (2012) 'Media Dynamics and the Lessons of History: The "Gutenberg Parenthesis" as Restoration Topos.' In J. Hartley, J. Burgess and A. Bruns, eds. *A Companion to New Media Dynamics*. Malden, MA and Oxford: Wiley-Blackwell, Chapter 3.

Phillipson, N. (2010) *Adam Smith: An Enlightened Life*. USA: Yale University Press; UK: Penguin Books.

Pirsig, R. (1974) *Zen and the Art of Motorcycle Maintenance: An Inquiry into Values*. New York: Bantam Books.

Rathbun, L. (2000) 'The Ciceronian Rhetoric of John Quincy Adams.' *Rhetorica: A Journal of the History of Rhetoric*, 18(2): 175–215.

Rettberg, J. W. (2008) *Blogging*. Cambridge: Polity Press.

Reuters (2012) 'China claims success in curbing racy entertainment.' *Chicago Tribune*, January 4: www.chicagotribune.com/entertainment/sns-rt-us-china-television-regulatortre8030uc-20120104,0,7398370.story.

Schudson, M. (1998) *The Good Citizen: A History of American Civic Life*. NY: The Free Press.

Scribner, S. and M. Cole (1981) *The Psychology of Literacy*. Cambridge, MA: Harvard University Press.

Soukup, P. (2007) '*Orality and Literacy* 25 Years Later.' *Communication Research Trends*, 26:4, 3–20.

Street, B. (1984) *Literacy in Theory and Practice*. Cambridge: Cambridge University Press.

Svehla, L. (2006) 'The Supremacy of the Image: Urban Students and the Idea of Secondary Orality.' *EAPSU Online: A Journal of Critical and Creative Work*, vol 3, 104–28: www.eapsu.net/PDFs/vol3.pdf.

Tawney, R. H. (1998, first published 1926) *Religion and the Rise of Capitalism*. New Brunswick, NJ: Transaction Publishers.

Wilson, E. O. (1998) *Consilience: The Unity of Knowledge*. NY: Knopf.
Wolfe, T. (2000, originally published 1965) 'What if he is right?' In J. Hartley and R. Pearson (eds), *American Cultural Studies: A Reader*. Oxford: Oxford University Press, 22–31 [also published in Wolfe's *The Pump House Gang* (New York: Bantam Books, 1969: 105–33)].

# INDEX FOR HARTLEY CHAPTERS

Made in the USA
Coppell, TX
06 May 2024

32077833R00148